THE GREAT PRETENDER

ABOUT THE AUTHOR

Nick Perry spent his childhood in rural Dorset. He was educated at Parkstone Sea Training School and left at fifteen for a job at ATV in London. He then travelled around Europe for a while and moved from job to job back in London until he came into a small inheritance. On impulse, he and his brother bought a hill farm in North Wales, which is where his first book, *Peaks and Troughs*, takes place. After seven years living on the breadline, he took his family on a new adventure in Greece, the subject of his second book, *Escape to Ikaria*. He now lives with his wife in Wiltshire.

THE GREAT PRETENDER

A CATALOGUE OF CHAOS
AND CREATIVITY

NICK PERRY

First published in Great Britain in 2019 by Polygon, an imprint of Birlinn Ltd.

West Newington House
10 Newington Road
Edinburgh
EH9 1QS

www.polygonbooks.co.uk

ISBN 978 1 84697 470 0
eBook ISBN 978 1 78885 192 3

Design and typesetting by Studio Monachino

Printed and bound in Great Britain by Clays Ltd, Elcograf S.p.A.

To Mike Townsend, who only once in eighteen years said,
'It's an impissibolity.' (sic)

✦ 1 ✦

It was down in the valley below the village of Frampton Mansell in Gloucestershire, watching the slow, ungainly flight of a heron rising from a flooded meadow on a still September morning, that I decided it was time to get on with it. No more living from hand to mouth and just getting by, I told myself as I stood under the ivy-clad red-brick arches of Brunel's railway viaduct and the sun spread over the hills across the valley. This was it.

So I moved into a 1940s single-storey stable block that housed a solitary Shire horse called Pearl. She was a large grey beast who seemed to enjoy my company, neighing when I arrived every morning with a pocket full of apples and a packet of Polos. The stable block, with its mossy roof and shabby pebbledashed walls, was one of many buildings on what had once been a working farm, Puckmill, close to the Thames Severn Canal that snaked its way through the Golden Valley, passed the Daneway pub and disappeared into the Sapperton tunnel. It was one of these stables, measuring no more than sixteen foot by twelve, that became my workshop, and the place where I began my business. It was owned by Celia Foxton, a friend of many years, who had recently bought the farm.

'Rent it from me if you want, for say sixty pounds a month, including electricity. So long as you can muck out Pearl's stable and give her half a bale of hay every day.'

'I can do that.'

Frampton Mansell is a small village of mellow Cotswold stone cottages on the steep slopes of the Golden Valley. At its centre is the seventeenth-century Crown Inn and a few hundred yards away St Luke's church, built by Lord Bathurst in 1843. The single-track lane that winds steeply down through the village requires patient drivers to find passing places; for those of a certain age suffering stiff necks, reversing can be an arduous task. And at the bottom is Brunel's viaduct, completed the same year as St Luke's. Here, through one of its arches, began the long stony drive to Puckmill's old farmhouse, where Celia lived.

It was 1981; I was thirty-four with four children. Our last, Belah, born three years before, trailed behind Seth who had just turned six, and our twins, Sam and Lysta, with eleven years on the clock. Then there was Ros, my Welsh wife, ahead of us all at thirty-eight.

We'd been a restless family; there was a non-conformity that ran through the bloodline and we had difficulty fitting into everyday life. We were trying to adjust to living next door to neighbours in a street of semi-detached houses in Cirencester after farming for seven years in the Welsh hills, where we had led an isolated life when it came to other people. Then we moved to Ikaria, a Greek island in the Aegean, where I'd worked as a fisherman and a gardener in a remote monastery while Ros taught the children their school work in the garden under eucalyptus trees full of the sound of cicadas. It hadn't exactly been a conventional life.

Till recently, I'd been working at the Brass Rubbing Centre pouring polyester resin into silicone moulds to make do-it-yourself kits for children. My younger brother, Jack, still worked there, having come down from the hills above Capel Curig where he'd been a shepherd for nearly ten years. His wife Corinna, who, unlike Jack, enjoyed being part of the human race, had heard about the vacancy. I couldn't believe it when Jack took the job, after spending so long wandering alone with Meg, his Border Collie, in the rugged landscapes of North Wales. And as for myself, well, I'd no idea where I was heading at the time, so I joined him in what was no more than a cottage industry.

After just a week and seeing no future in it, I said to him, 'Jack, what's happened to us? Why are we working here?'

'Well, I've got to stick it out for a while. Corinna's pregnant.'

I lasted three months before I handed in my notice, after realising that you could make a mould of whatever you chose, and surely something much more interesting than brass rubbing kits for children. Exactly what I didn't know, but before I left I made a mould of one of our door knobs, only because we needed two, and Ros hadn't been able to find a match. It fitted perfectly, and Ros was astonished that I had shown some DIY skills.

Jack wasn't surprised that I'd had enough even after such a short time.

'What are you going to do?'

'I really don't know. I feel as though I'm not going to fit in anywhere.'

I was never ideal employee material; in fact I was unemployable. Working under someone else who was making the decisions never suited me. At least if things go wrong and you're the boss you've only yourself to blame.

It was an intuitive thing, the beginning of a new phase, a force urging me to follow a different path. I needed to be single-minded, to make money and not be distracted. The biggest obstacle I had to overcome was myself. 'Do not allow your mind to wander' became my new mantra.

And then it came to me, in one of those moments coming out of sleep when images seem to be fading into the daylight and yet are still possible to catch, like a hand plunging into a pond and grabbing a tadpole. Of course – it was obvious. Replicas, that's what I should be making, but replicas of what?

So I gathered the family around to tell them my plan. I wanted them to know we were entering a new era. I just hoped they'd take me seriously. I had a history of various projects that had ended in failure, such as trying to talk hardened Welsh farmers into becoming organic, or convince the people of Caernarvon that they were ready for a health food shop.

'It's the future,' I had told them.

'Health food shop? What sort of talk is that, boyo? We've got three bloody greengrocers already.'

'I've got something very important to tell you,' I said now, which I thought would get everyone's attention. But before I could start, Sam asked me how long we were going to go on living in a house that was too small for us.

'Yes, Dad,' Lysta and Seth agreed, wanting to be off, seeking a new adventure in another country.

'Why can't we go and live in Egypt?' said Lysta. I knew immediately why she had put forward that idea. Greg, a Canadian friend we'd met on Ikaria, had travelled there and sent us postcards telling us what a remarkable country it was and suggesting we join him.

Sam couldn't understand why we didn't just leave, as we did when we went to Ikaria, and see what happened when we got there. Ros too said she would be quite happy if we upped sticks and went in search of something new. I was facing a rebellion and, completely out of character, found myself trying to talk some practical sense: that once we had some money in the bank, we could go on our travels again.

'We're broke. Why do you think your mother goes to jumble sales every week?'

'She'd go anyway. She loves them,' said Lysta dismissively.

'Listen to me. I have the makings of a new business. We can make a lot of money,' I told them. 'We had no money on Ikaria, even though I worked every day, while all of you had a long holiday in the sun.'

When I at last managed to explain my idea, which I'd hoped would be met with some enthusiasm, they grudgingly

4

accepted it, but repeated that living in a semi-detached house in a Cotswold town was not for them, which I well understood.

'Well, for a while we'll have to make a few adjustments and fit in with our new surroundings.' Three years was all I needed, I said, knowing that is a long time in a child's life, but thinking their dissatisfactions would be forgotten once they'd settled into their new school. Although Ros agreed, in the months that followed it was she who felt the most displaced, and she showed little interest in anything beyond the four walls of our house.

Meanwhile, I became completely absorbed in what could be done with that obnoxious sticky liquid, a refined by-product of oil – resin. I'd already learnt how to make moulds of little ornaments with silicone rubber. This was done by adding various filler powders and then mixing it to the right consistency. That was the easy part; if it was so simple everyone would be doing it. The hard part was to make the perfect replica.

Silicone is so sensitive it will reproduce every minute mark on any surface: your fingerprints, even the miniature veins in an oak leaf. The mould will hold this memory for hundreds of castings, using just a few penceworth of resin. That was the sum total of my knowledge. What I needed to discover was how to give the pieces I had in mind the aged look of a centuries-old antique.

In the beginning of a new cycle in one's life, it's uncanny how one can be invisibly nudged in the right direction; how your luck can change. As was illustrated by Dr Harvey, after he'd diagnosed my infected ingrowing toenail and I'd lost the prescription he'd given me for antibiotics. I knew he lived in Victoria Road so went and knocked on his door, hoping he could give me a replacement. He showed me into his sitting room, where I was immediately drawn to a collection of beautifully carved ivories in a glass cabinet, particularly a finely detailed piece of several rats in a cornsack. He told me the carvings were Japanese and called netsukes, and that he'd started collecting them while practising medicine in the Far East. I explained to generous Dr Harvey what I was up to, though I probably went too far when I said the techniques I was developing were going to make me an extremely rich man. He was so intrigued he said I could borrow the rats, on the understanding that they wouldn't be damaged. I'd found the first vital prerequisite for my venture – an exquisite piece to replicate.

I became so obsessed Ros and the children hardly saw me. Of course I always went home for supper; eating together was a ritual we never liked to miss. But then I was out again, driving the twenty minutes to the workshop to continue my experiments. Pearl now knew the odd hours I kept and neighed quite differently in the evenings, constantly scraping her hoof, knowing another snack was on its way. I always fed her, whatever time I turned up, and spent a few minutes with her. I don't know why I felt it necessary to tell her what I was up to; maybe it concerned me that she must be bored, leaning out of the stable half-door, with only the trains passing on the viaduct to break the monotony of her solitary night life.

To make instant antiques, I needed some sort of stain, which I was certain you couldn't buy off the shelf because it didn't exist. There was no alternative: I would have to find the secret formula through trial and error. As I fed Pearl an apple and stroked her neck, I heard myself thinking out loud, 'I have to become an alchemist.'

During those night hours working alone I wondered whether I was pursuing delusional dreams, losing my foothold in reality. Well, you would, spending so long alone beneath a single fluorescent tube that attracted an array of dancing insects, as if in a strange solitary confinement.

Things changed when Ros asked me to go to the chemist to get some cough medicine for Lysta; hardly the place you would have imagined for an illuminating meeting, but it was Walter Pepper, the pharmacist, who showed me the path. I happened to mention to him in passing what I was up to and that probably a chemist would have the answer.

He was a thin, pale man in his mid-sixties with a somewhat ghostly look, his hair the colour of an early morning cloud that the light passed through. However, there was a keen look in his eye that showed he was more than just a man in a white coat standing behind the counter. I also had a strange sensation that we'd met before and he was coming back into my life.

Of course, I exaggerated the importance of my endeavours. I'd heard that one should never undersell oneself so I told him I was in search of the Holy Grail, but it was all hush-hush for commercial reasons. This raised his eyebrows and curiosity enough to ask me what it was that I needed to find out.

'I'm trying to make instant antiques. Replicas, to be precise,' I whispered, to give it more emphasis.

He closed the shop at six o'clock, and over a cup of tea in a quiet little café in Black Jack Street I revealed my plan. And the more he heard, the more interested and excited he became. When Doreen, the café owner, who obviously knew Walter, came and told us it was closing time, he bribed her to let us stay another half hour by buying a couple of slices of her chocolate gateau.

'I cannot begin to tell you how much this means to me. As a young man I was fascinated by patinations to be put on to decorative arts. I wanted to work in a bronze foundry, but my father wouldn't have it.'

'We were meant to meet,' I said. 'But how do you think you can help me?'

'I know the periodic table and many chemical formulas.'

'That sounds good, but I don't know what it means.'

And I wouldn't, not that evening, as Doreen was impatiently ushering us towards the door.

'Walter,' she said, 'I don't think I've ever heard you talk so much, and for so long.'

'That makes two of us,' he said, smiling.

We parted, and as I walked home I was convinced that with Walter's knowledge and my enthusiasm there was a chance I had the makings of a real business. That evening after the children had gone to bed I said to Ros, 'Isn't it strange how three little mundane things can alter your life?'

'What do you mean?'

'An ingrowing toenail, a lost prescription, and Lysta needing some cough medicine.'

A week later, as I lay in bed with Ros, the telephone rang.

'It must be something serious for someone to be ringing at this time of night. You'd better go and answer it.'

Which I did, and listened to the quiet tones of Walter Pepper speaking softly into the mouthpiece, as if he didn't want to be overheard. He sounded like a spy in a John le Carré novel, calling in with some vital information.

'Can you get hold of a fish kettle?' he asked. I thought he was speaking in code. No one had ever said that to me before.

'Did you say a fish kettle?' I whispered back.

'That is you, Mr Perry?'

'Yes, but call me Nick.'

'Can you get hold of a fish kettle?'

'I don't know.'

'Well, we need one. I have the answer.'

Then he put the phone down, so I went back to bed where Ros was anxiously waiting to hear who had called.

'Walter Pepper wants a fish kettle. He says he knows how to turn my netsukes into instant antiques.'

Two days later I managed to find one in *Exchange and Mart*, on the Isle of Skye of all places. An old lady called Mrs MacGrogan living in a crofter's cottage had cooked her salmon in it for over thirty years. We settled on eighteen pounds, cheaper than the postage to get it delivered to me. It looked like a large oval aluminium saucepan with a lid. I carried it round to Walter's Georgian house in Dollar Street and down into the basement. He was listening to Eric Clapton's 'Layla', eager and excited, wearing a rubber apron and Marigold gloves, saying we must thank Timothy Cook's verruca for his amazing discovery. Apparently, Timothy's mother had asked for something to deal with the ugly growth that had suddenly appeared on the underside of her son's large toe, and this was the result. 'To Timothy Cook's verruca,' I said, pretending to raise a glass.

Walter held up a sachet of purple crystals under the bare light bulb and slowly emptied the contents into the fish kettle. He'd been heating up a large container of water on an old oven and kept checking the temperature until it reached precisely twenty-five degrees, when he poured it carefully over the potassium permanganate, which he told me was the chemical name of the crystals.

I passed him the dozen casts I'd made of the delicate cornsack. One at a time he submerged them into the steaming dark liquid. This was an incredible moment of anticipation, the hope of a breakthrough so exciting me that I began to sweat, a side effect of some psychological state I had not experienced before. Walter slowly counted down the seconds on his wristwatch. At the precise moment he reached zero, he sank his hand into the fish kettle and then held out in front of me the first cornsack, covered in a light brown coating similar in colour to the original. I gasped.

'Perfect!'

But Walter wasn't completely satisfied, and proceeded to take out the remaining pieces at carefully timed intervals. Each one had a slightly different depth of colour.

'I think the finish is too even,' he said. 'They don't have the worn look of objects that have been handled thousands of times over the past two hundred years.'

'You're quite right,' I said, although I doubted whether anyone else would have spotted it.

But Walter was insistent, convinced that if we put them next to the original there was a subtle difference that an expert's discerning eye would detect.

'This one's pretty close, though I think it needs to go through another process. But it's been a good night's work.'

'Let me take it with me. I have more things to do.'

'Don't pick it up with your bare hands. It will stain your fingers like nicotine. People will think you're a heavy smoker.'

That night Walter became a friend. I hadn't expected him to be so interested in what I was up to, but when we went and had a drink in the Oddfellows in Chester Street it became obvious how lonely he was, and that what I was pursuing could fill some of the empty hours in his life. It led to the inevitable question of money, which we delicately danced around for a few minutes before he asked me if I needed an investment, something that hadn't entered my head.

'How much do you want?' he asked.

'Not a lot . . . in fact nothing at all,' I said uncertainly.

'Well, you can't build a business without any capital,' he said, sipping his ginger beer; he didn't indulge in alcohol. 'I want to help you get started. I have nothing else going on nowadays, not since my wife died.'

'You know so much you could certainly help me, but I can't afford to pay you, not at this stage.'

'There's something about you. Maybe it's your infectious enthusiasm, but I do feel I could be of use,' he said, giving me an open, receptive look, free of cynicism. He could easily have had doubts; I had no experience, just the energetic drive of a young man, and we were opposites in so many ways. Walter had lived a conventional life and was coming to the end of a successful career.

'You know, I'd have thought you'd be a classical man, someone who liked Mozart, not Eric Clapton.'

'You're right, but it's never too late to be surprised by yourself. It's a new beginning, and I'm excited about the journey we're embarking on.'

'Let's meet next week and come to an agreement on how we can work together,' I said.

The next day I collected the fish kettle from him, bought two jars of potassium permanganate and went back to the workshop to perfect the finish I needed for my rats in a cornsack. Pearl gave me welcoming neighs, leaning over her stable door, as if she had become genuinely interested in my experiments. I had a bag of apples and every time I took a break I gave her one, and usually a couple of Polos as well. As I stood back contemplating the esoteric world I had entered, she chewed on her mints, grinding them down between her teeth. How she could make such a meal out of a single Polo always amused me.

I was realising that nothing gained ever comes easily and all knowledge has to be fought for. Around me on my workbench were tins of waxes, different gauges of wire wool, bottles of acetone and thinners for the stains I was playing around with. Unfortunately, I completely forgot to slip on the Marigolds before putting my bare hand into the permanganate. It looked as if half my arm had been up a cow's backside and it was impossible to remove this embarrassing stain; too late, I remembered that Walter had warned me to always wear a pair of gloves. Only after three days of continual washing in hot soapy water did the colour gradually begin to fade. Ros found it revolting and so did the children when we sat down to supper.

'Dad, can't you wear a glove when we're eating? You're putting me off my food,' Lysta said.

'Being an alchemist has its drawbacks,' I said. 'There's always a price to pay in pursuit of the ultimate goal.'

'What is the ultimate goal?' asked Sam.

'Success and money. Things we all need. Remember, I'm not doing it just for me, but for all of us.'

This was met with a general scepticism by my family. Ros gave me a mild reassuring smile, or maybe it was a look from someone resigned to the fact that what I was involved in would have to run its course.

Ros told me Sundays had to be a family day after I'd suggested that Sam could help me by mixing up the resin using a Black and Decker drill which I'd adapted with a special propeller. It was a long job and I said I would double his pocket money, because I knew he was saving up to buy a bicycle, some flashy thing with drop handlebars. But Ros insisted I took one day off a week. I reminded her that when we were farming in North Wales I had worked seven days a week.

'But you're not farming now.'

So I conceded, knowing she was right: Belah wanted help assembling some furniture for her doll's house; Seth was keen on cricket and I'd promised him some bowling practice. Lysta was at that age when girls like to stay with each other on a Saturday night and why should Ros always be the one to go and pick her up on a Sunday morning, while Sam was keen that I go and watch him playing football for the Cirencester Under

Twelves. And then there was Ros, who never complained that I might be neglecting her. It was when she said 'We never seem to have time for ourselves' that I realised I'd got completely wrapped up in my obsession to the exclusion of everything else. Of course I had to take Sundays off. So they became sacrosanct, and difficult as it was to turn my brain off, we spent them together as a family.

But on Mondays I was out of bed at six, creeping downstairs, leaving Ros sleeping. In my search to track down the hidden secrets of those old crafts, I spent a lot of time in the library, my head buried in the pages of master craftsmen who had perfected their art in cold sheds without the comforts of the modern world. It was here, in a book on old English furniture, that I came across rottenstone, a fine limestone powder used as a polish. The words leapt off the page; this was exactly what I was looking for, the missing ingredient, and I knew I had to get some.

Walter was familiar with rottenstone and agreed to buy a bag of it, believing it could provide the answer. It's a grey dust, so fine that with just the slightest breath it floats into the air. Applying it with delicate strokes of a half-inch paintbrush over the rats in a cornsack, I was amazed to see their glossiness immediately disappearing, giving them the perfect, aged look they had been lacking. It was impossible to tell the difference between the replica and the original piece: we had done it!

The first thing I did was produce my replica at the supper table, placing it next to the original in front of the whole family.

'Which is the oldest?' I asked them. 'And which one was made five minutes ago?'

There was complete silence. 'Can we pick them up?' asked Sam.

'You can do what you like with them.'

Ros genuinely couldn't tell them apart. 'It's quite remark-able,' she said.

'Which one is it, Dad?' asked Lysta.

'Do you know, I don't think I can tell myself.'

'Does it mean we're going to make a lot of money?' was what Sam wanted to know.

'Yes, and more than that, it means when we have saved enough we can travel the world.'

'Is it still going to take three years?' asked Seth rather glumly.

'I'm afraid so, but it will pass quickly if you don't think about it.'

Over the next four months I built up a range of Japanese carvings, all of them from Dr Harvey's collection. He was so impressed by the quality of the work, he couldn't tell the difference either. And I didn't have to pay him. He was happy to have three replicas in exchange for lending me the originals.

The journey really had begun, and now I was ready to find out if there was a market for my netsukes. I'd worked out all my costings, and if I could make a profit of five pounds on each one, then I had the makings of a viable business.

❧ 2 ❦

At last the time had arrived. I'd worked incessantly, and having taken only Christmas Day off now had enough product to sell at the Birmingham rag market. I'd already driven up there to take a look; it was a weekly market held every Monday where people sold furniture, jewellery, old postcards, second-hand clothes, military memorabilia . . . you name it, you could find it there, mostly on the stalls of traders who had come down from the north.

Despite my telling her it wasn't necessary, Ros got up to see me off at five o'clock on a freezing January morning. I hadn't slept for much of the night, revved up, nervous and excited. Then there was the cold fear that the day would bring total failure, that all the work I'd done was the result of an incredible self-deception, and today life would slap me in the face and teach me the hard lesson that I was nothing but a fool.

Ros gave me a thermos of coffee, and as we hugged on the doorstep I could feel in her embrace a kind of tense hope, a will, that after all the effort we would succeed.

The car wouldn't start, even though I had the choke out, and as I kept turning the ignition the battery began to fade and eventually died. I said to Ros I'd give it one more go, although I'd probably already flooded the engine. That last try failed too and I realised we were doomed. I was not going to Birmingham today. Ros was still standing on the doorstep in her dressing gown, shivering.

'We could bump-start it,' she said.

'What, the two of us?'

Then, with defeat staring us in the face, who should come purring round the corner but Ben Warriner, happily whistling in his electric milk float, bottles clinking. Ros joined him at the back of the car and together they pushed the Fiat down Chester Street. The old girl finally fired up, and with my foot flat to the boards I sped off in a great surge into the starlit night. I shouldn't have beeped the horn, not at that time in the morning, but I wanted to thank Ros and Ben while I could still see them waving in the rear-view mirror.

The motorway was quiet, just lorries in the slow lane, so I kept my foot on the throttle and, with the Fiat needing a good run, did a steady eighty mph. I got to the market ten minutes early, despite the delayed start, and queued up behind Ford Transits and estate cars pulling trailers, all piled high with furniture precariously tied on to roof racks. No one was out on the frosty pavement wheeler-dealing. Everyone sat in their cars with the windows slightly open, having an early cigarette, exuding blue tobacco smoke into the cold morning air.

Inside, I set up the table for my stall and draped a purple curtain over it, the very one that used to hang in my grandmother's bedroom. Next I placed a wooden tiered display stand in the centre, a professional touch to show off the netsukes to their full effect. Then I just waited in the vast, freezing building; a bare, forbidding place without any heating. To get any warmth into it would be impossible. It was a harsh environment to do any business in, let alone to put a hand in your pocket and pull out some cash. I didn't know what to expect; all I felt was what the hell am I doing here?

For the first few minutes I just stood there rubbing my hands together, stamping my feet, trying to keep my blood pumping. Who on earth would want to come out at this time of day? Surely no one was that hungry to make a pound.

But I was wrong. When the great steel shutters rolled up at least a couple of dozen hardy types appeared, moving with purpose. They were all dressed as if they were going out for a

16

day in Siberia, wearing bearskin hats, balaclavas, thick heavy coats, and scarves wrapped several times around their necks. Some wore great fur boots like those worn by trappers out in the Canadian Rockies, and all of them walked with a heavy, purposeful tread, sniffing out a bargain.

The need to wheel and deal cannot be suppressed; it's in the blood and drives you on. The inner satisfaction that rushes through you when you've bought something for a pound and know you can sell it for two. That's what everyone was chasing as they pored over the stalls, picking up what interested them, holding it up in the fluorescent light to examine it with a beady eye before coming up with an offer. And then the cold smirk when they heard the asking price, which no one ever paid but haggled over instead, some seriously, others in a light-hearted fashion. We all have our individual ways of conducting a business transaction, but everyone seeks the same result: to make a profit.

The downtrodden were there as well, coming in from sleeping rough, searching out the tea trolley, hoping for a warming cup of soup. What a diverse bunch walked past my stall that first morning, most of them without two pennies to rub together. Lonely souls wanting to engage me in chat, many with their stories, some speaking of their great achievements before the cruel vagaries of fate had struck them down and now living on benefits that they drank away, all of them victims of a long run of bad luck.

And walking past them as if they didn't exist came an expensively dressed, elegant woman wearing a brown suede hat with a bright red band, a coat belted at the waist showing off her slim figure. She stood out; no one dressed up in the rag market. All you needed were large pockets to hide bundles of cash. Her name was Isobel, and she immediately admired my netsukes.

'Adorable,' she said, picking up the rats in a cornsack, smiling warmly as she held them in the palm of her gloved hand.

Retired now after many years in the diplomatic service, she told me that the finest Japanese carvings came from Kyoto in the eighteenth century, and shared more of her knowledge for the next twenty minutes.

I had to ask. 'What is it that draws you to the rag market?' She looked completely out of place.

'I come every week. I find it absolutely fascinating, and now I have discovered you,' she said, with a slightly seductive tone in her voice.

Isobel became my first ever customer, spending thirty-five pounds on five netsukes.

'They're far too cheap,' she said. 'You should charge a lot more. Not to me though, of course,' she added, with a twinkle in her eye. 'I'll come next week. You really have made my day.'

Opposite me was a woman selling Art Deco jewellery. She was doing good business, and I could tell that all those who gathered around her stall were regular customers. Most of them had eye-glasses and examined everything two inches from their noses. She stashed a lot of cash away in her money belt, and no wonder: she hadn't stopped since the market opened. Mid-morning, she came over and introduced herself as Aileen. Wearing a torn anorak and a bobble hat, she looked rather masculine and lacked the feminine touch, which I felt when we shook hands; there was a man's clasp to hers.

'There's always a lull now. Everyone disappears for a cup of tea.'

'You've been busy,' I said.

'I've been coming for years, so I have my regulars.'

'Your clientele.'

'Sounds a bit posh.'

At that point we were joined by Graeme, her partner. They lived in Lutterworth, a place I'd never heard of, and had no children, just a Jack Russell tied up under the stall. That's what Graeme told me, his heavy-lidded eyes appearing half closed and giving him a mean look, which was harsh of Mother Nature, for the rest of his face was warm and friendly. He dealt in pocket watches, and he and Aileen spent most of the week driving around looking for stock to buy.

'Do you manage to make a living from it?' I asked.

'We'd like to, but it's impossible. I'm a barmaid pulling pints three nights a week.'

'Why do you deal in pocket watches?' I asked Graeme.

'I don't know. I'm not obsessed with them, I can't repair them, and most of the ones I buy don't work.'

'He doesn't like to tell the story,' Aileen chipped in, 'he thinks it makes him sound cocky, but once he bought an old stationmaster's watch after driving all the way to Devon and made six hundred pounds. Some of them fetch a high price, but you've got to know your stuff.'

'It rarely happens, but isn't that what we're all after, searching for hidden treasure?'

They were keen to know what I was up to. 'Are they antiques? They look genuine.'

'Replicas,' I said, as Graeme began picking them up, scrutinising each one under his eye-glass.

'Well, you could have fooled me,' said Aileen. They both believed I'd be successful. 'They've been faking jewellery for years, but not ivories. What a clever idea. All you have to do is keep making the same stuff, and I suppose you don't even have any competitors. We're out all week searching for something to buy.'

As I was packing away the stock I hadn't sold, I was approached by a dealer no bigger than a jockey. He was wearing a sea captain's hat, a polo-neck pullover and white bell-bottom trousers. I had to take a second look; he reminded me of a cartoon character. He was from Manchester, not that his accent gave him away, and was certainly sure of himself.

'You're a first timer, aren't you?' He was probably thinking he could put one over on me. 'I've been watching you and I think we can do some business. Are you interested?'

'Of course. Who are you?'

'They call me Sifta, but it's not my real name.'

'Yes, I can see why. You look like the chap in the salt adverts.'

'I've heard that a thousand times. Now, are you interested? I can sell your stuff up north.'

'You mean you'd be my sort of agent?'

'Not really. Give me your best trade price and whatever I sell I'll pay you every Monday. SOR, of course.'

'What does that mean?'

'Sale or return.'

'How do I know I can trust you?'

'Ask anyone. I've been coming here for five years, so take it or leave it.'

'Okay. Why not?' What had I got to lose? So I gave him all the stock I had, quoting the same price I'd been charging everyone that morning, seven pounds each.

'Is that the best you can do?'

'Yes. I can't go any cheaper than that.'

'What's your retail price?'

'I'm not sure. Something like fifteen pounds,' which didn't sound convincing and Sifta knew it.

'You're making this up as you go along.'

'Well, what do you think the retail price should be?'

'Twenty-five at least.'

'What?'

'This is quality. Can't you see that your pieces look like the real McCoy?'

'I've never understood that expression. Who exactly is the real McCoy?'

I packed each of the netsukes into a little parcel of bubble wrap, and after Sifta had filled a carrier bag he stood there staring at me.

'What's up?' I said.

'The little matter of a list and the prices you're charging me.'

'Of course.' I wrote one on the back of a receipt I found crumpled up in my trouser pocket.

'See you next Monday,' he said, and sauntered away. What a strange character. He seemed to have walked off the pages of a comic book. Cocky as well, no doubt compensating for his lack of inches.

I counted the cash I had taken, all one hundred and forty pounds of it. I hadn't realised it was that much. Not bad for a morning's work, although in reality it wasn't: it had taken months to reach this point. I was about to leave when Aileen came over and said, 'I wouldn't do that if I were you.'

'Do what?'

'Count your money out like that in full view of everyone. You're asking for trouble.'

'Why?'

'You'll get mugged.' A warning I heeded, and as I walked to the car everyone suddenly looked suspicious to me, as if they were eyeing me up, waiting for the right moment to pounce and rob me of my morning's takings. One of the homeless tramps approached me with his hand out, asking if I could stretch to a cup of tea. I searched for some loose change and when I could only come up with 10p he turned away, muttering in disgust, 'Tighter than a fish's arse.'

When I got home I emptied my pockets on the kitchen table, and apart from Belah, who was washing a plastic doll in a bubble bath, everyone gathered around.

'Count it,' I said to Sam.

'Are we rich?' asked Lysta.

'We're heading in the right direction,' I said, thoroughly enjoying the moment, glad that Ros and the children could see that I had not been wasting my time.

'A hundred and forty pounds,' said Sam.

'It can take people two weeks to make that sort of money,' I told them, 'and I made it in just one morning.'

Ros suggested we put a hundred pounds in the bank and start saving up for our next adventure.

'Yes, Egypt!' said Lysta, punching the air.

At six o'clock I went to see Walter and told him the news. I was more than a little excited, in fact it was hard to suppress exactly what I was feeling. We were on our way. At last, we were going to make some money.

'This is just the beginning,' I told him. 'But we need to expand the range. The stall looked half empty with just those few netsukes.'

'I have a surprise for you,' he said, opening a large cardboard box. 'Do you know what scrimshaw is?'

'No. It sounds like someone's surname, an old-fashioned one. Mr Scrimshaw, headmaster.'

'No, nothing like that,' Walter said, taking out several individually wrapped parcels which he undid one by one, laying in front of me six whale's teeth. He went on to tell me that whaling men had carved them for their loved ones back home to while away the slack hours becalmed on faraway oceans.

The engravings depicted the men at work, up in the crow's nest, or unfurling the sails; the ships they had sailed in, the

Royal George, the *Eagle*, the *Vicksburg* and the *Dakota*, fighting the waves on stormy seas. Some showed dramatic chases: whales with tail fins rising, men in smaller boats aiming harpoons. It was a brutal way to make a living, but in those days no one questioned the morality of it, any more than they worried about the trade in ivory. Then there were engravings for sweethearts left behind, of a girl's name and an arrow through a heart: 'To you dear Susan, to when we meet again.' Two immediately stood out as moneyspinners, one a finely etched portrait of Napoleon in his tricorn hat, and the other of Rachel Pringle, a well-known buxom lady who accommodated the lonely sailors in Barbados. Most of them looked as if they had been etched with a blunt needle, probably the same one they used to repair torn sails after a storm. Touching as some of the images were, they lacked a delicate hand.

'This is scrimshaw.'

'I know people will collect these,' I said to Walter. 'Where did you get them? What's the deal we have to do?'

'I told you about the old friend I was at university with? His grandfather was a whaler and brought them back whenever he had shore leave. He wants nothing in return, but I think we should give him some replicas.'

'And what do you want, Walter? All I ever give you are my grateful thanks. It doesn't feel right.'

'Wait and see. I'm planning on retiring in six months. Later this week I'm talking to someone about taking over the pharmacy.'

I was convinced I was on my way to making a fortune. Tomorrow I needed a long, uninterrupted day casting the netsukes and making moulds of the scrimshaw. And I would take my record player out to the workshop and put the twin speakers on opposite walls. I'd be jammin' all day to Bob Marley.

When I got home I found Ros sitting alone at the kitchen table, the children in bed, thank goodness.

'I'm sorry, Ros. I know it's late, but I've some great news.'

'I don't think we can go on much longer,' was all she said. It was enough to tell me our savings were running out and we were heading towards a financial crisis.

'But what about today? We're on our way now. I'll be bringing in money every week.'

'All you've done is gradually empty the coffers, and we've bills to pay. Maybe you should get a part-time job.'

'I'll borrow some money from my mother.'

'There's more going out than coming in, that's the problem.'

The next evening when I met Walter he could see I was subdued. 'You don't seem yourself tonight,' he said.

I told him we were running out of money, Ros was fed up and I needed to get a job. He immediately offered to lend me a thousand pounds. 'Pay me back when the business can afford it.'

'Are you sure?'

'Of course. We're in this together, and the sooner we start selling some scrimshaw the better.'

I banked Walter's loan and told Ros the money would soon be rolling in. Brave words, I knew, but said to reassure her. That evening I sent Sam to the Friar Tuck fish and chip shop in Dyer Street to celebrate the breathing space Walter had given us, rallying the troops, telling them we were close to a major victory.

'Yes, Dad, we're all in this together. We know.'

'I'm a man not given to repeating himself.'

'We've heard that before, Dad.'

We were eating our suppers out of the newspaper, after Lysta said it would save on the washing up.

'I know we're hard up, and it's good to save water, but I want a plate with some tomato sauce.'

'Dad, use your fingers. It's what we did when we lived in caves.'

'That was thousands of years ago, and they didn't have newspapers then.'

Ros came to the table with a handful of receipts. 'I found these in a pair of your trousers. Are you going to file them away?'

I had kept all my invoices in a goldfish bowl since the creature's mysterious disappearance. The subject came up from time to time and had never been resolved.

'It can't just vanish into thin air,' I said to Seth. 'Somebody knows what happened to it.'

'Dad, supposing a nameless person had taken a bath with the goldfish and Nemo had gone down the plughole,' said Lysta, who always liked to point me in the right direction with subtle hints when someone was under suspicion.

'It wasn't the plughole, it was the overflow pipe,' said Seth, anxious his sister be accurate about the facts.

'Is that true, Seth? Can we at last solve the mystery?'

'It was a freak accident.'

Our household pets had become free range. Lysta's hamster had escaped its cage and now lived under the floorboards; we could hear it scratching at night. She allowed her two guinea pigs to run around the sitting room, using it as a theme park and climbing up the curtains before finishing up on the coffee table to enjoy a bowl of crisps.

The only pet I got on with was Hank, our blue budgerigar, who spent most of his time looking at himself in the mirror and jumping up and down on his perch to peck on a bell. He had a strange impediment: unable to sing, he repetitively hummed the first few bars of 'It's A Long Way To Tipperary'. I had no idea how this tune got stuck in his head.

Ros and I had a new sleeping arrangement, one that suited us both. I followed her to bed half an hour after she had gone upstairs, as she was fed up with me tossing and turning. I could never just switch off and damp down what was passing through my brain. While everyone slept I kept thinking about scrimshaw, more ideas spinning around me in the darkness, like planes banked up, waiting to come into land.

❧ 3 ❧

My mother lived in Bath, about forty-five minutes from Cirencester. She was an unusual woman who lived alone but attracted men, not only because she was good-looking, but also because she was a good listener and a sympathetic soul. Consequently, she had built up a following of retired gentlemen who escorted her to art galleries and lectures. She never refused an invitation to an exhibition or to hear an expert talking on any subject, whether it was the history of the Roman Empire or the Icelandic Cod Wars, as long as it was followed by tea and cake. She had a sweet tooth and was never more than fifty yards from a Bakewell tart.

She had always been a loving mother and supported me with an exuberance that knew no bounds. Nothing was beyond reach, everything was attainable, but she couldn't suppress her laughter when I told her she could well end up being the mother of a millionaire.

'It's not that funny; I'm being serious.'

'You're on the road to riches,' she said, and couldn't wait to tell me that I could rent a stall for ten pounds at the antiques market in Bath every Wednesday.

'I've spoken to Mr Capstick-Dale, the man who runs it, and he assures me he has stalls available. You will come, won't you?'

'Of course. It's an opportunity not to be missed, and, despite your amused reaction, another step on the journey to becoming a millionaire in three years and then travelling the world.'

'That's marvellous. But be realistic, darling: give yourself five years.'

'I'll meet you on Wednesday at eleven.'

'Stay for lunch; we'll finish it off with a lemon drizzle cake.

And then could you take some bookshelves to Roger for me? He only lives in Julian Road.'

For the rest of the week I worked frantically, casting netsukes to replenish my stock. And as I waited for them to cure (by that I mean harden), I poured silicone over the whale's teeth. Such was my concentration and involvement in what I was doing that when I took a break and walked outside, it was as if I had entered some other, disconnected world, far removed from the hours spent alone casting and de-moulding.

When I got home in the evenings the family said I smelt of resin; I couldn't smell it myself, putting their reaction down to an over-evolved olfactory nerve, one of those dominant genes that is usually found in police sniffer dogs. The children said I stank and Ros insisted I undress outside in the back porch, after which I ran through the house in my vest and pants and took a shower before covering myself in Old Spice, an aftershave you could smell coming down the street a hundred yards away.

It had always been agreed that supper was the time when we could speak our minds and get anything off our chests. Ros and I thought it important that children should be both seen and heard and needed to be encouraged to express themselves. We hoped they'd carry the self-confidence it would give them into their adult lives. Not that we dwelt on it; I usually said, 'Spit it out, then; let's hear what you've got to say.'

'We have to save money Dad,' Lysta said, in a very matter of fact way. They had obviously been talking about it, probably after lights out. Sam and Lysta shared the same room in bunk beds, while Seth was only feet away in a little annexe. The thing that astonished me was the sense they were talking, although it had the hallmarks of Ros all over it.

'We will, and then move on,' I promised them.

'You tell him, Mum.'

'No, I'll tell him,' said Sam.

'What is it?'

'We want to move. We don't like living here.'

'Oh . . . I wasn't expecting that.'

'I would prefer to be living out in the country,' Ros confessed. 'I don't think we're suited to living in a town.'

'No, Dad, we aren't,' said Lysta emphatically, which suggested she'd not budge on the subject.

'We haven't got the money,' I said. 'Why do you think we're living in a semi-detached? Because that's all we could afford.'

'Can't we sell up and start a new life somewhere?' said Sam. 'We could live in Canada. It's huge, and they're part of the Commonwealth and speak English.'

'The first thing to do is to make some money, then anything is possible,' I said.

It was pretty miserable to hear that my family wasn't happy where we were living. What was worse, there was nothing I could do about it, except become financially successful. If I didn't we would be going nowhere. I fell back on some amateur dramatics.

'Trust me,' I said. 'Give your father a chance. I'm on my way to becoming a millionaire, do you hear me? A millionaire!'

Five o'clock, Monday morning, when most of the human race was asleep under their eiderdowns. I'd revved up the Fiat the night before and put a blanket over the engine. I had also laid cardboard over the windscreen and bought some de-icer just in case. I'd managed to replace all my stock of netsukes and loaded everything into the boot. Ros had bought me a bear-skin hat at a church jumble sale that made me look like a Russian peasant. I was wearing two pairs of socks and my old farming coat. Ros handed me a thermos of vegetable soup and stood on the doorstep putting her hands together as if seeking divine intervention, but it wasn't necessary.

My preparation paid off, and the engine fired up on only the second attempt. I was on my way. Lying next to me on the passenger seat was my cassette player; the car radio had broken long ago. I cruised out of Cirencester towards the M5 listening to Bob Seger and the Silver Bullet Band singing 'Still The Same', one of those tracks I played over and over again. I was in a completely different frame of mind from my first trip last week, knowing what to expect this time. I had to attract more dealers, which I knew would only happen if they saw more activity going on around the stall.

The temperature was up a few degrees when I arrived, traders already walking up and down the pavement, shining torches, peering into one another's vehicles before the doors were opened at seven o'clock. Any dealing beforehand was strictly forbidden and broke the trading by-laws. But no one seemed to care, some already lifting furniture off roof racks. A Transit van with Dutch number plates full of jukeboxes and slot machines had stirred the interest of a few dealers, who were shouting to be heard as they tried to out-bid one another. It was similar to a pack of wolves moving in on the kill: it's every man for himself when demand exceeds supply.

All this I could see as I sat in the Fiat changing tapes, trying to find Dire Straits' 'Telegraph Road'. Aileen walked past carrying her Jack Russell. Graeme, smoking a Hamlet cigar, shouted out 'Good luck' to me, crossing his fingers as the doors were slowly wound upwards.

After I'd set up the stall I only had to wait five minutes before I was approached by a diminutive figure wearing a flat cap, with a remarkable similarity to Barney Rubble in *The Flintstones*. He was carrying a collection of walking sticks in a leather golf bag over his shoulder. He introduced himself as Frank Webb in a rich Brummie accent and produced a wooden carving of a swan's head from his pocket.

'All right, kid, can you make this?' he asked, shoving it into my hand.

'Don't see why not,' I replied, almost indifferently. It was part of my new strategy not to appear too keen.

'Can you do it for two quid and make it look like mahogany?'

That I had to think about, and hummed and hawed for a minute, practising a bit of method acting, putting on a dubious look.

'Sifta said you could do it for two quid.'

Which I knew he hadn't, and if he had it was a darn right lie.

'I can do it for three and not a penny less.' I wasn't too good at haggling; I wanted to concede and get the business, but if there was no profit in it, what was the point? We were joined then by one of the great unwashed with black, greasy hair, carrying a Gladstone bag. He was a shadowy figure, like a Victorian prowler and someone you would run away from in a dark alley. That was my first impression of Gerald, until I heard his Brummie accent and realised he was Frank's sidekick.

'He can do it for three, Gerald,' I heard Frank say to him under his breath.

'Did I hear that right, two pounds fifty, was that what you said?'

'No, Frank was right. Three pounds is the best I can do.'

'I must get my ears waxed,' said Gerald, turning to Frank. 'I'm sure I heard him say two pounds fifty.'

'Or was it two seventy-five? I don't think I heard him either,' said Frank.

I wasn't sure if I was involved in a business transaction or listening to a comedy duo rehearsing some new material.

Then Sifta turned up and slapped me on the shoulder, telling me of the countless opportunities there could be with Frank and Gerald. 'They sell at all the big fairs: Charnock Richard, Newark, Ardingly,' he said, handing me eighty pounds in cash in front of them. 'That's for you and it's just the beginning.'

'Do it for two pounds fifty,' said Gerald.

'Three pounds,' I said. 'That's my final offer.'

They agreed and ordered twenty swan heads for their walking sticks. I said I would bring them next week, even though I hadn't got any mahogany stain and I could only cast three a day.

Sifta wanted to take all the netsukes I had, but it wasn't even eight o'clock and I told him I could only give him what stock I had left when the market closed at one.

'Make more of the stuff. You've got to grab the opportunity now.'

No sooner had they all moved on than the Dutch guy selling jukeboxes came over, tall and rugged, wearing a leather jacket, a thick moustache covering his top lip. He wore cowboy boots and had a tattoo that spelt out someone's name across his knuckles, but they were never still long enough to be able to read what it said.

'I'm Kase, from Amsterdam. I come over three or four times a year,' he said, after a rather robust handshake. 'If you make all this yourself, you could be useful to me.'

'I do, down in Gloucestershire,' I told this Dutchman who was probably selling jukeboxes all over the world, mostly to millionaires.

'Well, find me a Wurlitzer and you'll be a friend for life.'

Not only was he likeable, but he was also successful and had a network of people throughout America and Europe looking out for musical memorabilia. He shipped in his jukeboxes from the States and hired them out for parties, or to film companies; they were even on cruise liners. When I told him what I was trying to achieve, he could see it had possibilities.

'What is it you really want? That's what you have to ask yourself.'

'I want to make the best replicas in the world.'

It certainly made him think. An intense look came over him as he paced up and down, rubbing his chin, and he nearly collided with Isobel, who greeted me with a warm, brightly lipsticked smile. She wasn't alone.

'This is my friend Rosemary from Solihull,' she said, introducing me to a middle-aged lady who looked like a librarian, with blue-rinsed hair and a great deal of face powder. Both she and Isobel were overdressed in the sparse surroundings of the rag market. 'I've told Rosemary all about you and she's going to become a regular customer, aren't you, Rosemary?'

Meanwhile Kase continued to pace up and down, somewhat distracting my visitors.

'Has that man got a lot on his mind?' Isobel asked.

'Yes, but I couldn't tell you what.'

Rosemary, who was captain of the Solihull Bowls Club, seemed keen to speak to me. She was clearly impatient to get through the small talk and having to listen to Isobel giving the impression we knew one another well.

'Do you know what an okimono is?'

'Yes, I do. A Japanese decorative carving.'

'Well, if you're interested, I have a superb example of a reclining boar,' she said, unwrapping a wooden carving from a parcel of yellow crepe paper. 'Don't you think it's beautiful?'

'I do . . . are you offering it to me to make a replica?'

'Yes, but first we need to come to an arrangement, don't we?' she said, turning to Isobel and giving her a look that showed they were in cahoots. I realised that this could happen a lot, people coming with pieces to be reproduced. I needed to have a standard response rather than negotiate every time.

'Well, if we can reach an agreement, and on the understanding that I can sell the piece wherever I choose, I'll give you the first three I produce free of charge by way of payment.'

I thought I stated it very clearly and gave the impression that I knew what I was talking about. I felt rather pleased with myself.

'Fine,' Rosemary said, and turned her attention to the netsukes I was selling. She bought four of them for seven pounds each. I wanted to ask more but couldn't, not with Isobel there.

Kase, who had been hovering and getting more agitated all this time, finally interrupted us. He was so keen to discuss an idea that he swung me round and put both hands on my shoulders.

'Can you keep a secret?' he said, his piercing blue eyes staring into mine. I found myself hoping he wasn't mad before I answered.

'Of course I can. I've never had any trouble in the past.'

'We'll come back later,' said Isobel indignantly. 'This gentleman obviously has something of the utmost urgency to say to you.'

He bombarded me with a series of questions, where did I live, what were my mould-making skills, could I airbrush, could I make larger pieces. After finally satisfying himself, he said he'd like to come to the workshop in a month's time.

'I shall bring you something that will change your life.'

It was big talk that I doubted would come to anything. He followed it up with a hug, pulling my head into his chest.

'I like you. I've got a good feeling about you.'

We exchanged telephone numbers and he stood staring at me for a few seconds, a huge smile spreading across his face. Aileen opposite had seen what was happening and when he eventually left she shouted, 'What was that all about? Has he fallen in love with you?'

The rest of the morning wasn't busy, just a steady trickle of people coming to the stall, most of them time-wasters wanting to talk about themselves and the hardships they had to endure. Aileen said if I gave them a sympathetic ear I'd never get rid of them, and they were bad for business. 'If you give them money they'll keep coming back and they'll put people off coming to the stall,' she shouted over to me.

Another fast-talking dealer came to see if there was anything we could get going together, a Scouser from the Wirral who had a shop in Birkenhead selling stripped pine. Initially it was difficult to keep my eyes off him: his face was covered with a mass of little white circles, as if he had a rare pigment deficiency. He told me these blemishes were the result of acid burns from years of stripping pine.

'Self-inflicted,' he said brazenly, passing it off as no more than a hazard of the job. 'I need ornaments; statues to display on my dressers. I'm fed up with Delft dinner plates.'

'I'll come up with something,' I said, never wanting to stop a door from opening.

As I was packing up, Sifta appeared to see how many netsukes I could give him, and cursed when I said I only had twelve left.

'You've got to increase production. No one's going to get rich on these meagre offerings.'

That night, I told Ros I had a job vacancy, or rather a vacancy to be filled. 'I need someone who is easy-going, pays attention to detail and can use a paintbrush.'

'Have you anyone in mind?'

'Yes . . . I was thinking of you.'

'You're joking, of course.'

'Not at all.'

'What about Belah?' she asked.

'She can come out to the workshop and play with her doll's house all day.'

It was early spring, with the daffodils flowering, and new-born lambs running around the fields of Frampton Mansell. Ros and I had been working together for over a month, taking the twenty-minute drive to Puckmill each morning, out in the countryside where we were both happy to be. What had once been a chaotic workshop with drums of resin and acetone lying around the place had now been tidied up and everything given a home.

We paid a pensioner, Tom Minety, to put up some shelves and build a couple of workbenches. Every Sunday he rang the bells in the village church and led the local ramblers on walks along the many canals to be found in Gloucestershire. He rambled vocally, too, and never started work until he'd had a cup of tea and a chat. His claim to fame was that he had once swum the English Channel covered in goose fat, a feat he reminded us of at least every other day. 'Did I tell you I once swam the English Channel?' He had many irritating traits and you wondered how his wife of nearly forty years had endured them for so long. He thought out loud, mumbling to himself as he measured up pieces of wood, 'Now where is that damn pencil?' when it was usually behind his ear. He had another annoying habit of finishing your sentences for you. The only time we were spared it was when he used the circular disc to sand down the MDF worktops, meticulously checking everything with a spirit level, after I had told him I needed flat surfaces, critical when you're filling moulds.

Unfortunately, he became besotted with Ros, and after he had finished working for us he dropped in every day under false pretences, such as suddenly finding a spare tin of emulsion and offering to paint the shelves free of charge, when all he really wanted to do was ogle Ros and engage her in the most trivial conversation.

To break up the working day Ros and I walked along the canal at lunchtime, Belah on my shoulders. We'd eat a picnic by the side of the towpath and throw bread to two swans who were building a nest nearby. Puckmill was situated below the village, quiet and remote. My nearest neighbour, Dr Booth, lived on the other side of the viaduct with his wife and four children.

Now that the grass was growing again, Celia asked me if I would walk Pearl out into the field behind the workshop in the morning and bring her back in each evening. I'd break up a bale of hay for her too. I enjoyed these little agricultural interludes, even though my mind was always on work. Whoever said the first million is the hardest was probably right. And the first ten thousand is even harder.

I'd rented a stall in the Bath antiques market every Wednesday and could hardly keep up with demand. My mother made me packed lunches and always came with one of her gentlemen friends. Although she didn't know it, she was an extremely good saleswoman, praising my replicas to those she brought to the stall, pointing out the quality of the workmanship.

'Am I right, darling, that this piece of scrimshaw was originally engraved by a Napoleonic prisoner of war?'

That's when I whispered in her ear, 'Mother, less of the darling please; it undermines my professionalism.'

She was proud to show me off as a skilled artisan. If she'd been on commission I'd be owing her a fair bit. My mother had natural, unconscious flair and her admirers were happy to put their hands in their pockets.

Now I was making a range of scrimshaw and over thirty different netsukes, Ros could see just how much cash we were taking and offered to keep the books, knowing full well that I was still stuffing invoices into the goldfish bowl.

'It will get out of hand if we don't do something about it now. We need to get an accountant.'

It was something I'd kept putting off, using the excuse that we hadn't been trading for a year. That made no difference to Ros, who knew that one day the tax man would come calling.

'And you need to get into the habit of keeping petrol receipts.'

Walter Pepper came to visit me at the workshop. It was the first time he had been out to Frampton Mansell, and we'd agreed that now he had finally completed the sale of the pharmacy we would talk about how he could get more involved in the business, which I had recently registered at Companies House, trading as Puckmill Studios, my mother's suggestion. He drove into the yard in a Subaru pick-up, which I hadn't been expecting, wearing jeans and a lumberjack's shirt. Used to seeing him immaculately dressed with not a hair out of place, I'd never imagined him looking so casual, his hair blown into a white heap like a breaking wave.

I showed him round, meeting Ros as she swept a pile of horse droppings down the centre aisle. We took it in turns to muck out Pearl and put fresh bedding in her stall. He was impressed and nodded agreeably, clearly seeing some structure in our modest set-up, although he did have one reservation.

'I'm not sure about the horse. It doesn't seem to create the right image.'

'She's not ours; she came with the workshop.'

We went up to the Crown Inn, sat in the saloon bar and set about discussing the future. I needed Walter around me for all sorts of reasons, not just experimenting with new finishes and helping me with product development. I also hoped he could keep me on track, stop me pursuing things that I probably shouldn't. It was the story of my life, my brother Jack liked to remind me, and why, he said, I would never become a millionaire: I'd soon get bored and then distracted when something else presented itself. Walter might not have been flamboyant, but he had a more measured approach than my own and I liked to think he wouldn't be wasting his time with a complete idiot.

He was also a quiet, intelligent man and had a precise way of summing things up. He'd handed over the pharmacy to a newly qualified chemist from Gloucester and was now retired from a profession he had followed for thirty-five years. He never mentioned the deal he had done, but he was obviously comfortably off.

Over a couple of prawn cocktails and chocolate chip ice creams we spoke honestly to each other and found a way forward that we were both happy with. I would be Head of Production and Sales, a grand title I know, but two roles I was at home with, although I struggled with the early morning starts. Walter would work in his basement perfecting the finishes we needed to expand the ranges. I bestowed upon him the title Master of Chemistry and Alchemy, making it sound as if we had a laboratory.

We'd have weekly meetings in the Crown and give one another a full report on what we'd been up to. He insisted he'd only put in invoices for expenses, saying it was unrealistic to talk about any other kind of remuneration until the business could afford it.

'You know,' he said, 'I really think we can do it. I can't tell you how excited I am, I have a new meaning and purpose in my life.'

Kase from Amsterdam rang; it had been so long since we'd met in the rag market that I thought it had all just been talk. Especially when he'd told me he was bringing me something that would change my life. Words are a cheap commodity in the markets, where people talk themselves up into something that they're plainly not.

He was leaving in the morning, taking a boat from the Hook of Holland to Harwich. He had nowhere to stay, so I booked him into the Crown. They let him sleep in, and he didn't appear until eleven o'clock, looking rough and unshaven. He was driving a Volvo estate and had a woman with him who turned out to be his wife Eartha, blonde, slim and attractive, with a tiny waist like the girl in the Nimble advert who floated away under a hot air balloon. 'She flies like a bird in the sky.' She got out of the car eating a Ryvita, flicked back her hair, and kissed me on both cheeks. She was relaxed, breathing in the air, flinging her arms open in an exaggerated gesture. 'It is so beautiful here, these rolling hills and this great bridge.'

'Viaduct,' I said.

'In Holland you can see for miles, nothing but flat open countryside,' she told me. 'This is a special place, I can feel it.'

Kase seemed indifferent to Eartha's delight and I could sense his impatience. After I'd introduced them to Ros and Belah, Eartha couldn't wait to take up Ros's invitation to go for a walk along the canal. When they'd gone Kase ushered me to the back of the car.

'This is it, then,' he said, unwrapping from a blanket a dog about two feet high, with its head at a slight angle. I recognised it immediately.

'That's Nipper.' The emblem of His Master's Voice records.

'Exactly. And I want you to make two hundred of them for me.'

'What!'

'I have two hundred reproduction horn record players coming from India. Can you make a replica for me?'

'Yes, I think so, but you should have warned me. I haven't made anything this size before.'

'You have to match the colour perfectly. No one must spot the difference.'

I needed to think about it. I couldn't commit to something I might not be able to fulfil.

'It's very heavy. Do I have to match the weight?'

'Yes. Everything has to be identical.'

'I'm really not sure, Kase. I'll have to play around with it, and it will take time.'

'You have three months. That's when the record players arrive in Rotterdam.'

'We haven't talked about money,' I said.

'I'll make it easy for you. Five hundred pounds up front to make your moulds and send me a perfect sample. Then for each one I will give you thirty-five pounds.'

I had serious doubts about being able to do the job, but he had come all the way from Amsterdam and I didn't want to disappoint him. As I hesitated, he took an envelope from the Volvo's glove compartment and counted out five hundred pounds in cash. I should have said the job was hopelessly beyond me, but I couldn't bring myself to say it. I heard the words within, but never uttered them.

'Come,' he said, slapping me on the back. 'Let's find the girls and go for a walk in this beautiful valley of yours.'

During lunch in the Crown, Eartha told us about the exciting life they led, going to the States three times a year, driving around Europe buying and selling jukeboxes and music memorabilia. They had a storage warehouse outside Amsterdam, and once a year they held an auction there, inviting dealers from all over the world.

Kase was successful all right, and he made a great impression on me. It was his knowledge of the market he dealt in, nothing less than an encyclopaedia of the jukebox, and then of course his worldwide network of dealers and collectors, gradually accumulated over the past fifteen years. He was so certain about everything; he knew the costs down to the last penny, and the profit he was making. When I thought about how far he'd come to see me, I realised it had to be worth his while. He was probably a millionaire; well, if he could do it, so could I.

So the next night over supper I gave Ros and the children an update on Puckmill Studios. I told them they were all shareholders in the company and the future looked brighter than Venus.

'Why Venus?' asked Ros.

'Because I didn't want to use a cliché like very rosy indeed. We have an exciting product development programme . . .'

Sam interrupted me. 'We don't know what that means, Dad.'

'Well, it means money is coming our way, and we're on course to make a lot of it.'

'How much longer is it going to take?' asked Lysta, having heard it all before.

'Probably two years, give or take a month.'

'Then what?'

'Then the whole world opens up for us, and we begin our travels again.'

'How much money have we got in the bank?' Seth wanted to know.

'Ros, how much do you think?' I asked, not having a clue myself.

'A little less than a million. In fact a lot less.'
'Tell us, Ros. How much have we got?'
'Just over eight thousand pounds.'
'Well, that's better than having an overdraft.'

Some strange individuals came into my life whenever I was selling from the stall. All of them had one thing in common: the burning desire to make money. It was the diversity of what people dealt in that never ceased to surprise me. I soon realised there was a customer for everything, whether it was a thimble or a disused Jumbo jet. I met that one in Bath; he dismantled aeroplane interiors and sold everything he found there, including the seats. The thimble dealer was Betty Entwhistle, a fierce lady from Bognor Regis, who despite having suffered a stroke still had the willpower to search out rare examples in every street market within reach. She was a collector, and collectors are addicts, no different from those who need to go out and find their drugs.

Usually it was nothing more than curiosity that brought people over to my stall for a chat. Because I was doing something different, they came to see what I was up to; no one else was selling replicas. Most of the dealers working the markets had an interesting story to tell. I heard about the deals they had done, when money had been lost, or how they'd managed to come out on the right side by refusing to budge and standing their ground, squeezing a few pounds of profit from a deal about to go dead on them. A lot of the time I didn't sell anything, but I was forming relationships and gradually I built up a network of leads, hoping something might come my way through the grapevine.

That's why I didn't hesitate when Frank Webb asked me to make a detour and pay him a visit at his house in the Hagley Road on my way home from the rag market. Although I saw

Frank every week, he was not an extrovert, keeping himself hidden, a man of few words. He lived alone in a 1930s semi-detached, one of the identical-looking rows that went on for hundreds of yards. All I knew about him was that he and Gerald 'Greasy' Gadd had some kind of partnership, driving around the Midlands on a motorbike and sidecar, selling walking sticks and military paraphernalia. Fred Flintstone and Barney Rubble on a day out, wearing crash helmets.

When he opened the front door, I was immediately hit by the damp, musty smell of a house that hadn't been cleaned for years. Frank didn't look like someone who would go around the place with a feather duster. An overweight tabby squeezed through the cat flap with a mouse wriggling between its teeth, even though the door was wide open.

He offered me a cup of tea in the kitchen, clearing away a multitude of foil trays that came from eating nothing but takeaways. An earwig was slowly making its way across the floor and a fridge droned on in the corner, a continuous hum that I could still hear when we moved into the sitting room.

Frank hadn't warned me of what lay ahead, or rather below, because beneath us, weaving in and out of the furniture, was a model railway, travelling through a rural landscape of green fields and hillsides where sheep and cattle grazed.

'I made it all out of papier maché,' he said in his Brummie tones.

On the sideboard were train timetables, books on the history of the age of steam, and the complete works of Ian Allan, the great god of trainspotting. Through the door I could see a signal at the bottom of the stairs. The sheer scale of it, the whole sophisticated layout, with all the attention to detail, must have taken him years to complete. There were coloured posters on the walls of seaside resorts: *Welcome to Torquay, the English Riviera.*

'Come with me,' he said, and we followed the track along the hallway into a bedroom where the scenery changed dramatically as the rails passed beside the lochs of Scotland, below great snowy mountains peaks. The line then turned back on itself and made its way through towns and tunnels, children waving from a bridge, and out into the English countryside. I had walked back into another age, into the 1950s, when I too had been a child.

'So, this is your world, Frank.'

He took off his jacket and put on his porter's waistcoat, pulled out a pocket watch and blew on a tin whistle. 'Let's go and sit down,' he said.

And we did, on an uncomfortable sofa whose springs pushed into my backside, waiting for the 2.27 goods train from Waterloo to pass below us on its way to Bournemouth West. The cat sat watching as the train sped past carrying a dead mouse in one of the wagons.

In a garden shed no more than ten foot by six, Frank made his walking sticks under an eighty-watt light bulb, wearing his flat cap and keeping his tea warm on a paraffin stove. Several used tea bags hung from clothes pegs above him. He said, in passing, he could get three cups from one bag. There was a solitary photograph on the wall of a young boy and a soldier leaning out of the cab of a steam engine. I guessed it was Frank with his father, but I didn't ask, and although he could see me looking at it he said nothing.

'Do you know why I asked you here today?'

'I was wondering.'

He took from a drawer the most exquisite miniature wooden carvings of milk churns, corn sacks, trunks and suitcases, even one of a hat box. All things you would have once seen on station platforms.

'Did you carve these, Frank?'

'Yes. They took months,' he said. 'But it would only take you days to make them for me.'

It wasn't going to help me become a millionaire, but I agreed to take on the job. It was hard to price it accurately and I knew Frank would quibble no matter what I said. I quoted him three hundred pounds because the work would be so fiddly and he only wanted ten of each. In the end we agreed on two hundred and sixty pounds and I really had no idea whether I would make a profit or a loss.

I was struggling to overcome the difficulties of making Nipper the HMV dog for Kase. I had made the mould; it was the casting that was causing all the trouble. He was far too heavy. Thank goodness Tom Minety kept dropping by, with ever more ridiculous reasons why he needed to have a quick word with Ros. When he turned up that morning on the pretext that Ros might be interested in some onion sets, he heard me cursing and casually remarked that he had once helped build a slush-casting machine in his days working for Ryton Engineering over in Stonehouse.

Within half an hour I was talking to Reg, the very man who had designed and made the machine, which he called a tumble caster. Not cheap at eight hundred pounds, but I ordered one. I had no alternative. I was going to have to squeeze some more money out of Kase; I was already out of pocket on the job.

Later that day I had my weekly meeting with Walter up in the Crown. I noticed he hadn't shaved and had dirt under his fingernails. Whenever I saw him his appearance had altered, as if in his later life he was finding new characters within himself. His days of being a pharmacist were long behind him, and for the first time he ordered a pint of Wadworth 6X.

He was keen to tell me about the trip he'd made to

Kidderminster to visit Schloetters, a large German company which had developed a technique to electroplate metal finishes on to resin.

'This is a big breakthrough for us. It opens up many opportunities.'

'How, exactly?'

He took from his bag a book of Art Deco statues made of ivory and bronze: beautiful figures from the 1920s in various poses on onyx and marble bases.

'This is where the money is,' he said. 'Take a good look. The originals cost thousands.'

'But how do we get our hands on them?'

'We go to auctions and after we've made our replicas we sell the originals on. It's as simple as that.'

'And who has that kind of money?' I asked.

'Me. I'll fund it.'

That was a lot for me to take in; this was a side of Walter I hadn't seen before. He was beginning to sound like me, not the person I'd hoped would keep me firmly focused. The man was changing in front of me, as if a metamorphosis was taking place, or maybe this side of him had been suppressed for years and was now asserting itself. He was rushing into things too quickly. Could I really take on all this work? We might be a business, but in reality I was no more than a one man band with his wife. And I already had Kase breathing down my neck for his Nippers. But the last thing I wanted to do was dampen Walter's enthusiasm by appearing faint-hearted. I wouldn't have been able to live with myself. So I dived in. Which sums up my life, really.

'Okay, If you're prepared to finance it, let's do it.'

Walter had certainly done his homework; he produced a copy of the *Antiques Trade Gazette* that listed all the upcoming auctions.

'Leave it with me. Now I must be on my way. I'm working on a formula for a bronze patination to apply to polyester resin.'

That night at the supper table I let slip accidentally-on-purpose that I was still on target to become a millionaire within two years.

'What you really mean, Dad, is two and a half years, because you said that a few weeks ago,' said Sam.

'Think you're pretty smart, don't you?' I said.

'He's only speaking the truth,' butted in Ros. But she did agree we were making some money.

'Enough for me to go on a school trip to the Science Museum?' asked Lysta.

'Of course,' I replied, 'And to buy an ice cream if you want.'

'The school's going camping in the Quantocks for a week. Can I put my name down for it?' asked Seth, not to be left out, seeing the generous spirit I was in.

'Sounds painful, but why not? Any other requests?' I asked.

'Dad, the curtains in our room let the light in at four o'clock in the morning. Can we buy a new pair, please?' Lysta again.

'Belah, is there anything you'd like?' I asked our youngest daughter, who was not only extremely lovely but, at three years old, undemanding.

'She could do with some lighting in her doll's house,' said Lysta.

Luckily the doorbell rang and Sam, Lysta and Seth ran to see who it could be, sure it was one of their friends. But it wasn't.

'Someone called Mike Townsend for you, Dad,' said Lysta.

I hadn't seen Mike for months, not since I'd worked with him at the Brass Rubbing Centre.

'Mike, come in. Welcome to the house of fun.'

He seemed apprehensive, looking down Chester Street,

making sure he hadn't been followed. 'Can we talk on our own somewhere?' he asked.

'We could go and have a pint in the Oddfellows,' I suggested.

'No. Someone might see us and put two and two together.'

What on earth was he talking about, this young man whom I didn't know well and had only worked with for a couple of months? So we sat in the living room, asking the children not to disturb us, and he told me he wanted to leave his job. Although he was only twenty he needed a change; the Brass Rubbing Centre was the only place he'd worked since leaving school at sixteen. He could make moulds and casts. He was a Gloucestershire boy and had a soft burr to his words, a gentle turn of phrase, and an unassuming way of asking me if there was any chance I could offer him something.

He'd told no one he had come to see me, because he was worried that if anyone found out they would sack him.

'So what? Then you could come and work for me anyway,' I said. 'How much have I got to pay you?' I knew I needed him.

'Could you stretch to eighty pounds a week? At the moment, after tax and National Insurance, I take home fifty-six pounds.'

Mike handed in the statutory two weeks' notice and joined me in Frampton Mansell: my first employee and the beginning of a new phase in the expansion of Puckmill Studios, replica makers extraordinaire.

Mike could turn his hand to almost anything. So when Reg delivered the tumble caster, it was to Mike he explained the hidden secrets: how to get the best out of a device that consisted of an A and a B frame, one going in the opposite direction to the other. What did I know about machinery? My job title was Head of Production and Sales, I said, tongue in cheek, but Mike took it seriously and I could tell he wasn't joking when he asked me what his was. So I made him Chief Mould Maker and Tumble Caster.

When we finished the first Nipper dog I staggered from the workshop and lay in the grass, filled with two sensations: relief and sheer delight at being freed from an awful anxiety, the weight of which I had felt each night before going to sleep. Now it had all been lifted away, or rather had floated away like the passing clouds. I put together a roll-up for a moment of quiet reflection. Tenacity was what we needed to succeed, and I felt we'd taken an evolutionary step. The triumph which Mike and I had pulled off would keep me going. My self-belief was intact and that night I rang Kase to tell him the good news. We despatched the Nipper by courier and would hear back from him in three days.

I wasn't seeing a lot of Jack; from what my mother told me he was practically running the Brass Rubbing Centre. Corinna was a mother now and our lives had moved on from the days we shared together farming in North Wales.

The children seemed to have settled down after the initial rumblings of discontent. Having made friends, they hadn't asked for a while when we'd be moving on. My family life went on around me while my thoughts orbited another planet full of creative explosions whenever I discovered some new chemical formula, or an old recipe that I could use to give a particular piece the correct patination to satisfy the eye of the beholder. There's a lot to be said for old wives' tales, for there's usually a grain of truth lurking beneath the surface. Various waxes, vinegar, tea bags, even yoghurt I experimented with in my never-ending search for the right finish, all to forward my simple ambition to become a millionaire.

Only Sam, who had photographs of Formula 1 racing cars on his bedroom wall, said he wouldn't consider me a success until we had a Ferrari. I told him I'd never have a Ferrari, no matter how rich I was.

'If you had the choice, what car would you buy?'

'Probably a Ford Capri with a pair of cow horns on the bonnet. And I'd wear a Stetson and drive around the country singing "Next thing you know, old Nick's a millionaire".'

Mike had become an important member of the team. I use the word team loosely, because there were only four of us. He was vital, if I'm honest, because he was happy to have a go at anything I threw at him and met every challenge with enthusiasm. He joined the weekly meetings with Walter; they knew each other anyway, Walter being the nearest chemist to where Mike had been living since the day he was born.

Walter told us he had been to an auction in Bath and bought a bronze and ivory Art Deco statue for over three thousand pounds, sculpted by a Parisian artist called Chiparus and entitled *Footsteps*. She stood on a veined marble base, about eighteen inches high. As we considered the best way to make the piece, I suddenly realised that although we might well be able to reproduce the figure, the marble base was another matter. We hadn't thought of that, and we certainly couldn't replicate marble.

So I went to a monumental mason, Dyke & Son in Victoria Road in Cirencester, who had great slabs of different marbles piled high in the back yard. I took the original base with me, and was met by a monosyllabic chap as charmless as his overalls. Not blessed with a sense of humour, he exuded a miserable lack of interest.

'We carve headstones,' he said dourly. 'This isn't our kind of work.' But he went off and returned with a fragment of marble which was remarkably close to what I was looking for. After a brief discussion, he agreed to make me half a dozen for thirty pounds each. I had no idea if that was expensive, but I agreed as I knew how keen Walter was to test the market.

At half past eleven, when we were all asleep, Kase rang and woke up the whole household. The phone stopped before Sam, Lysta or I had reached it, and on our way back upstairs it began to ring again.

'I'll get it,' I said.

'It's me, Kase.'

'Do you know what the time is?'

'Twelve thirty. We're an hour ahead of you.'

'Well, eleven thirty's still late. I go to bed at ten.'

'Sorry, but I had to tell you what a brilliant job you've done. Go ahead and make the two hundred Nippers.'

'I need more money up front to buy all the materials we need.'

'Of course. Give me your bank details and I'll wire the money over. I'll ring you in two days.'

Belah was awake, and crawled into bed between us and wriggled constantly. I didn't know how Ros wasn't disturbed by all her fidgeting.

'Dad, are you awake?'

'No.'

'I am. Will you tell me a story?'

'Shall I tell you about the boy who grew up to be a millionaire?'

'Is it a fairy story?'

'It started off as a fairy story, and then it became true.'

❧ 5 ❧

It was June and we needed more space in the stable, which wasn't a stable any more because Pearl was now outside grazing in one of the fields, spending most of her time leaning over the gate hoping ramblers passing on the footpath would put an apple in her mouth. With her gone, it felt as though we had a real workshop. Ros and I would go down at lunch time every day to see her, lifting Belah up to stroke her face; she was too frightened to hold out her hand and give her a Polo.

Celia had applied to the council and been given permission for change of use of the stable to a light industrial unit. The Booths, our nearest neighbours on the other side of the viaduct, didn't object, although it did occasionally get noisy when the compressor charged up in the lavatory at the end of the building.

We were making money but expanding all the time, so what was coming into the bank was leaving just as quickly; I was already thinking we would soon need to buy another tumble caster.

Derek Tindall, a major wholesaler of antique reproductions from Bermondsey, who shipped a lot of stuff to the States and sent a buyer to the rag market each week, got in touch and drove up to the workshop in his vintage Bentley with the roof down. He was from the East End of London – 'All right, son, you know what I mean?' – and must have been in his mid-fifties. My first impression, when he climbed out of the car wearing a well-tailored dark sports jacket with the top button of his shirt undone, revealing a glimpse of a gold chain, was that he took care of his appearance. He ran the Antiques Warehouse and had a large showroom managed by his sidekick Archie, who had come along with him.

Before we even shook hands, Derek took off his jacket and drew in several deep breaths.

'I like it. I like it a lot.'

'Do you mean the viaduct?' I said, as he seemed to be looking up at it.

'No, son, just a little word that fills the lungs.'

'Could it be air?' Archie wanted to know.

'I always said you could win Mastermind if you engaged your brain.'

'We fancied a nice day out in the Cotswolds,' said Archie, a tall man in a camel-hair coat, with a scar below his left eye. He had dyed hair, although only in his early forties, and several rings on his fingers. He talked a lot, and after he'd done so for several minutes about all the money we could make in America, Derek said, 'Now you know why his nickname's Rent-a-gob.'

Archie ignored him and moved towards me, cracking his knuckles and raising his shoulders threateningly when I began to laugh.

'Don't take him too seriously,' said Derek. 'You're lucky. I've got to drive back to London with the bugger.'

Derek had a unique turn of phrase, a vocabulary all of his own. He was a wit, a poet and, as he put it, full of the flange.

'What does flange mean?' I asked him.

'A kind of syrupy bullshit that dribbles off a silvery tongue,' said Archie in his heavy smoker's harsh voice.

They'd brought with them a range of advertising figures, taking from the boot of the Bentley a toucan advertising Guinness, a Penfold golfer and a dapper little chap called the Meltonian Man promoting shoe polish. They'd all have to be produced in the tumble caster; now I knew we'd have to get another one.

Then we walked round the workshop and met Mike, who greeted them in his Gloucestershire accent.

'Afternoon, gents. Not seen you round these parts before.'

Archie tried to mimic him. ''Cos, me old cock, we ain't been round these parts before.'

'Where you from, then?' asked Mike.

'London, mate. A big place down in the south-east.'

'That's miles away. I've never left Gloucestershire in all my life.'

'Funny place to have a workshop, at the bottom of a country lane,' said Derek, as if there was something suspicious about it.

'Yeah, surrounded by cows and sheep.'

Thank goodness Ros had taken Belah down to have lunch with Celia. I could tell Derek and Archie weren't getting the impression that we were a serious business. I took them to the Crown, where they knocked back a couple of glasses of red wine and told me that I was never going to make 'big bucks' unless I employed more people. They were looking for someone who could supply enough stuff to fill shipping containers.

'This is a big opportunity, but you could never meet the demand,' sneered Archie.

'Hardly a hive of industry, just you and a country bumpkin,' said Derek.

'You'd be surprised. What you see here is not the complete set-up. Far from it.'

'Don't tell me you've got a research and development unit hidden away,' laughed Archie.

'We have a scientific laboratory, run by a retired pharmacist perfecting finishes on several other products,' I told them, which, after all, was very close to the truth.

'Like what?' asked Derek.

'I'm sorry. That would be revealing trade secrets.'

'You're good at the flange, I must say,' said Derek, a smile creeping across his face.

I knew they were trying to undermine me, so having deflected their flippant remarks I asked how many of the advertising figures they wanted with all the indifference I could muster, which wasn't a lot when confronted by a couple of East End wide boys.

'If the price is right, give us fifty of each, and that's just for starters,' Derek said. 'I'll put the dosh where my mouth is. Would a grand see you all right on it?'

I could feel my heart rate increase dramatically and just hoped my expression hadn't given anything away. 'Yes . . . yes,' I said thoughtfully, 'that should just about cover it,' and added, 'for starters,' delivered with such coolness that they gave one another a quick glance. But from then on, their tone changed. Having begun to take me seriously, Archie delivered a threat.

'If you don't come up with the goods, we'll come calling,' he said, leaning across the table and lighting a cigar.

I probably should have stepped back, or at least asked for some time to consider what they were proposing, but I didn't. Instead, I said we'd take on the job.

After Derek had given me two envelopes, each containing five hundred pounds, and they'd driven off, fear and a sense of dread flooded through me. It was the same feeling that had kept me awake through all those nights of anxiety over Kase's Nipper dogs. Why did I keep taking risks, and should we be dealing with these two hoods from the underworld anyway? I went back to the workshop and told Mike what I'd agreed; he simply shrugged his shoulders.

'I'm happy to work nights. They were nice folk. Unusual in their talk.'

After that, I couldn't sleep, wasn't even tired, and took to sitting in the shed at the bottom of our garden. I liked the sense of being enclosed, staring through the little window at a patch of night sky, beneath millions of stars twinkling in a vast universe, while everyone else was in bed.

It helped me think, not about burning questions such as 'What the hell are we all doing here?' but much bigger issues than that, like where could I find someone who was an airbrush artist? All the advertising figures had to be painted, as did the Nippers and the Chiparus statue, which we'd now cast; I'd already picked up the marble bases from Dyke & Son. Puckmill Studios was growing; the netsukes and the scrimshaw were selling out every week at the rag market and in Bath. I decided to put an advert in all the newsagents in Cirencester, by which I mean postcards in the windows.

Wanted, someone with artistic flair and a steady hand to join an expanding company. Must be able to use an airbrush and have their own car. Salary negotiable.

That's what I came up with after sitting for an hour in the shed. It had been far from a waste of time, and to my daily mantra 'No matter what, I must not be distracted' I added 'We mustn't take on any more work'.

At breakfast, I wrote out the postcards advertising our job vacancy and asked Sam if he could put them in the newsagents' windows after school.

'Any chance of a pound, Dad?'

'Can't you do it for love?'

'Not really. I need the money.'

'I used to like you. You've changed.'

'Give him a pound,' said Ros.

'Where did you get this attitude from?'

'From you, Dad. You said if you're going to make money, you've got to be able to sniff out a business opportunity.'

Well, that put me in my place, and he was right, so I gave him a pound.

'Dad, while you're talking about money,' said Lysta, 'can I ask you about our pocket money?'

At which point the phone rang. Lysta grabbed it as always, believing every call was going to be for her. But not this time; it was my oldest friend Rob calling from Chorley. He told me that he and Kate were leaving Lancashire and thinking of moving down our way. Did I have a job I could offer him? I certainly did have a job, and the perfect one, because Rob was an artist.

'When can you come?'

'At the weekend, if that's okay. Can we stay?'

'We'll fit you in somewhere.'

It was great news. Rob had worked with me on the farm in North Wales, mucking out the pigs. I knew he would be more than capable of doing a good job with an airbrush.

'Don't worry about the postcards, Sam. I think we have just filled the job vacancy.'

'What about the pound?'

'Keep it.'

'And the pocket money, Dad?' asked Lysta.

'You can have an extra fifty pence a week.'

Meanwhile in the background, but always playing a key role, Walter had taken some of our resin casts up to Schloetters in Kidderminster to see if they could put metallic finishes on our figurines. They had successfully electroplated copper, tin and nickel on to our samples. This was another major step forward. They really looked as if they were made of metal, when what you were holding in your hand was polyester resin with a metallic surface coating. It was a complicated process, each cast having to be suspended in nine different tanks containing various acids and chemicals at specific temperatures. Walter and I had a long hard talk: maybe this was a step too soon. It required more capital expenditure, probably several thousands of pounds, and who would be responsible for it? But when I suggested finding a subcontractor, Schloetters said they knew of no one else doing such work. Plenty of companies were chrome-plating plastics such as car bumpers, but that finish was far too bright and garish and wouldn't suit us. We needed an antique look.

Finally, it was agreed that Schloetters would continue to do trials for us free of charge on the understanding that if they could perfect the finishes we needed we would set up our own electroplating facility. Walter was in his element; having been a chemist, he knew the shop talk and they welcomed him with open arms whenever he visited to take notes.

Rob and Kate had been and gone, after spending the weekend in Cirencester. Rob was keen to come and work with us; the only problem was they had to sell their house in Chorley, which could take months, after which Kate, who was a schoolteacher, would have to give a term's notice. I couldn't wait that long.

'Can't Rob start now and stay here with us, and go back to Chorley at the weekends?' I suggested. 'We need each other.'

'Where's he going to sleep?' said Lysta, who had been listening to every word.

'He can sleep on the sofa bed in the sitting room.'

And so it was agreed. It would be like the old days, the two of us working together again, only now we would not be chasing pigs across a Welsh landscape.

I needed to take stock, go to the garden shed and gather my thoughts. The children were always curious about this, me traipsing off to the bottom of the garden, not understanding why I had to be on my own for a while. Sam and Seth would creep up on me and bang on the door. 'Dad, Spurs are playing on TV. Why don't you come and watch the match?'

'I will in a minute.'

'What are you doing in there?'

'Thinking.'

'Thinking about what?'

'Whether I'm in control of everything.' I was far from certain.

'How long now, Dad, until you're a millionaire?' Sam asked me this every week when he saw the cash on the kitchen table after I'd been to the markets. Dealers were turning up with pieces they wanted made, and our reputation was spreading. I was bringing home hundreds of pounds, and the children had become more demanding, wanting to decorate their rooms and buy a video recorder. But when Ros told me that all the money we were making was being spent, I wondered if I was in danger of being nothing but a busy fool.

'If you stopped spending so much money, perhaps we could start saving some,' Ros said, which shut everyone up, until I came up with the analogy that after the Big Bang the universe went on expanding for a while, and that's what was happening at Puckmill. A mass expansion was taking place and then everything would settle down.

'Do you understand?' I said to all of them.

'Whatever you say, Dad.'

Mike had cast all the samples of the advertising figures for Derek Tindall and passed them on to Rob, who now showed me the finished articles. He could have been airbrushing all his life, such was the quality of his work; he showed a natural flair. There's a huge satisfaction when something you've attempted to produce turns out better than you'd imagined. We were a successful little team, working in a converted stable without any training, making it up as we went along.

When Derek received his samples, he was so excited he wanted to drive up that day and discuss all sorts of other opportunities. It was unusual for me to dampen anyone's spirits, but I think I had woken up to the fact that we were unique. I didn't want to be working at such a pace, dancing to the tune of others. Listening to Derek, I realised it is far easier to place an order than fulfil it. They would all have to wait, and if I said we needed paying for fifty per cent of the order up front, then maybe we could build up a buffer in the bank. It was the first time I felt that our customers needed us just as much as we needed them. Ros noticed it, telling me I seemed more confident, and obviously pleased that I was no longer being dragged into making promises that were hard to keep.

Walter came out to the workshop with the electroplated *Footsteps* figure, or rather the sequined dress, because the piece was made in several parts that had to be assembled before we mounted it onto the marble base. We had cast her face, hands and feet separately in an ivory finish. Using a scalpel, Rob had cut the finest delicate cracks into the surface of the ivory to give it the right aged appearance, and now he added a greenish tint to highlight the sequins on her dress. He had discovered that spraying one lacquer on top of another gave the effect of a crackled surface, and when he had finished our statue looked identical to the original.

Assembling the piece took the whole afternoon. It was one of those jobs that was painstakingly slow, needing our full attention, until, finally, she was glued into the base. And then one last thing, a dusting with rottenstone. When we stood back and looked at the piece from every angle, we couldn't fault it. Here it was, our first Art Deco statue, the most expensive piece we'd made. I estimated it had cost fifty-five pounds, although I couldn't be entirely accurate, because we hadn't paid Schloetters for plating the dress.

Now we had to decide the best way to sell them, which was certainly not on market stalls. Walter suggested we should start by putting this one in a Bath auction house to see how much interest there would be from the public. It was a work of art, after all.

We described it as 'after the style of Chiparus' in the catalogue and put no reserve price on it, just hoping two people would bid against each other. I dressed for the occasion in my only suit, pinstriped with turn-ups and large lapels. Ros thought I would have looked trendy back in the sixties, but not now. And sitting next to me Walter, after years of conformity, was wearing a leather jacket and looked like an old biker.

'Walter, are you being Marlon Brando today?'

If he was full of nervous excitement he kept it hidden. He had a bag of acid drops that he sucked continuously. We seemed to be waiting for ever, and as I returned with two cups of tea I could see him sitting amongst the audience, his head tilted back, staring into some other world. It came over me again that I owed him more than a big thank you and had never properly expressed my gratitude.

'Now lot 345, a lovely piece after the style of Chiparus,' said the auctioneer. 'A beautiful Art Deco statue, who'll start me at a hundred?' No one did. 'Surely fifty, come on, someone . . . yes, fifty, I have fifty, sixty, seventy, yes, eighty, ninety, the lady in the scarf. Come on, this is far too cheap, a hundred, yes, at last. Is that it? A hundred and ten? Any advance on a hundred and ten? A hundred and twenty. Come on, someone, a hundred and thirty, yes to the gentleman with the silk cravat. Come on, you lovely people, these pieces don't turn up every day. Can I tempt anyone else? No? Is that it? Going, going, gone. Sold for a hundred and thirty pounds.'

'Well, it was a struggle, but it was a profit,' I said, turning to Walter.

'We should be pleased. If we could make fifty pounds on each piece that's good business.'

'Let's hope you get your money back on the original.'

We sat in a café outside the abbey listening to a busker singing Bob Dylan's 'Like a Rolling Stone'.

'Walter,' I said, 'are you happy with everything?'

'With everything?'

'What we're doing . . . your part in it all.'

'Couldn't be happier. I have a life I'm completely engrossed in.'

'What about the money?' I asked.

'I'm not doing it for the money. I'm more than comfortable.'

'I'm so grateful for all your generosity.'

'And me for yours.'

'I don't understand.'

'You will one day.'

I was engrossed in my work, following the same routine every day, but with a little awareness I should have seen what was staring me in the face. When Ros announced that she was going to start leaving early, catching the bus that left Frampton Mansell at three o'clock, I didn't understand why. There were several reasons, she told me, that I'd have to wake up to. First, she didn't like getting home after the children had returned from school.

'It makes me uneasy, it always has, although they've never complained about it. Also, if I got home earlier we wouldn't have to eat so late. The children get hungry and fill themselves up on snacks.'

She wasn't angry, but when I asked her why she hadn't mentioned any of this before she said it was because I needed her out at the workshop.

'And it's not where I want Belah to be for most of the day. Things have to change. I'm the mother of four children.'

'You're quite right. I should have seen it,' I said, and put my arms around her. Ros had made sacrifices for the business, and now I needed to manage without her. 'I'll find somebody else. If only you had told me sooner, Ros. I can tell you've had enough.'

I'd miss her out at Puckmill, for the way she worked around me; all the little things that miraculously happened by themselves, or so it appeared. She had streamlined her area so that everything was neat and tidy and within arm's reach: economy of movement, she called it.

A sadness came over me as I remembered the night when, after several glasses of Shiraz, I'd said she could be Head of Stains and Finishing, and she couldn't stop laughing, telling me I was a fool, pretending I was interviewing her for a proper job.

'There's something else you need to know, and you're not going to like it.'

'Tell me. Let's clear the air.'

'We need to register for VAT, and get a proper bookkeeper. Another thing that should have been sorted out.'

'Is that too much for you?'

'It's not that it's too much, but we need to find someone for one day a week to do the books and fill in a quarterly VAT return.'

'I'm sorry, Ros.'

'It's just the way you are. We need a reliable person who will look after the clerical side of the business, and it's not your wife.'

In the Bath antiques market I'd made friends with an unusual man who moved through the world in the most unhurried, leisurely way, as if the stressful pace of modern living was no concern of his and he lived in a bygone era. The days when a gentleman would lift his hat, open shop doors and say good morning to women he passed on the street. I was drawn to him, because opposites attract. He had an aura of calmness and it was hard to imagine him ever being ruffled.

His name was Quentin Saffell and he dealt in antique tins. The outer persona he showed the world was no pretence, and what was also remarkable was he could only have been in his early thirties. He had a kind, giving face, his dark hair was already thinning, and he was in the process of growing a goatee beard. He chewed pine nuts, which he kept in his jacket pocket; as if unconsciously, he'd take two or three at a time between his fingers and put them into his mouth. He had an authoritative air and was an expert on tins, often invited to speak on the subject to collectors and people who brought along their prized possessions for him to value.

He lived above his shop in the London Road with his wife Jo, who tap-danced on Tuesday evenings, while Quentin sat in his chair in front of the fire cataloguing his tins. He sent newsletters to dealers all over the world. It was Quentin who introduced me to Thelma, a bookkeeper he highly recommended. The very person I needed to sort out the paperwork for Puckmill Studios.

I arranged an appointment with her and went to her house in Camden Terrace. When I rang the bell, a wet nose pushed itself through the brass flap and its canine owner yapped incessantly until the door opened. A long-haired terrier leapt up at me several times before Thelma scooped it up in her arms, telling me there was nothing for me to worry about. 'Let him lick your hand and then he'll know who you are.'

Thelma was a middle-aged, expansive lady and looked exactly as I had imagined. Solid, with horn-rimmed glasses and greying hair, in which a yellowy streak was the result, I guessed, of the cigarettes she smoked as she pored over the invoices on her desk. She had two moles on her forehead, and somehow there was no doubting she was a bookkeeper.

We went up to her sitting room where she was drying her underwear on a clothes horse: large white articles which she folded in front of me, not the slightest bit embarrassed that I was privy to these garments. There was a Bechstein piano in the corner covered with piles of sheet music and a vase of flowers which were dropping their petals. She cleared away folders from the sofa and, patting a cushion, invited me to sit down.

She had shut the dog outside and it continuously scratched at the door as I told her what I needed her to do. She already had part-time work but could fit me in easily. I would pay her five pounds an hour and every quarter I would come and sign the VAT declaration form. Before I left she told me she was also the church organist.

'You don't happen to sing, do you?' she asked.

'Yes, often. I can sing the whole of Bob Marley's "Redemption Song" unaccompanied.'

'I'm afraid I don't know it.'

'Why do you ask?'

'We're short of a few people in the church choir.'

'I can sing "Onward Christian Soldiers" and I know a lot of carols, "O Come, All Ye Faithful", stuff like that.'

'Could you possibly come for an audition on Thursday evening?'

'I very much doubt it. I live nearly an hour away.'

'Perhaps it's best I'm just your bookkeeper.'

When I got home that night Lysta told me Derek Tindall had rung. He'd said it was urgent.

'He has a funny way of talking. I didn't understand a lot of what he was saying.'

'He's a cockney from the East End of London.'

'He asked me if I was your bricks and mortar.'

'Daughter. It's rhyming slang.'

When I got through to Derek, he immediately told me he owned a dozen greyhounds and had a dog running at Wimbledon that evening so only had time to tell me he needed to see me soon. Something big was developing. 'I've got to go, son. There's a monkey riding on the bitch.'

'What?'

'I've put a bet of five hundred pounds on her,' and he hung up.

I sat and talked to Ros, asking her how she felt about everything. Sam, Lysta and Seth were doing well at school and never mentioned that we should be moving on. They had their friends, while in September Belah would be starting at the kindergarten. Was she happy to be living in Cirencester, did she think we had done the right thing moving here?

'It's too soon to give you an answer. We're all putting up with it for a while, until you've made your million.'

'And if I don't?'

By the look on Ros's face I could tell she had a lot more to say.

'I think we should change the subject,' she said.

There was one more call that night. My mother informed me she wouldn't be able to see me on Wednesday. 'I'm taking an unexpected break in Cumbria. Well, the two of us are.'

'The two of you?'

'I'm not going to lie to you . . . with Peter.'

'I get confused. Which one is Peter?'

'Oh, stop it. You know perfectly well who he is. He came to the stall last week and introduced himself as my dancing partner.'

'Oh yes. The chap you do the tango with.'

'Actually it's the foxtrot, but yes, him. We're going to give it a try . . . you know, a week alone together.'

'What, in a tent?'

'Don't be silly. In a guest house. It's nothing serious.'

'Send me a postcard.'

'Of course. Anyway, I must be off now. Love to you all.'

That was my mother. Now in her late fifties, still hoping the right man would turn up. I remembered when she went on a walking holiday with Herbert through the Swiss cantons, collecting wild flowers and singing 'Edelweiss'. She was certain it would last for ever, until he spent every evening for the next two weeks pressing flowers in a notebook.

6

In the gradual waking of a summer's day, before the sun had risen above the Golden Valley, when I'd driven down from the village and not met a single car on the winding lane, I couldn't turn my back on it. Not just open the workshop door and get on with removing casts from moulds, which was always the first job of any morning. So I'd walk down to the canal, scattering the wood pigeons, watching the whitest swans glide, my mind going back to those farming days in North Wales, the peace you feel when you're out alone before the world has woken.

By the time I'd walked back, the sun would have flooded through the arches of the viaduct and it was difficult to connect with what was really going on in my life. How strange it was to be doing what I was doing, making replicas out here in the countryside and wanting to be a millionaire with 'All right, my son?' Derek Tindall and his sidekick Archie on their way from the East End of London. They arrived at eleven in a red Bristol 411 Series 4 with a crate of champagne on the back seat.

'What are you celebrating?' I asked.

'A nice little touch with a certain greyhound at Walthamstow last night.'

'Another line of income we indulge in,' said Archie, with an irritating smugness.

'How much did you win?'

'That's the one question you never ask,' Derek let me know; I'd obviously breached gambling etiquette. 'It's a world you know nothing about. All I can tell you is he races under the name of Passing Wind, and his pet name is Bert.'

'Can we get on with why we're here?' said Archie. 'Which is about your future, my boy.'

'I've added to the workforce,' I told them. 'This is the finest airbrush artist in the country and my oldest friend, Rob.'

'Put it there, son,' said Derek, offering his hand, while Archie just nodded, not wanting to appear the slightest bit friendly. I was tempted to introduce him as 'Rent-a-gob' but didn't think it would go down too well.

Mike was removing the Guinness toucan mould from the tumble caster and I asked him if he would give Derek and Archie a demonstration, so they could see what was involved in the manufacture of these complicated pieces.

'The stuff stinks,' said Archie.

'That's polyester resin. It's the styrene you can smell.'

Mike wasn't used to being the centre of attention but rose to the occasion admirably. Unfortunately, halfway through his running commentary, which he delivered in his finest Gloucestershire accent, Derek turned a whiter shade of pale and made a fast exit through the door.

'I've seen enough,' he said, bent double over Pearl's water trough, gasping for fresh air.

'It's because you're not used to it,' I said.

'I don't want to get bloody used to it. How can you breathe in that smell all day?'

'Now you know what goes into making these pieces for you.'

'Which is why we're here, son,' said Archie, coughing into his handkerchief. 'So let's go up to that little pub of yours and have a quiet chat about things.'

We ended up sitting in there for two hours, only because I just happened to mention how busy we were, with people offering me work every day. It wasn't premeditated, but it set the tone. They spent most of the time trying to convince me they had more than enough work for me and I didn't need to take on anything else. I'd never felt in such a position of strength with these two big wheeler-dealers. I had something they needed, and without any competition I knew there was nowhere else they could turn.

What happened next was one of those unexplainable things that always seem to happen to someone else: a lucky break. Completely by chance I found myself in the right place at the right time, sitting there that day in the Crown in Frampton Mansell.

'What's the big development that's brought you here today?' I asked Derek.

They fell silent and looked at each other as Derek searched in his pockets for the car keys before handing them to Archie. 'Go and get it, then.'

When Archie returned and took an Art Deco statue from an old leather suitcase and placed it on the table in front of me I managed not to react, although I was stunned by the coincidence.

'Can you make this for us?' Derek asked.

'It's the *Charleston Dancer* sculpted by Ferdinand Preiss,' said Archie, 'not bleedin' cheap at five grand. Now give us a price to make a hundred of 'em.'

I wasn't sure how to respond. Did I dare tell them about the Chiparus *Footsteps* figure?

So I let them ramble on, rolling out the clichés: this was going to be big business, and if I played my cards right I could have a slice of the action.

'Sounds interesting,' I said, deliberately underplaying it.

'This, my boy, is the next big thing. Art Deco's coming back into fashion. Now, give us a straight answer. Can you do it?'

'I've already made an Art Deco statue.' I'd finally shown them I was ahead of their game. And I knew it would give me the upper hand with Archie, who liked to talk down to me.

'What did you say?'

'Not this one, but *Footsteps* by Chiparus.'

That shut them up, and the two of them disappeared to the bar and stayed there deep in conversation, drinking red wine.

While they were gone, Ivor, the village postmaster, came and sat down with me.

'I've seen that type before on *The Sweeney*. They look like gangsters,' he whispered to me.

'They're not gangsters, Ivor, just a couple of businessmen from London.'

'I'll inform Neighbourhood Watch. They look suspicious to me.'

'They'll be gone in an hour. They're not up to anything.'

'Eyes like a hawk, that's me. I've already taken down their number plate and the tax disc is out of date.'

Ivor not only ran the post office from his terraced house, he also had a taxi business, making a steady income from running the village children to and from school. He and his wife Janet had lived in Frampton Mansell most of their lives, and of all the residents in this small Cotswold village they had been here the longest. Whenever I took parcels and letters to be posted, I'd often sit in their front room and have a cup of tea with them, dunking a shortbread biscuit. Even if I was only buying stamps, it always took half an hour to get out of the place, but that was village life, and everyone liked to chat. Ivor considered himself a bit of a sleuth, but never quite put two and two together; there was too much supposition that led him wide of the mark. I liked him, but many people in the village said he stuck his nose into other people's business. If there was ever a break-in and Constable Slinn cycled over from Sapperton, Ivor would be there offering his help. He knew what I was up to under the viaduct and had made it plain what he thought. 'You should be offering jobs to people in the village, help the local economy.' And he was right. 'What about Ade Tucker? He's out of work. Give him something to do.'

When Derek and Archie returned to the table, you might have expected Ivor to politely make his excuses and be on his way, but no, not Ivor, he had to tell them their tax disc had expired.

'What's it got to do with you, old timer?' said Archie.

'Just letting you know.'

'We don't need to know, so take my advice and be on your way, *comprendi*?'

'There's no need for that attitude. I thought you might have forgotten to renew it.'

'Well, we haven't.'

'I'll leave you to it then,' Ivor said, but not until he'd taken out his notebook and pretended to scribble something in it.

'We've got a plan,' said Derek, when he'd gone. 'I might have got you wrong. You've grown in my estimation. You're no country bumpkin.'

'What's the plan, then?' I said.

'We're going to put a lot of dosh into this,' said Archie, with gritted teeth, a flicker of a cold smile making his unlit cigar quiver on his bottom lip. Derek calmly told me that every Art Deco statue was to be exclusively for them.

'We have to control the market, and when to release them. We can't have Art Deco statues turning up everywhere; it will weaken the price. Do you understand?'

'Do you get our point?' said Archie, leaning towards me.

'Yes, quite clearly.'

'Good. We're making progress.'

'One question,' I said.

'What?'

'How much will you give me as an up-front payment? Because without that, nothing will happen. You're asking a lot from me. It's almost as if you're taking over my whole business.'

I thought they would have to go back to the bar and discuss it further, but they didn't.

'We'll give you ten grand,' said Derek, 'to get the ball rolling.'

'It'll take months before you see any money back. I don't even know where to source the marble and onyx bases,' I said, having been told plainly at Dyke & Son that it wasn't their type of work.

'We can help you with that. We already buy marble and onyx table tops from a quarry in Pakistan.'

'Give me forty-eight hours. I'll have to talk to the team before I give you my decision,' I said, with an aloofness that was out of character for me.

After supper that night I told Ros I needed an hour with Walter, because something big was happening.

'Not again. Something big's always happening,' she said sarcastically.

'This time it really is big.'

'Have you made an appointment yet to see the accountant Celia recommended?'

'I'll ring him tomorrow.'

Just as I was about to leave, Lysta came into the kitchen. 'Dad, do you think I'm interesting?'

'Of course,' I said, putting on my shoes, my mind elsewhere. 'Why do you ask?'

'Because I've met someone, and we like each other.'

'But you're only twelve.'

'So what?'

'Because I didn't have my first girlfriend until I was sixteen.'

'He's not a boyfriend, just someone who is going to walk home with me.'

'God, you're growing up.'

'We do have sex education at school.'

'Going back to your original question, do I think you're interesting, you are in many ways. For a start, you've formed opinions about what you believe in, like why you became a vegetarian, and you're very good at the art of conversation, and observing people.'

'Thanks, Dad. That will really help when I walk home with Jason tomorrow.'

'And you're a good listener,' I said, rushing out of the front door.

Walter wasn't expecting me, frustratingly stuck on a clue in the *Times* jumbo crossword.

'I never finish it.'

'What is it? Not that I'm any good at crosswords.'

'Nitty gritty . . . four, three, five.'

'Should be easy, but nothing comes to mind.'

'Sorry. I can tell you've come to see me for a reason.'

'Do you mind if I distract you for a while? I have a lot to tell you.'

'Pull up a chair. Let's hear the latest.'

I told him all about the possibility that Derek and Archie presented for the massive expansion of Puckmill Studios. All evening we discussed what they were proposing. Walter's main concern was they would take control of the business and we'd be working for them in everything but name.

'You're right. We could lose our freedom,' I agreed.

'And what's more, you would still have all the overheads of running your own business when those two had taken over.'

'So what do we do?'

'Agree to make six Art Deco statues for them and in a year's time review the agreement. Tell them if it's not working for both parties, either can walk away.'

'I fear they'll muscle their way in, but everything you've said makes sense.'

'One thing's for certain, though,' said Walter. 'You're going to have to employ more people.'

'I'm so glad I came over. I needed to get down to the nuts and bolts of it all.'

'Nuts and bolts! Of course! Well done. Staring me right in the face.'

'I don't understand.'

'The clue . . . nitty gritty.'

The rag market in the summer months was a lot less painful than in the depths of winter. In all the weeks I'd been going, no matter what the temperature, Frank Webb dressed as if it was January. His only concession to the warmer weather was to remove his flat cap and put a handkerchief in the breast pocket of his jacket which he used to dab his sweaty brow, but he never took off his mittens. Gerald 'Greasy' Gadd, on the other hand, wore an outrageously loud Hawaiian shirt several sizes too big, while still walking around the market carrying his Gladstone bag. Spitting images of Barney and Fred.

We'd made Frank his miniature models of luggage and milk churns, but I had to tell him it was unlikely I'd be able to cast the church he wanted as the centrepiece of Wapping Sodbury, a village he had built out of balsa wood. He'd made up the name in his make-believe world.

'There's no money in it, I'm afraid, Frank. I finished that last job out of pocket.' He tempted me then by offering me his walking sticks at a discounted price.

'I'd be interested if I could sell them in the Bath antiques market.'

'Then you can make my church for me?'

'All right, Frank. I don't know why I'm so good to you.'

We were interrupted then by Adelola, a rather striking Nigerian woman who had come to the stall the previous week. She was wearing a full-length, bright blue and yellow dress and a pair of large gold earrings. I remembered her name and that she'd been very interested in the rhino horn that I'd recently added to the range, which showed a herd of rhinos drinking on a riverbank. She was keen to tell me about the horn's potency as an aphrodisiac. I said that I'd heard this was a common belief in some African countries, but that in England you could pick up something in the chemist that was probably far more effective and some poor rhino hadn't been killed for it.

'You know, this make my husband very sick, and you should give me my money back,' she said, taking the half-ground-down rhino horn from her bag.

'There's been a terrible misunderstanding,' I said, astonished. 'It's not a real rhino horn.'

'If it is not real then what animal does it come from?'

'It doesn't come from any animal. It's polyester resin, like a plastic.'

'You mean the powder I have put in my husband's tea is plastic?'

'I'm very sorry. I'll give you your money back.'

I had never suggested it was a real rhino horn, but what else could I do? Aileen on the stall opposite, who had heard the whole conversation, told me she'd once sold some decorative hairpins to an African lady who had cut them down and stuck them through her nose. Thank goodness Adelola had gone by the time Isobel, my most regular and reliable customer, turned up. Always immaculately dressed, she now liked to tell me stories of her past life, usually about her time spent in India working for the British embassy in Delhi.

She told me she kept all the netsukes she'd bought in a glass cabinet and then asked if I'd care to call round after the market one day and give my honest opinion on how she had displayed them. I desperately searched for a reason that would prevent me from doing so. 'I could show you my old photograph albums,' she said, laughing, 'pictures of Ted and me riding elephants, and the beautiful summer residence we stayed at in Simla.'

'Soon,' I said, rather than refuse her. I liked her and was grateful to her and didn't want to lose a good customer, or the many friends she brought to the stall, who usually felt obliged to buy something from me. She was showing off our friendship and the well-to-do women she introduced to me all said, 'I've heard so much about you.' But I had to keep a healthy distance from her, not that I could ever imagine a lady of such refinement seducing a man. To me she seemed more the sort of woman who would coyly succumb to flattery in a drawing room, listening to a piano recital. Nevertheless, she was lonely, and kept telling me she thought the work I was doing was fascinating.

So it was becoming difficult at times; there was a familiarity that was getting a bit too close for comfort. She was at least thirty years older than me, and although I found her interesting, something told me she had ideas that were far removed from showing me her display cabinet.

It took several attempts to phone Derek, for as soon as I'd dialled the number I kept replacing the receiver. Frankly, I was nervous, and I wanted what I had to say to flow without hesitancy, as if unrehearsed. And I felt disappointed in myself that I'd allowed it to become an ordeal. Also, I was hoping I wouldn't have to speak to Archie, who always unnerved me. But when Derek finally answered, it went much better than I'd expected, and although I had made notes I didn't need them. He listened silently, never butting in once, and agreed to everything. Not that he said he thought it was a brilliant idea, just 'Let's give it a go then', and that the five thousand pounds up front was okay.

I sat alone for a few minutes and let the tension I'd been feeling drain away. Derek had no alternative, and now, with money in the bank, we could afford to employ someone from the village. Something I was pleased about, even though it could only stretch as far as one individual.

When wholesalers who ran proper businesses got to hear about us and preferred to ring me to place their orders, I knew it was time to get a telephone at Puckmill; until now I had made all my calls at home in the evenings. It hadn't seemed necessary to have one at the workshop, because we weren't dealing with people who worked from nine to five, just stallholders, wheeler-dealers, and traders who were out all day walking the markets. Some of them would call from the pub in the evening, which annoyed Ros, as it was often during supper.

So I installed an old red telephone box outside the workshop. Plum's Emporium up in Preston had one, circa 1960, and wanted three hundred pounds for it, which I offset against the statues of silent film stars, such as Charlie Chaplin and Laurel and Hardy, that we were making for them. They delivered it on a low loader and it took six of us to manoeuvre it into position. It became my office; a bit cramped, but my paperwork was minimal, and we hadn't grown enough to have a filing system. Besides, all the money we took was in cash, what Derek and Archie called 'instant bliss'.

But the proper wholesalers were a different breed and wanted invoices and thirty days' credit. They were legitimate, VAT registered, and played by the rules. I had to start writing out receipts in duplicate and keep records of all the transactions, which I took over to Thelma in Bath. With a wagging finger she said I'd also have to play the game now and get VAT registered. Of course she was right, but to issue an invoice to the likes of Frank and Sifta, and all those who came to the Birmingham rag market and Bath, well, they'd laugh me out of the place.

I'd given Ade Tucker, who lived in the village, a job casting all the smaller stuff we made, the netsuke and scrimshaw, and the walking-stick heads. The day he came down to the workshop he was wearing a tie with a knot that appeared to be strangling him. I told him to loosen it and undo the top button of his shirt. He gave a great sigh of relief as an Adam's apple the size of a gobstopper popped out. He handed me an envelope with *Mr Perry* written on the front. It was a reference from Ivor saying he'd known Adrian since the day he was born, and he was an honest boy with a likeable personality. He had once been a boy scout, and during bob-a-job week always did more than was expected of him, which is what he would do for Puckmill Studios, *Yours sincerely*, *Ivor*.

Unfortunately, it began to rain, and I had to interview him in the telephone box, face to face, except that Ade was six inches shorter than me, so I talked to the top of his head. I wanted to ask him which shampoo he used but didn't. He was only eighteen, nervous, and breathing quite heavily, so the windows misted up. I'd barely started the interview, or had a chance to tell him that we were market leaders in our field – a phrase I had stolen from Walter who had used it recently – before Rob interrupted us, needing to ring the garage to find out whether his old VW had got through its MOT. As Ade walked away in the pouring rain, I shouted after him, 'I can give you fifty pounds a week. Can you start on Monday?'

'Yes,' was all he said, not even a thank you.

It was the first interview I'd conducted; Rob and Mike had

just walked into their jobs. Ade probably went home and told his mother that he wasn't sure what he had let himself in for.

The business was changing rapidly, our reputation still spreading, as more and more people saw the work we were doing. Marco Spinetti, an Italian playboy who worked the Portobello market in London and drove an E-type Jaguar, turned up at the workshop unannounced with an Irish wolfhound sitting in the passenger seat.

'How did you find us?' was the first thing I asked.

'It doesn't matter. I know a lot of people. All that matters to me is whether you want to make a lot of money.'

How many times had I heard that?

'Heh, this is a lovely part of the country, but the man in the post office, he asks me many questions, as if he is a policeman.'

'Ivor,' I said, 'be careful of him. I hope your tax disc isn't out of date.'

'I told him I was an Italian here on business and this upsets him.'

'I don't know why it should.'

'I tell you why, because we fight with the Germans in the war, that is why.'

'He lives in the past. Now tell me why you're here.'

And so I began listening to another idea that would supposedly lead to riches beyond my imagination. I knew what was coming: that this was all 'top secret' and no one must know about it. I wasn't far wrong.

'This you must keep to yourself at all costs.'

'Of course,' I said, 'at all costs, on my mother's grave.' Not that my mother was dead, far from it; I was having lunch with her the next day. But I thought the Italians liked that sort of thing, coming from a matriarchal society.

'Car mascots.'

That was it, and by the way he said it I could tell he expected an astonished response, so I gave it to him. 'Car mascots!'

'Yes, exactly. Bentley, Alfa Romeo, Rolls-Royce, so, so many, all these beautiful old cars have a car mascot, and worth a pretty penny.'

'But they're made of metal. We only make things in polyester resin.'

'I will bring them to you, these mascots, and you make reproductions to look like antiques.'

'I don't know. We're so busy.'

'How can you say no? I have come all the way from London, and please give Lola a drink. My sweet dog, please. Look at her tongue, how it hangs from her mouth.'

As Lola drank one bowl of water and then started on another, Marco counted out five hundred pounds and forced it into my jacket pocket with a theatrical pleading look.

'Bring me the mascots,' I said resignedly.

'This is wonderful for both of us,' he said, moving towards me with his arms outstretched.

'Please don't kiss me. I know what you Italians are like.'

So he hugged me, which was bad enough.

'Now, please, I must make a telephone call to my people.'

'I hope you don't mean the Mafia.'

'Heh, they are Sicilian. I am bona fide Italian from the Amalfi coast.'

I left him to make his phone call and went to help Ade unload the Fordamix lorry delivering another ton of filler powder. Most commercial vehicles were too wide to get down the single winding lane from the village, built when the mode of transport was horse and cart, so in the Crown one night I had bribed old Rex Horton, a dairy farmer on his fourth pint, to rent us his Land Rover and trailer so we could get the deliveries that came on a juggernaut down to Puckmill.

Marco tapped me on the shoulder. 'I cannot use your phone. Someone is in there, and he won't stop talking. You tell him I need it urgently.'

'Hey, who are you? This is a private phone,' I said indignantly.

'Doris, I didn't mean that . . .' the man said, then putting his hand over the receiver and turning towards me. 'Do you mind?' He was middle-aged, wearing a bobble hat and a pair of shorts. 'Please, this is a sensitive matter,' he said, affronted that I should have interrupted him.

'You don't understand. This is not a public phone. Didn't you notice you didn't pay for the call?'

'Please give me one more minute, and I'll pay whatever I owe you.'

So I did, and as he was paying me I said, 'You're a member of the Chalford Ramblers Club, aren't you?'

'What gives you that impression?'

'A pair of shorts, a rucksack and the walking boots you're wearing.'

'Well, yes, I am.'

'This has happened before. Please tell your members this is a private telephone, and from now on could you please use the one outside the church in the village.'

7

Over supper, Lysta announced that Belah was very keen to have a rabbit, which really meant she was. Of course, she already knew of one needing a home, a schoolfriend having six of them to provide for. Because all our previous pets had made a run for it and disappeared, Ros and I put our feet down and said those days were over. Half an hour later we conceded, on the understanding it lived in the garden shed, the sanctuary where I went to collect my thoughts and check on my sanity.

'It can run around in the garden and eat the lawn rather than be cooped up in a hutch all day,' I told them, which they agreed to.

So Silo, a little grey and white thing that would sit in our hands and eat lettuce leaves, moved into the garden shed. I became quite attached to him and stroked him continuously as he sat on my lap. It had a calming effect on my racing brain, and meant I could reflect on the tremendous effort necessary to become a millionaire.

In all the time I had known Thelma, she had never once asked about my business, other than the most obvious things, like invoices and receipts and a record of my cash sales. So it came as a complete surprise when at the end of one of our quarterly meetings she asked if she could have a word with me. She closed the lever arch files and stacked them on the bookshelf, folded away the clothes horse, after removing certain articles of her outsize underwear, and rearranged the cushions on the sofa. As we sat down next to each other she said, 'I have a friend I think you might be able to help with her new business venture.'

'I thought you were going to ask me to join the choir.'

'No, certainly not. This is a serious question.'

'Sorry, Thelma. I naturally assumed it had something to do with the church.'

'Can you make skeletons?' she asked, with such an intense look that it tightened all her facial muscles. I realised I had to alter my tone and pay attention.

'Do you mean can I make every bone in the human body?'

'That is precisely what I'm asking you.'

'Why?'

'For teaching hospitals and GP practices. You'd be surprised how many institutions need a skeleton.'

The idea appealed to me: bones made from polyester resin. But would it be lucrative? I told Thelma it might be, and to organise a meeting with her friend.

'I'll suggest Beatrice gets directly in touch with you.'

At that point Thelma's Jack Russell began scratching at the door. 'He hates me being in here, especially with a man. He gets terribly jealous. I'll have to let him in.'

'I've never asked you his name.'

'Chippy.'

Who, like a creature gone berserk, charged around the room, jumping over furniture, finally running along the piano keys and leaping up into Thelma's arms. It was time for me to leave.

'By the way, have I got enough money to buy a van?'

'Yes, you probably have, but I suggest you consider hire purchase.'

'I need a van and a driver to start doing weekly deliveries to the wholesalers.'

'I noticed you're doing a lot of business with Dutch Connection and Tindall's Reproductions, also Hancock's Wholesale.'

'You're right, Thelma, and it's growing. I need to look after them.'

At which point Chippy stood in front of me and began to growl aggressively.

'There's nothing going on,' she said, picking him up and consoling him with a series of gentle strokes. 'Let's go and find that old bra you like to chew on.'

Isobel arrived at the stall carrying two cups of tea and a slice of her homemade chocolate gateau wrapped in Bacofoil. She was closing in on me and could no longer say 'So what's new this week?' because there wasn't anything, most of our time at Puckmill being now spent fulfilling orders. Not just for the dealers, but also for our regular customers, who had begun to collect netsuke and scrimshaw, so we couldn't produce new pieces. It meant my conversations with Isobel took a new direction, of a more intimate nature. She knew I was married, but it didn't seem to deter her, and she suggested we should have lunch after I left the rag market. I began searching for excuses and then told her the truth, that when I left the market I drove back to the workshop and did an afternoon's work. Just as I was preparing to tell her that she could help me a lot by finding ivory carvings for me to mould, two Brummies turned up and started taking various pewter items from a cardboard box. One of them tapped me on the shoulder.

'Are you Nick?'

So I couldn't finish what I was saying, and with a look of disappointment Isobel walked away. I wanted to go after her and wondered if that was the last I would see of her.

'I'm Baz, and this is Chaucer.'

'That's an unusual name.'

'It's a nickname I was given at school.'

'It's because he tells tales,' said Baz, who was wearing a pair of overalls and an Aston Villa scarf.

'It's not because you're from Canterbury?'

'No. I'm from Long Eaton.'

'We run a pewter factory over in Digbeth and need your help with a project we've just taken on.'

They showed me a range of hip flasks, on which they wanted to attach engraved ivory inserts of old English hunting scenes.

'We have an in-house artist, but can you cast them for us with an antique finish?'

'Of course. It's what we do every day of the week,' I said rather cockily.

It suddenly occurred to me that maybe I could subcontract Marco Spinetti's car mascots to them. I didn't know why I'd agreed to take that job on in the first place; it was obvious they should be cast in pewter.

'I think I have some work for you too,' I told them. 'I'm here every Monday. Why don't we meet next week?'

'Of course. We'll give you a guided tour.'

I was about to leave when Sifta appeared, pushing what looked like a railway porter's trolley full of bundles of clothes.

'Bet you thought I wasn't going to turn up.'

'It had crossed my mind.'

'I've been at an auction at the BBC Pebble Mill studios.'

'What have you bought? Looks like a load of old rags.'

'They're not rags. They're the costumes from the Kenny Everett and Ken Dodd TV shows.'

'Who'd want to buy those?'

'You've no imagination, have you?' said Sifta. 'Fancy-dress parties for a start. Have a look at this.' He held up a pair of striped trousers with braces attached. 'You know who wore these, don't you?'

'No.'

'One of the Diddy men. And look at this.' He showed me a stockinette garment that looked like a spring onion. 'You'd look good in this.'

'I don't think it's me.'

He then brought out wigs and dresses, clowns' uniforms, ridiculous hats, and a range of pantomime costumes we could have a lot of fun with at home. The children always liked dressing up.

'Go on then, give me a couple of bundles. You can knock it off what you owe me.'

Sifta came with me to the car and chucked the clothing into the boot.

'You should change this car of yours. It's becoming a rust bucket. Surely you're making enough to buy a van?'

'You're right. I'll start looking for something.'

'I know someone flogging a Transit. Let me have a word with him.'

'Throw in the spring onion,' I said. 'I fancy that for a laugh.'

'Only if you put it on now and drive down the motorway wearing it.'

'I'll try it on, but I'm not going to wear it home.'

Not only was it an extremely tight fit, I also had great difficulty getting my arms through the two little slits cut into the sides. The hardest part was pulling it down far enough so that my face could look out through the circular hole. As for the tufty bits on top of my head, I looked like a strange plant that had arrived from another planet.

Sifta said he'd give me a fiver to keep it on. Which unfortunately I did, or rather had to: I couldn't get out of the thing. And the farce didn't end there. As I left the motorway, I noticed I needed to get petrol and had to pull into the Shell garage and fill the tank still dressed in it, which turned a head or two. One lady gave me such a strange look that I told her I was doing it for charity. She must have believed me, because she gave me a pound.

Ros eventually cut me out of it and after supper the children spent the rest of the evening parading about the house in various costumes.

Kase phoned to say he had transferred the last of the money due for the Nippers, all three thousand five hundred pounds of it. I had thought that with the job complete I wouldn't hear from him for a while, but I was wrong. He went on to ask if we could make some huge musical instruments for a nightclub in New York.

'How huge is huge?'

'Six feet long, but lightweight; they've got to be suspended from the ceiling. I need a guitar, a saxophone, a trumpet and a double bass.'

'How am I going to price that up?'

'That's your problem.'

'It's going to run into thousands. How many do you need?'

'Just one of each to begin with, but I'll probably want more. And I'll own the moulds, so exclusively for me.'

We'd have to make them out of fibreglass, something we hadn't done before at Puckmill.

It was Marco Spinetti who gave us the lead, after he had turned up with half a dozen car mascots, which I now told him we could make out of metal, believing that Baz and Chaucer could do the job for us.

The maestro of all fibreglass worked out in the film studios at Shepperton and was a close friend of Marco's. He had made props for all sorts of successful films, including *Raiders of the Lost Ark*. He also designed and fitted the window displays for Fortnum & Mason in Piccadilly. He was our man, Marco said, and gave me his telephone number.

'He'll do anything for me. If he asks for a code word, just say Lavazza.'

'Why would he ask for a code word?'

'He doesn't like time wasters. This is a very important man.'

'What's his name?'

'Rod Holt.'

Marco Spinetti had so built up this man that I felt I'd have to inflate my own importance, fearing he might just put the phone down on me. So I started by telling him we specialised in making the finest replicas and had developed bronze patinas that could be applied to the surface of polyester resins. He didn't say a word, just let me ramble on, until I finally said, 'Shall I shut up now? Have you heard enough?'

'Fascinating,' he said.

'Oh, by the way, I forgot to say Lavazza.'

'That's Marco's idea of a joke. It's my favourite coffee, since he introduced me to it.'

He was so impressed he wanted to come to the workshop, a long journey, all the way from Brentwood in Essex. He said he would teach us how to use fibreglass and that he could offer us lots of casting work.

I called a summit meeting, our first ever at the Crown in Frampton Mansell: Walter, Mike, Rob, Ade and myself, with one subject on the agenda, the further expansion of Puckmill Studios. Vital decisions needed to be taken and we'd have to increase our numbers.

It was decided that evening after much discussion that we needed two people who could both tumble cast and use an airbrush. Flexibility, that was the thing. It was obvious that people who could do more than one job would help us expand the business, even though it meant increasing our overheads. Mike put his big Gloucestershire foot down and insisted he should take on the fibreglass work, as well as being the mould maker. It made sense; he liked to be left on his own, without anyone looking over his shoulder. It was agreed we'd buy a van to do the Friday deliveries to the wholesalers in London and Manchester. And I'd also use it to go to the rag market on a Monday and Bath every Wednesday.

I didn't take Sifta up on buying the Ford Transit, after he told me some 'new age travellers' had toured the country in it, and with ninety thousand miles on the clock I wondered how much life was left in it. So I bought a year-old Citroën C15 van for five thousand pounds from Lacey and Thompson, a local garage. I didn't go for hire purchase as Thelma had suggested, because I had the cash.

There was just one problem: we didn't have anyone to drive it. Then Mike said he knew a chap who lived a few miles away, over in Coates, who was looking for a job. He described him as multitalented and technically minded and able to turn his hand to anything.

'He's our man,' I said. 'What's his name?'

'Johnny Allard.'

'It's got a good ring to it. Invite him to the workshop.'

At last I contacted the accountant Celia had told us about, and he came to pay me a visit. Simon Fisher was tall and distinguished, and far too young to have a mop of white hair. Celia told me that as an undergraduate he'd rowed for Cambridge and was not your everyday accountant; he wore jeans and T-shirts. She was certain I would get on with him. From a tin of Golden Virginia he offered me one of his ready rolled cigarettes, then took one for himself. In the wind that funnelled its way through the arches of the viaduct he struggled to light it, and out of frustration he knelt behind the door of his Audi before he was successful.

'Now, where were we?' he said at last, drawing deeply on his roll-up.

'We weren't anywhere,' I replied. I could tell straight away by the look on his face that he was not impressed by what he saw. 'Let me take you into the stockroom so you can see exactly what we make.'

Silently he picked up various samples of our finished work. 'You make all this amazing stuff here, in this hovel of a place?' he said, shaking his head.

'Why are you so surprised?'

'Show me round the workshop. I want to see all the processes it takes to finally have a finished product.'

We spent half an hour going through it all, speaking to everyone. He took his time before he said that he'd never seen such a primitive set-up and was horrified by our working conditions.

'Where are the extractor fans? None of you are wearing face masks when you're paint spraying. You don't have a single fire extinguisher, and I doubt you've got a first aid box. God, if Health and Safety saw you they'd close you down.'

'We keep the windows open,' I said.

'Well, you can't in the winter. And what do you do about heating?'

'I'm going to get some infrared heaters. Apparently, they just heat the body and not the room.'

'I've never heard of that before,' he said, genuinely astonished, staring at me as if he couldn't believe any of it.

'Okay, I'll make some changes . . . I promise.'

'You'd better. If the council suddenly decide to pay you a visit I don't know what they'll do.'

'Simon, I'm sorry, but I thought your visit today was about taking me on as a client.'

'Of course I will; I've never seen anything like it. But I really am in a state of shock.'

'Would you like some paracetamol? I can get some from the medicine cabinet.'

'Very funny.'

Some other neighbours at Puckmill, about half a mile away down at Baker's Mill, were Martin and Daphne Neville. In their fifties, they were an unusual couple who kept otters, and nowhere was too far for them to travel for an engagement to show off these tame creatures. Once, in their kitchen, one of them called Bee opened the fridge door and after stealing some cheddar cheese went and lay on her back in the stream, eating it between her paws. There wasn't a school in Gloucestershire where she had not been to entertain the children. Daphne had written a book about Bee and made several television appearances with her. Bee would climb all over her and was quite happy to sit on her head. Daphne had once been an actress and loved the show-business life; having the otters kept her in the limelight.

One Sunday morning Mike and I were working at Puckmill, having recently taken on a job for Derek and Archie who urgently needed six swordfish for a seafood restaurant in the King's Road, when who should come strolling up, carrying a microphone and a tape recorder, but Daphne.

'We need to speak,' she told me with some urgency.

'What's it about, Daphne? I'm a bit busy at the moment,' which she could obviously see as I loaded another swordfish into our Citroën van.

'The BBC are thinking of bringing back the radio programme *Down Your Way*.'

'That's good news, but what has it got to do with me?'

'I'm auditioning for it and need to interview you.'

'Why me? Only my mother thinks I'm interesting.'

'You're wrong. People would be fascinated by what you're doing, out here in deepest rural England, making replicas under a Brunel viaduct.'

Fifteen minutes later, with the van full of swordfish and Mike throwing a frisbee for his dog Buttons, I leant up against the doorway of the workshop as Daphne walked towards me with the tape recorder and a prepared script.

'Good morning, everyone. It's a glorious sunny day down here in the village of Frampton Mansell in the county of Gloucestershire. And who is it that I should just happen to come across in this beautiful valley but Nick Perry. Hidden away beneath a Brunel viaduct on Puckmill Farm, he runs a very unusual business, making replicas of the most amazing works of art, which I believe you export all over the world, including America.'

'Oo, aarh, I do, that be quite right.'

'You don't have to speak in the local dialect.'

'Oh, sorry. I got carried away by your introduction.'

'I'll edit that out, let me continue. Which I believe you export all around the world.'

'Yes, we have been very successful in the United States, and in several countries across Europe.'

'And I understand you employ people from the village, thus helping the local economy?'

'Yes, and we spend a bit of it in the pub.'

'Ha, ha, ha, on the odd pint of cider or two.'

'Yes, ha, ha, ha.'

'Perhaps you can describe for the listeners what it is you make.'

'Well, we specialise in making polyester resin replicas of Japanese ivory carvings, which do not involve the killing of an animal to get hold of its tusks. We also make replicas of scrimshaw, the name given to the art of engraving on whales' teeth.'

'I can tell you're a very contented man. And in this day and age, when other villages are losing their shops and post offices, you are helping Frampton Mansell to thrive.'

'In a very small way, I suppose we are.'

'It's little businesses like yours that should be considered for the Queen's Award to Industry.'

'Oh, Daphne, I don't think that will ever happen.'

'And your ambitions, Nick? Do you have any?'

'Yes, to become a millionaire, live an outrageous life and die a happy man.'

'I think we might have to edit that out. It's not in keeping with the simple honest folk we meet on *Down Your Way*.'

'But I was being honest.'

'I think I've got enough. If not, I'll have to rearrange a few words.'

My mother Dinah would always come and see me at the Bath antiques market. There was a café in Bartlett Street where she insisted we went for lunch, and because Quentin Saffell was willing to keep an eye on my stall I was usually able to sneak off for half an hour. It was during these lunches that she kept me up to date with the men in her life, all of them gentlemen. Despite her fading beauty, she still had an attractive sparkle, not only in her eyes but in her personality as well. Her diary was full, and whenever she planned a Sunday lunch with us it was weeks before she could fit us in.

'You have no idea just how exhausting it all is.'

'Being popular, you mean?'

'Most men need sympathy and reassurance when they get to a certain age.'

'You should open a clinic,' I suggested.

'Don't be sarcastic. I'm being serious.'

'Why have you never remarried? You've had so many proposals.'

'That's easy. Men snore, and I'd never give up my independence. Life is so much easier when you have only yourself to cook for.'

'Is this leading somewhere?' I asked.

She was continuously stirring her cup of coffee, which was

usually a clue that something was playing on her mind.

'It's Peter, the chap I spent a week with in Cumbria.'

'He wants to marry you.'

'No, the flat above me is for sale and he's considering buying it.'

'And you're not keen on that.'

'No, I'm not!'

That's as far as our conversation went. Quentin came in to tell me Thelma and Beatrice were looking for me at the stall. Beatrice was the one who wanted me to make skeletons for her; I had completely forgotten they'd arranged a meeting.

She had long blonde hair that she kept brushing back from her face and I detected an Australian accent. She told me her husband was a doctor, well connected in the medical world, and they'd done their market research.

'How many bones are there in the human body?' I asked her.

'Two hundred and six,' she said, without a moment's hesitation.

Which shut me up completely. In fact, to such an extent that for a minute I could offer no response whatsoever. The word ludicrous came to mind. If there had been a chair nearby I would have sat down.

'Two hundred and six, you say?' I managed at last.

'Yes.'

'It's impossible, absolutely impossible, for me to make a single skeleton,' I told her.

'Why? You sound so emphatic.'

'You have already stated it: two hundred and six bones. Our set-up couldn't start to handle the job. You need to find someone who specialises in injection moulding.'

'How disappointing. With the investment I've just received, what am I going to do?'

'I could make the skull for you, but that's about it.'

'Okay, I'll bring you one, so you can make a cast for me.'

'A skull will be no problem, but I really don't know anyone who can help you with the rest.'

When Johnny Allard walked into the workshop, I knew within five minutes he was the right person for us. A mustachioed young man with jet black hair, he'd walked from Coates, which must have taken half an hour. He was, as Mike had said, multitalented. In fact, he gave me a long list, not just of what he could turn his hand to, but also how good he was at them all; he certainly didn't suffer from under-selling himself. But his biggest asset was that he could sculpt, and as soon as the words were out of his mouth I asked him if he could make us some six-foot-long musical instruments.

'Yeah, why not?'

'When can you start?'

'How much are you paying?'

'Will you work full time and join the team?'

'You'll have to pick me up each day and drop me home.'

'Okay, you're on. I'll give you eighty pounds a week.'

That night, in the Oddfellows in Chester Street, I told Walter we now had a sculptor and could start creating our own pieces. And for his part, Walter had completed all the electroplating experiments with Schloetters in Kidderminster and said that soon we should start doing it in-house.

After I got home, Ros told me Derek Tindall had rung and a shipment of onyx and marble was arriving the next day from Pakistan.

8

'Concentrate on what you've already got,' Simon Fisher said to me in the Crown as we were having lunch. 'Stop searching. This imaginary product that's going to bring you all the riches you've ever dreamed of, it doesn't exist.'

'I don't know what you're talking about.'

'Someone has to reel you in. It's a mirage. You'll never reach it.'

I was only half listening, because I could see a hot air balloon descending rapidly into one of the fields below the pub. A basket full of people bouncing a few times before rolling over on its side was quite distracting.

'You're right, of course,' I said, my mind elsewhere, as Rex Horton's herd of Friesians stampeded, or rather lolloped, across the grass and encircled the balloon. Then the intercity train on its way to Stroud, which always blasted its horn before crossing the viaduct, scattered the cows in all directions; it was hard to pay attention to a single word Simon was saying.

'There's bedlam going on out there,' I said, but Simon, who had his back to the debacle taking place, thought I was talking about the state of the world.

'You've carved out a nice little niche for yourself, and with the knowledge you've acquired you should soon be able to make a good living.'

'I've learnt a little, that's all. Just about put a foot on the first rung of the ladder towards success.'

'You've done a lot in a very short time.'

'I've set myself a target.'

'What's that?'

'To become a millionaire, and I've only got two years left to do it.'

'That's impossible.'

'What makes you say that?'

'You're going to make a million working in a converted stable in a farmyard?'

'It's not where it's made but what you make that's the crucial thing.'

'You need a state-of-the-art facility with a production line for that to happen.'

Our conversation continued while five dishevelled people picked themselves up and staggered towards the Crown. As they walked into the snug, they looked as if they'd spent a rough night in a hedge. The barman, who was pulling pints, didn't comment on their appearance, and greeting them with a polite smile said, 'What can I get you?'

'Five whiskies, please . . . actually, make them doubles.'

I'd finally made Frank Webb the model church for his imaginary village of Wapping Sodbury. I should have charged him at least a hundred and fifty pounds for it, but instead settled for thirty walking sticks. He hated parting with cash, though in other ways he was a generous man.

'Not once, Frank, has a penny left your hand and found its way into my pocket.'

'That is a figment of your stagnation.'

'It's called denial, Frank.'

Greasy Gerald, who was standing nearby, said it was easier to get blood out of a scone.

'Don't you mean stone?'

'No, scone,' said Gerald.

'Have it your own way.'

'He's got money all right, stashed somewhere in that house of his. They'll find it one day under the floorboards after they've brought him out in a coffin.'

Anyway, I was on the right side of the deal, selling the walking sticks for nine pounds each. Frank, alias Barney

Rubble, always with mischievousness in his eyes and an appealing boyishness, was his own man and wouldn't budge an inch once he had made up his mind. I was always close to a smile when we were in conversation. But we only ever talked about walking sticks and the real love of his life, his model railway. He often invited me to call in at his house on the Hagley Road, tempting me with the chance to be a guard on one of the trains. And he was serious when he asked me to attend the first service to be held in the church of Wapping Sodbury, to which I agreed.

With dextrous fingers and a miniature screwdriver, he'd managed to fit a little repetitive tape recording of church bells to ring out across his papier mâché countryside. For some reason, a sense of sadness suddenly flooded over me as I listened to it and I felt a terrible loneliness in him. He shared this world with no one, living in the past. He never spoke of his parents or his childhood.

'You see, it's now complete, my England of the 1950s, when bread was tuppence a loaf, there were hardly any motor cars and Mother made me my Ovaltine.'

Whenever Derek and Archie turned up at Puckmill they always arrived in a different car, this time a Daimler.

'How many cars have you got, Derek?' I asked.

'I've got a warehouse full of 'em, and they all need a run from time to time.'

'We've shipped the *Charleston Dancer*s. Now here's the next piece for you,' said Archie, handing me a bronze by Bruno Zach on a malachite base, a topless girl holding a riding crop, wearing knee-length boots.

'By the way, I read the *Antiques Trade Gazette*,' I remarked, to let them know I was aware of the prices Art Deco statues were fetching.

'What's your point?' said Derek.

'That in a certain London auction house a *Charleston Dancer* sold for eight thousand pounds and it looked remarkably like one we made.'

'Many of the originals were made as limited editions,' said Archie, trying to throw me off the scent.

'Not this one.'

'How do you know?'

'Because I recognised the marble base.'

'You make good money out of us, so I wouldn't ask too many questions.'

'You told me you were selling them across the States, not in London.'

'Oh, let's tell him the truth,' said Derek, knowing that if they didn't it would be even harder to talk themselves out of a deeper mess.

As I'd suspected, they'd sold one of the *Charleston Dancer*s as an original and deceived not only the auction house, but the buyer. Their excuse was they were testing the market; all the rest had been shipped to America. Never once had it crossed my mind to mislead a customer of ours. It would have been not only dishonest but also self-defeating, since what I was trying to achieve was to get Puckmill known for the quality of its replicas.

'I'm going to up my price from the hundred and twenty pounds you're paying now to a hundred and fifty. But if you intend to sell them as originals, you can find yourselves another manufacturer.'

'Who do you think you bloody are?' said Archie, grabbing me by the shirt collar.

'Leave him alone, Archie. We don't want to fall out over this,' said Derek, removing Archie from my lapels. 'Look, let's start this conversation again. We agree to pay you a hundred and fifty, and we won't sell the statues in London as originals. Please price up the Bruno Zach for us. All right, Archie?' He patted his partner gently on the shoulder. 'Now why don't you apologise to Nick.'

Archie couldn't bring himself to do that verbally, managing only to give me the slightest nod of his head.

'We all need each other, let's remember that.'

Derek then opened the boot of the Daimler and showed me another six advertising figures they wanted made: a Dunlop golfer, a pirate smoking shag, an ice-cream girl holding a cornet, a Kilkof frog advertising cough medicine, a Johnnie Walker figure striding along clasping a walking stick, and a large Robertson's Golden Shred golliwog.

'Can you price them up and make fifty of each for us?'

When Mike appeared, chewing on a piece of straw and twanging his braces, I knew he'd be on the end of some ridiculing remarks from Archie.

'Afternoon, gents. I'd tip me hat but I ain't got one,' said Mike, in an exaggerated drawl.

'Look who we've got 'ere, old Wurzel himself.' Archie always had to mimic Mike's Gloucestershire accent.

'Got some news for the two of you.'

''Ere, and what might that be?'

'He's coming round the corner any moment now.'

The Booths' Rottweiler, Haggler, casually wandered over from the other side of the viaduct, as he did from time to time.

'Don't run, just edge yourselves slowly to the car,' I said, which they did as I distracted Haggler with one of the many deflated footballs he had burst.

As they drove off, Derek wound down the window to tell me we had a big future together. 'We haven't even begun yet,' he shouted.

Even after they had disappeared I could hear them

continuously sounding their horn, disturbing the villagers of Frampton Mansell.

Mike said to me, 'You know it's a show I put on for them, don't you?'

'What?'

'Talking Gloucestershire.'

'Really? I hadn't noticed.'

When Ros said that she had never heard me mention the word holiday and wondered if it was in my vocabulary, I knew exactly what was coming. The children were breaking up for the summer in two weeks.

'We could go camping,' she suggested.

'What, all of us in a tent!' I said, horrified at the thought.

'I was thinking we could go to Dorset and show the children where you spent your childhood.'

'You mean where I used to roam wild and free across the Purbeck Hills?'

'That's not quite the image your mother has given me. More of a trainspotter sitting on a platform with a packed lunch.'

'Only because I told her that's what I was up to.'

'So, what do you think of a camping holiday? You can show us what you learnt when you were a boy scout and spent a weekend on Brownsea Island.'

'I think we should stay in a guest house. I can't see us surviving a week in a tent.'

'I'll do the cooking, Dad,' chipped in Sam. 'I'm top of the class in domestic science.'

'What's your speciality?'

'Eggs and bacon and baked beans on toast.'

'It's not really haute cuisine.'

'Sam can cook the breakfast, and we can eat out in the evenings,' said Ros.

'What about me?' said Seth. 'I made an omelette the other day.'

'Which you burnt, and it got stuck in the frying pan,' Lysta reminded him.

'You can make the tea in the mornings.'

'So, we're going. Does everyone agree?' They all put up their hands, reluctantly followed by me. I'd be worrying about Puckmill the whole time we were away. And it would be the first long journey we'd be making in the Peugeot 304, which we had recently bought from a neighbour in Chester Street.

I told the team at Puckmill during our tea break the next morning that I had been forced to take a holiday, and that while the managing director was away Rob would be acting as my deputy and would oversee the running of the place.

'Thanks for letting me know,' said Rob.

'Sorry. I only thought of it five minutes ago, but somebody's got to be in charge.'

'So I'm deputy managing director of Puckmill Studios.'

'Yes.'

'I thought you were Head of Production and Sales,' Mike said to me.

'I was, but I resigned from that position, and promoted myself to managing director.'

'So, what's my job title?' asked Mike, looking confused.

'Well, it hasn't really changed, I've just added another position. Chief Mould Maker and Tumble Caster and Senior Maintenance Officer.'

'And I'm Head of Sculpting,' said Johnny Allard boastfully.

'And you, Ade, have replaced Ros as Head of Stains and Finishing.'

That had taken twenty minutes out of my life, just because I was going on holiday.

'One last thing, as we're talking about it,' said Rob. 'Where does Walter fit into all of this?'

'Walter Pepper has the most senior position as Master of Chemistry and Alchemy.'

At the Birmingham rag market the following Monday, I continued to do business with all my regular customers, including Frank and Gerald, who always disappeared and then returned two or three times to show me what they had bought from the other dealers. Gerald was wearing a tricorn hat and carrying a musket and told me they were acquisitions for the famous battles of the English Civil War he re-enacted on summer weekends. More to the man than meets the eye, I said to myself. As he was telling me how seriously everyone took these re-enactments, I saw Isobel a few yards away with her back towards me. I wondered whether she was coming to say hello, as she had done week after week.

'You're not listening to a word I'm saying,' said Gerald, who was going into the detail of how he got flattened under a drawbridge.

'I'm sorry, just give me a minute,' I said, leaving the stall and walking up to Isobel, who didn't know I was standing behind her until I said, 'Isobel.'

She turned quickly so that we came face to face. 'You gave me a fright.'

'How are you?' I said. 'I felt last week things were left up in the air a little.'

'Maybe I was being too friendly. Why don't we leave it at that.'

'Well, I hope you'll keep coming to the stall. I enjoy your company.'

'I took an interest in what you're doing, that's all,' she said dismissively.

'And I hope you'll continue to.'

'Goodbye for now, and good luck with your business.' There was a finality in her tone.

'Goodbye, Isobel. I'm sorry if I hurt your feelings.'

Gerald and Frank had wandered off again, and as I packed up the stall Sifta Sam came and told me he had just bought a hundred Dr Barnardo's collection boxes, those little cottages that I remembered from my childhood.

'Sifta, you are a man of curious tastes. What makes you think you can sell those?'

'Collectors, people who can spot an investment opportunity. They are becoming rare items.'

'Okay, I'll buy one. How much?'

'A pound, that's all.'

So I gave him a pound. 'Ninety-nine to go,' he said, 'and making fifty pence on each one. That's a tidy profit. And I did well on those Pebble Mill costumes,' he said. 'Now what netsukes have you got for me?'

Sifta was a man who knew how to survive, living off the scraps dropped by others, swimming in an ocean looking for what he could feed upon. He was a loner, but sure of himself, and, moving from market to market, bought and sold what would keep him afloat for a few more days. Who he really was, his thoughts about the world we lived in, I would probably never know. I saw him for a few minutes every week: a man of short sharp conversations whose eyes never met mine but scanned the wider background, always on the lookout.

Greasy Gerald had known him for over twenty years. They first met at Charnock Richard antiques market when Sifta tried to flog him a medal he claimed was from the Boer War and had haggled over the price all morning. Sifta drove an old Morris van and, being the size of a jockey, curled up and slept in the back two or three nights a week.

How different Frank Webb was. He wanted me to share his make-believe world, and if I'd accepted all his invitations to call in after I had left the rag market I'd never have made it back to Puckmill in the afternoons. He saw me as a schoolfriend who'd come round and play with him for a couple of hours. Aileen told me that once he had chatted up Dora, the lady who pushed the tea trolley around the market, not for any romantic reasons, but because he had found out that her late husband had a collection of old Great Western timetables.

When I walked into Baz and Chaucer's pewter factory in Digbeth, I could sense that they had recently cleaned the office and had probably just finished a few minutes ago; it smelt of Air Wick. Surely not for my benefit? Was I so important that they needed to impress me? There was an unnatural neatness to the place. I'd brought Marco Spinetti's car mascots with me and would be glad to offload the job.

Baz and Chaucer were cousins and had inherited the business from Baz's father, now retired to a bungalow on the south coast, fishing for whiting off Boscombe Pier. They gave me a complete tour of the factory, which consisted of a series of little rooms. It was an efficient set-up, churning out such items as thimbles, spoons, plates, drinking tankards, and the range of hip flasks that was the reason they'd wanted me to come in the first place. It was all about quantity, a numbers game. As soon as they had de-moulded the casts, the machines were filled again, day in, day out.

How painstakingly slow in comparison were our casting techniques at Puckmill. We'd be lucky to cast twice a day into our moulds, as we had to wait for them to cure. Polyester resin hardened gradually, while pewter, with a low melting point, solidified in a matter of minutes.

Baz and Chaucer, both in their mid-thirties, were ambitious and wanted to diversify, wishing to break into new markets with their own original products. They were bored and uninspired by everything they were manufacturing.

'We've been making virtually the same things for over a hundred years, since our grandfather started the business,' they told me.

'That is boring,' I said.

'Not just boring, but very boring,' said Chaucer.

'Here's the plan,' said Baz. 'We want to make a range of products that combine pewter and ivory, decorative pieces at the top end of the gift market.'

'Sounds like a good idea,' I said.

'We do all the major trade shows, including the Spring Gift Show here at the NEC, and we sell to Selfridges and Liberty's,' said Chaucer, who had already convinced me they were worth getting involved with.

'Well, if you want to start making new products, what about these car mascots?' I said.

They looked them over for five minutes and then somewhat reluctantly agreed to take on the job, I'm sure only because I'd agreed to make the inserts for their hip flasks.

'We would have to make them in several parts and then solder the pieces together. It's not going to be cheap,' said Chaucer, passing the Bentley mascot to Baz.

'You don't sound too keen.'

'Small runs don't really interest us, but to get something going with you we'll do it.'

'Can you put an antique finish on them, so they look like the real thing?'

'Let us play around and see what we can come up with.'

'I'll leave them with you. It's a job I never wanted; it would be a weight off my shoulders.'

After they'd given me the six masters of the English hunting scenes for their hip flasks engraved in wax, I headed home. I'd been up since five o'clock and it was now three thirty in the afternoon. I usually had the energy to go back to the workshop, but I didn't today. Instead I went to see Walter, who greeted me at his front door wearing a white space suit, a huge pair of goggles and a helmet with an air pipe running from it. He looked extra-terrestrial, like a visitor to our planet. As he lifted the helmet from his head he said, 'It's the fumes from the hydrosulphides. They're unbearable, as if you're breathing in a pile of rotten eggs.'

'I can smell it myself.'

'Come in, but we can't go down to the basement. It'll overwhelm you.'

'What are you experimenting with?'

'Those bronze patinas I was telling you about.'

'What's the latest on the electroplating?' I asked.

'Now I suggest you sit down, because this will be the biggest decision you have ever taken. This is the final frontier.'

'You sound like someone from *Star Trek*.'

'Well, it is, in a way. We are the first people to be doing it, going where no man has gone before.'

'I'm losing my sense of gravity. What are you talking about?'

'I think it's the final expansion we need to make, and then everything will be possible.'

We spoke for an hour, most of it about the practicalities of installing a plating shop. Then my least favourite subject, capital expenditure. Walter estimated ten thousand pounds, the largest outlay of my life. Buying Dyffryn Farm and its thirty-eight acres had only cost six thousand. Then someone would have to run the shop, which meant employing yet another person. I thought it was a step too far. It filled me with such apprehension that I started to backtrack on the whole idea and Walter could see it.

'I'll cover the cost, or rather lend the business the ten thousand pounds.'

'We've got the money in the bank, it's not that. But what's it going to give us?'

'That's the most important thing, of course. With electroplating we can make the most wonderful works of art, not just replicas of Art Deco statues but our own originals, limited editions, and sell them in the London art galleries.'

'You mean we are going to become modern artists?'

'Yes, when we've mastered the techniques,' said Walter, giving me the most penetrating look.

'We'll be the forerunners of a new idea in art.'

'You've got it!'

'What we're talking about has just given me an idea.'

'Tell me.'

'Are you familiar with the artist Beryl Cook?'

'Can't say I am.'

'She's extremely popular. We could sculpt some of the figures from her paintings.'

'Can you get in touch with her?' Walter asked me.

'All I know is that she lives in Plymouth.'

'Well, write to her and see what she says.'

After this exhilarating conversation, we fell into a becalmed silence; there was so much to consider.

'Those chemicals you're exposed to all day . . .' I said to Walter.

'Yes, what about them?'

'Are there any side effects . . . for instance, can they change your personality?'

'Probably, but why should I care at my age?'

Johnny Allard had finished sculpting the musical instruments, a mammoth task which he had stuck to every day for nearly two months. We had run out of space in the stables, after we'd allocated the last sixteen feet of it to our electroplating workshop. So now I had to rent half the barn opposite the workshop as well; there was no alternative. Johnny had to work somewhere, and besides, he was a messy worker, leaving his tools lying around the place. Celia had recently moved Pearl into the barn and stored bales of straw and hay for her at one end. What she hadn't told me was that she'd said her cleaner could stable her two donkeys in the barn as well, along with Pearl and the goats. I liked animals, but with our expansion they were now taking up too much space.

Haggler had got into the habit of strolling over every day, sniffing around as if he owned the place. He was now a fully grown Rottweiler whom you didn't mess with. When I grabbed him by the collar to walk him home he growled fiercely, and I started to worry he might attack one of us.

In reality we worked in a farmyard, a far cry from the professional workshop that Simon had said was necessary for producing works of art. The first reaction of many who came to Puckmill was one of astonishment: a group of hillbillies hidden away under a viaduct, exporting to countries around the world, with a quack quack here and a moo moo there. And that was the reaction we got from Rod Holt when he drove in to show us how to fibreglass the musical instruments.

'Wow! I thought I had a basic set-up. How do you survive in winter?'

'We put on more clothes,' I said.

'Is that it?'

'And bobble hats.'

Rod, at a guess, was in his early forties, with shoulder-length hair beginning to show signs of grey. No doubt once a raver in hippie London, he wore faded jeans and sunglasses.

'I bet you liked Led Zeppelin.'

'Petula Clark, actually.'

He spent the day with us, and indeed was a master craftsman. Not only that, he was generous-spirited and told us everything about how to make skin moulds and mix filler powders with gelcoat resins, a technique which must have taken him years to perfect.

As Marco had told me, he'd learnt his trade working at the Shepperton film studios and now also designed and installed all the window displays for Fortnum & Mason, replacing them four times a year for each season. He and a small team worked through the night to complete the transformation before the store opened at nine in the morning. He also designed schemes for Asprey's, the royal jewellers. I didn't know it then, but a long friendship began that day. I was glad when he said there were things we could do for him.

So Mike started to mould the largest pieces we had ever made. That night I rang Kase to tell him we would have one of each of his musical instruments ready in a month. This time, when the job was complete, we were to ship them straight to New York, to spare him the long trek to Puckmill.

Then came the difficult bit, the price, but Rod had told me what he would charge for such a job. Fifteen hundred pounds for each mould, one thousand two hundred and fifty each for the guitar and double bass, a thousand for the saxophone and eight hundred for the trumpet, a total of ten thousand three hundred pounds. If I'd priced it up, I'd have arrived at eight thousand.

'Don't be a fool to yourself. Who else is going to make them for him?' had been Rod's reaction.

'How much am I going to owe you?' asked Kase.

'Ten thousand three hundred pounds, to be precise.'

'Okay. I'll transfer over half of it now, and I'll settle what's outstanding when the shippers pick them up.'

Rod was right: you're the only loser if you sell yourself short. I estimated we had made at least six thousand pounds out of the job.

'I feel like splashing out tonight,' I said to Ros and the children.

'Fish and chips from the Friar Tuck?' said Sam.

'No, wilder than that. Let's go to the Wimpy Bar.'

'And milkshakes, Dad?' said Seth.

'Don't push your luck.'

It was Wednesday and at the Bath antiques market I told Quentin Saffell that on Saturday I was going to Dorset for a week. I asked him if he'd look after the stall for me if I gave him fifty quid. He said he would be happy to normally, but that cracks had started to appear in some of the walls of their house in the London Road and next Wednesday he had a chartered surveyor coming to inspect it. He was very worried that it could be subsidence.

'Why don't you ask your mother?'

'My mother? She'd talk too much, although she does have natural charm.'

'I find Dinah very engaging. There wouldn't be anyone better in my opinion, and she certainly has the sales patter.'

When she arrived at the stall, she always threw her arms around me and then, never discreetly, asked how much money I'd made. I never replied, it being something of a personal nature, but it was only because she wanted to hear how well I was doing. I could imagine her telling all the other stallholders just how much we were taking as soon as she sold anything. But she wasn't herself today, and looked anxious, as if something weighed heavily on her mind.

'I can tell something's wrong,' I said. 'What's up? You look worried.'

'I'm in a desperate situation,' she whispered. 'I have to talk to you.'

'You're not ill, are you?'

'No, it's far worse than that.'

'Well, we can talk about it over lunch,' I said.

'It can't wait until then. We must go now, somewhere quiet.'

I'd not seen her so agitated for a long time, so I asked Quentin if he would keep an eye on things while we went for a coffee. Sitting in a corner of Popjoys at the end of Bartlett Street, my mother told me about the situation she suddenly found herself in. Before she said a word, I knew a man would be involved.

'It's Peter,' she said. 'He's put in an offer on the flat above me. I'm going to have to move out.'

'Why? Have an arrangement; let him know when you're available.'

'You don't understand. It's too close for comfort; he's too needy for me.'

'Well, what do you want me to do about it?'

'Tell him I'm mad. That on the surface I might appear quite normal, but I'm unstable.'

'He'll see through that straight away.'

'Then tell him I'm a kleptomaniac and can't stop shoplifting.'

'Mum, come on, we can deal with this. You're getting into a panic.'

'We have to move quickly. They accepted his offer this morning. Come to the flat this afternoon. I'll make sure he's there and then I'll pop out, saying I've got to pick up a prescription.'

'So you don't want to see him any more, it's all over. Is that what you want me to say?'

'Of course not. I like him as a friend at a distance, just not living right on top of me.'

'I think that is exactly what you should tell him, not me.'

She began to stir her coffee repetitively in a clockwise motion, deep in thought.

'You're right. I panicked. I'll tell him.'

'Good. Now could you do something for me? Would you look after the stall for me next week while we're in Dorset?'

'Me? I couldn't. No, definitely not. I don't know the price of anything.'

'I'll write them all down for you. You'll love it, and I'll pay you commission.'

'I'm not interested in your money.'

It took five minutes to convince her, but I knew she would agree in the end. She rang me that evening; she had talked to Peter, and he'd decided to withdraw his offer rather than lose her friendship. It was how it had always been with my mother. She couldn't help it, she attracted men, and unless she altered her personality, which would be impossible, it would always go on happening. She needed to hang a sign on her back: *Available at odd times for friendship and walks in the park.*

⁂ 9 ⁂

It was late afternoon when we arrived at the campsite at Durdle Door, having stopped for lunch in Poole and quickly walked along the jetty where as a child I'd fished using a hand-line. No wonder I'd taken up trainspotting; I never caught anything but a crab. Then Ros had wandered around the pottery and bought six eggcups. It seemed an odd purchase, because I couldn't remember us ever eating boiled eggs.

We were greeted by Renata West, the camp commandant, dressed like a Wild West girl, wearing a neckerchief and a leather cowboy hat. She reminded me of Calamity Jane, though she stopped short of saying 'Howdy, folks, a mighty welcome to you all'. Her Scottie dog Bugle introduced himself by offering us his paw and then standing on his hind legs and walking backwards. This was obviously a well-rehearsed routine for new campers, who loved it of course. Renata gave us strict instructions not to give him any treats, saying he was a natural show-off and would move from tent to tent expecting to be rewarded.

She then pointed out the showers and let us know it would take about five minutes till the water ran hot, so some patience was required. Nearby was a concrete block of toilets, with a notice on each door telling us what was permissible to be flushed away, and another over the basins: *Please be aware of other campers and remember radios should be turned off at 10 p.m.*

I refrained from goose-stepping as I went to unload the car, before the farce of erecting the tent began. It had never been out of its packaging, so we weren't prepared for the ordeal that lay ahead. We struggled with it for over an hour, trying to make sense of the incomprehensible diagrams and falling into general disagreements as everyone thought they knew best. That was when our neighbours, fed up with our petty arguing, showed us how to erect a tent in under fifteen minutes. They didn't offer their help, or ask permission, but came over and put the whole thing up in silence. It was only later that I noticed their tent was identical to ours.

'Well, no wonder,' I said. 'It's easy when you've done it before.'

Strangely, as the week progressed, so did my fascination with those neighbours, Bernie Gillup and his wife Rita, who became known as the clockwork campers. They'd cycled from Derbyshire, covering twenty-five miles each day. They were a strapping couple, whose organised and mapped-out world intrigued me. Their daily routine unfolded with a frightening precision.

Every morning they used the seven o'clock pips on Radio 4 as their alarm and put the exact amount of water in a saucepan to come to the boil just as they returned from an early morning run around the campsite still in their pyjamas. After a quick breakfast, Bernie pumped up the tyres on their bikes and gave them a squeeze to check they were at the right pressure. Next, he placed their packed lunch and a neatly folded Ordnance Survey map in the saddlebag. After mounting their bicycles and counting down the seconds to dead on nine o'clock, they set off. I wondered if a mutual love of timekeeping had brought them together. Maybe they'd met and fallen for each other under a clock. Ros said I should look at my own behaviour, as I was showing a pathological interest in them.

After supper in a local pub, we went for a walk, watching the sun go down like a blood-red orange into the English Channel. My mind was never far from Puckmill, and when on some remote bridle path we happened to come upon a telephone box I said, 'Go on ahead. I'll catch up with you in a minute.'

'Dad, who decided to put a telephone box out here?' asked Sam, being a naturally inquisitive boy.

I didn't have any loose change, so made a reverse charge call to Rob. After agreeing that he'd pay for it, he said, 'I just mentioned to Kate, why hasn't he rung yet?'

'What's going on? Is everything all right?'

'You mean your business empire, or the state of the world?'

'Tell me quickly what's been happening.'

'Nothing. You've only been gone for a day.'

'So no disasters?'

'Only one. Ade's sliced off the top of his finger with a scalpel.'

'My God. Did you take him to A&E?'

'No. Mike bandaged him up, and because he can't hold a cotton bud is teaching him how to use the tumble caster.'

'Is that it?'

'Daphne Neville came over and said her otter's in season.'

'What's that got to do with us?'

'False pretences if you ask me. She calls by for any reason.'

'Yes, like last week, to warn us about the frogs shagging on the Chalford road. I'll ring in tomorrow if I'm near a call box.'

'Everything's fine. Leave it a couple of days. See if you've got it in you to enjoy a holiday.'

Halfway through our week, and the highlight so far, we visited Corfe Castle. Seth and Belah rolled down its steep green slopes just as I had as a child. By chance, the old steam engine, billowing great white clouds, crossed over the stone bridge on its way to Wareham.

'Go on, Dad, tell us again about your days as a trainspotter,' said Seth.

'No, they're too emotional. All those fish paste sandwiches, sitting on platforms.'

'What about when you waited at Lymington station all day, and the only train you saw was the one that took you back to

Brockenhurst six hours later?' Sam reminded me.

'I don't want to talk about it.'

'Let's go to the amusement arcade in Swanage where you put "Tell Laura I Love Her" on the jukebox,' Lysta suggested, which set me off, singing my own special version of that worldwide hit.

On the beach below Canford Cliffs, we spent an afternoon enjoying a 1950s holiday. I watched the children making sandcastles, playing badminton and running in and out of the waves before I took Belah on a walk along the promenade and we sat together eating a choc ice, watching the Isle of Wight ferry on its way to Bournemouth.

We agreed that evening we should cook ourselves a meal, using the Calor gas stove and then letting rip with some singing and dancing. So far Seth had successfully managed to make us a cup of tea in the mornings, which meant Ros and I could have a lie-in, or as much of one as is possible in a tent shared with four children. We applauded his efforts as he carefully stepped over his brother and sisters, still dreaming in their sleeping bags.

'You deserve it, having to bring us all up. It can't be that easy.'

Strange sympathy to hear from one of your own children.

We started by cooking the sausages, planning to follow up with the eggs and baked beans, juggling it all on the single gas burner. Everything was fine until the wind changed direction and engulfed the Gillups in a fatty blue smoke. Bernie, mild-mannered until now, rushed over and ran off with our frying pan of sausages and put them in the grass some twenty yards away.

'Bloody amateurs,' he said. 'Can't you read the wind?'

Lysta interrupted, telling me she had found the tape of Hank Williams' greatest hits.

'Those fumes get into your clothes. We'll have to go to the launderette. It's completely ruined our schedule.'

'I'll pay the cleaning bill, Bernie. I'm terribly sorry.'

'Well, I haven't got time to argue over it now. Wind is a changeable phenomenon, hence the need for weather vanes.'

'I can't disagree with that, Bernie.'

'Dad, what shall I put on first? "Straight To Hell" or "Crazed Country Rebel"?'

While all this was going on, Bugle stole in and scoffed the sausages. So we gave up on our campfire cooking and ended up eating scampi and chips in the Little Red Rooster.

The next day, as we were coming to the end of a longer than planned walk after following the wrong footpath, I noticed a telephone box gleaming in the rays of the setting sun. Belah was riding on my shoulders, but I put on a sudden spurt, hoping I could make the call before the others caught up. I'd been on the lookout all week for the chance to ring the workshop without Ros knowing; she wanted me to forget about Puckmill for a few days and be a family man.

'I can't help it, Ros,' I shouted back to her. 'I've got to make sure my business empire is surviving without me.'

'I always knew only a part of you would be here. Go and make your phone call.'

I ran on, Belah still on my shoulders, and when I got through to Mike I asked him, 'What's up?'

'I'm watching *Coronation Street* with Mum and Dad.'

'You're joking.'

'I used to watch *Crackerjack*, but I've grown out of it.'

'Okay, enough. What's going on? I've only got twenty pence here.'

'Well, this could be pretty big news. The Mary Rose Trading Company rang, wanting to know if we could make a replica of the ship's bell.'

'Wow! That *is* big news.'

'I told them our managing director is away for a week,

taking part in a sailing regatta, and you'd be in touch when you returned.'

'Ha ha, very funny. What else has been going on?'

'I saw an adder today. It went into the shed where we store all the onyx and marble.'

'Maybe it came in one of the crates from Pakistan.'

'No. When I mentioned it to Ivor he told me this place used to be known as Adder Valley.'

'You shouldn't have told Ivor. Now everyone will know about it.'

'There is something I forgot to tell you. The whole village is going to be without electricity next Friday, something to do with a problem in a substation.'

'What? For the whole day?'

'Yes. Rob reckons we should take it off, and have a long weekend.'

'I've got to go, Mike, my time's up. See you in a couple of days.'

I knocked on the door of Renata West's caravan to say goodbye, holding a bag of rubbish to show her we had left no litter. Lysta asked if she could take a photograph of us all with Bugle standing on his hind legs.

'There's no need for that,' said Renata, handing us a selection of postcards of her and Bugle at thirty pence each. 'Forty pence if you want one with an original paw print. He signs them every day with fresh mud.'

'Oh, Dad, with his paw print, please,' begged Belah.

I conceded without a word to this outrageous, sentimental con, and as we drove away, Renata waving us off with Bugle in her arms, I sang 'Whip crack away, whip crack away'. And so began the three-hour journey home to Cirencester.

Within five minutes of being back at Puckmill, I had Thelma on the phone telling me that a VAT inspector would be paying us a visit next month. I knew his immediate thought would be 'What on earth have I walked into here?', a perfectly reasonable reaction from the trained eye of one sniffing out any discrepancy in the profit and loss columns. For a start, my office was a telephone box, I told Thelma, who didn't believe me, having never visited Puckmill.

'Is that one of your jokes? Because if it isn't you need to get an office very quickly.'

'Can you come yourself? I need someone who'll give the place an air of authenticity, and besides, I wouldn't know what to say to him.'

'You'll have to pick me up.'

It completely deflected me from what I had thought was going to be an exciting morning speaking to the Mary Rose Trading Company in Portsmouth. Instead I went out and bought a 10x4 shed, which Mike promised to assemble before the VAT inspector arrived. We had less than three weeks to make the place look like a well-run, conventional business.

When I got back, Rob handed me a sheet of paper, telling me it was his report on what had been happening during my week off. 'Changes need to be made,' he said seriously. But I didn't get a chance to read it as Walter rang to say Schloetters would be delivering the chemicals next week and sending out a rep to help us set up the electroplating shop.

I'd only been back an hour when Haggler appeared with yet another burst football in his mouth, followed by Chris Booth, who as well as being our neighbour was also my GP.

'I thought you'd found out where he'd been escaping.'

'That was last week. Now he's learnt how to open the front gate.'

'He'll be skateboarding over next,' I said, trying to make light of it, but Ade was terrified of him. I told Chris that he might be a family pet, but he could be quite threatening when he was over here. 'He thinks the place belongs to him, and he shows his teeth and growls if anyone goes near him.'

Finally, in the afternoon I got a chance to ring Priscilla, the Keeper of Collections at the Mary Rose Trust. They were keen to meet us at the earliest opportunity to discuss making replicas of the ship's bell. Prince Charles, who was patron of the trust, had agreed to the idea of a limited edition of seven hundred and fifty, each one to be numbered and sold with a certificate signed by him. They were hoping it would interest American visitors and raise funds for the restoration work.

I assured them that we specialised in this sort of work, and I would come to Portsmouth next week with my head mould maker, a man of vast experience. A slight exaggeration, I knew, but Mike had learnt a hell of a lot at Puckmill.

'You will need to convince Margaret Rule, our senior archaeologist, that no damage will come to the bell.'

'Next Tuesday at ten a.m.?' I suggested.

'I'll make sure all the key people are here.'

I was aware that Mike had never left Gloucestershire, and although I had seen him talking confidently about tumble casting and mould making to the likes of Kase and Derek Tindall, that had been on his home territory. In the Oddfellows, while he crunched on some pork scratchings, I let him know people had commented on his professional approach to making moulds, and that it seemed to come naturally to him.

'I suppose it does now,' he said modestly.

'How would you feel if you had to demonstrate the art of mould making in front of other people?'

'What are you getting at, exactly?'

'Well, for instance, if we got the job making the *Mary Rose* bell. I don't think they're going to let us bring it back to Puckmill and mould it here; it's priceless.'

'I see what you mean. Being watched by total strangers,'

he said, withdrawing into a long silence and rolling a Golden Virginia cigarette.

'Would we have to stay away the night?' he asked eventually, blowing a cloud of smoke up towards the tobacco-stained ceiling.

'Longer than that. It will take at least three days.'

'Let me think about it.'

'We have to go there next Tuesday and decide whether to take on the job.'

When I got home Ros insisted I go and speak to Lysta.

'What's up?'

'She's absolutely refusing to do gymnastics any longer. She says it's a complete waste of time.'

'I thought she wanted to be a ballerina.'

'That was months ago. Now she wants a horse and to start riding lessons.'

'Daphne Neville's got a horse that leans over a gate all day. I'll have a word with her.'

Lysta walked into the kitchen then and told us she'd heard every word and wanted us to know straight away that despite what everyone said, it was nothing to do with her adolescence.

'Even Miss Holdenhurst, our Latin teacher, who can't remember where she's parked her car, says girls always get obsessed with horses in their adolescence. Dad, I'm fed up with being told what to do the whole time, and that everyone knows better than me. I just want to gallop through the countryside and enter gymkhanas, and to do that you need a horse.'

'No one seems to escape adolescence.' I said. 'It's the intensity that's the problem. Let me speak to Daphne. Maybe I can get Ivor to bring you out to Frampton Mansell after school.'

Then Derek rang, impatient as ever, but now I knew how to stand up to him. I switched on my newly found killer mode.

'You're not my only customer,' I told him.

'Why don't you sell me the business and work for me?'

'I'd never do that.'

'I've got a dog running at Walthamstow on Tuesday night. It's a sure thing. Why don't you come down? Can't be beat.'

'What's its name?'

'Lord Flange. I named him after you.'

'What do you mean?'

'You've got the flange, my boy. Lord Flange of the Cotswolds.'

I knew he was softening me up for something. 'I can't do Tuesday, but if you want to meet up I'm coming down the Saturday after next. I'm going to take a stall in the Portobello Road.'

'Good. See you then.'

I was going to Portobello Road because I had recently met Tom Greenfield, who had completely organised his life although only in his mid-twenties. He made enough in six months from his stall in the Portobello Road to escape the English winters and head for the Caribbean sun. He had the features of a Greek god, blond curly hair and a line of chat that made you believe every word he said. Well, I did, after he told me he had hitch-hiked round Europe for over a year on the proceeds of selling fifteen-hundred pairs of cufflinks made from hot and cold bath-tap inserts. He was a fast talker and assured me that getting a stall on the Portobello Road was a gold mine. From May until September the tourists flocked there, and the secret, he said, was to make something that fitted into a lady's handbag and I could sell for under a fiver.

'Of course, your netsukes and scrimshaw will sell well, but your big winner would be flogging English souvenirs.'

He was right; there was no end to the possibilities. 'Yes, mementos of our little old country for the Americans to take back home,' I said.

'In return for putting their dollars into our pockets.'

'You've got it.'

The stall next to Tom had become available, and although there was a long waiting list for any pitch Tom must have greased someone's palm with a backhander. I had to give him five hundred pounds as an upfront payment; he assured me I would make more than that every week. I had it in cash anyway, but what Tom really wanted out of the deal was me to make some ivory prayer balls for him.

He produced one from his pocket, beautifully carved, no bigger than a billiard ball; it could be opened into three segments and had a brass clasp at its centre. The delicate carving was of a religious scene, Christ on the cross surrounded by a crowd beneath him praying. Tom told me these rare pieces were carried by monks who knelt and prayed before them on their travels. The one he showed me was over six hundred years old.

'Please make me a thousand of these.'

'So you can go and spend your winter in the Bahamas,' I said.

Knowing we'd be without electricity the coming Friday, rather than have everyone sitting around, I announced that I'd close the workshop as there was absolutely nothing we could do without power. The forecast was for a warm summer's day and I rang my mother and suggested we walk beside the canal and have lunch in the Daneway pub.

'Are you unwell? It's not Mother's Day,' she said. 'I'd love to, but there's nothing wrong, is there?'

'No, I just thought you'd like a lovely quiet walk in the countryside.'

'You're not going to do any of those awful Norman Wisdom impersonations, are you? Mr Grimsdale! Mr Grimsdale!'

'Bring some suitable footwear; I'll meet you off the 10.57.'

I still went to Puckmill for a couple of hours before picking up my mother from Kemble station. I couldn't remember the last time she and I had been out in the country on a summer's day, certainly not since my childhood. As we walked along the towpath, we recalled a visit together to Cheddar Gorge during my school holidays, and a clotted cream tea.

'I took a photograph of you, up against a whitewashed wall. You had blonde hair then.'

'It was very hard for me in those days. Your father was an absolute bastard, and I had to bring up four children on my own.'

'It was difficult, I know, having to give us all the individual attention we demanded.'

'And I was working full time for the gas board.'

'Well, I think you did a bloody good job, especially with me. Look how well I've turned out.'

10

Mike and I walked into the building in the Portsmouth dockyard where the skeletal remains of the *Mary Rose* were being continually kept wet by the spray from several hoses.

'It makes you wonder, seeing the condition it's in, how they managed to get it off the seabed of the Solent without the whole thing disintegrating into thousands of pieces,' I said to Mike.

We were met by Priscilla, the Keeper of Collections, a refined lady who had an air of superiority, by which I mean looking down one's nose, that obviously went with the job. After all, the whole nation had witnessed the raising of this historic ship. So it was hardly surprising she was somewhat doubtful that two young men could possibly have the skill or expertise to mould and then make a replica of the *Mary Rose* bell. It probably didn't help that Mike was wearing his overalls and carrying a tool bag. He did look like someone coming to mend the boiler. I wasn't much better, in faded jeans and a denim jacket.

She showed us into a bare room with just a table and four chairs. It felt as though we were in a police station waiting to be interrogated.

'I'll be back shortly. Can I bring you a cup of tea?'

'That would be very nice. Would there be any chance of a biscuit?'

When we were on our own, Mike leant over and said, 'Do you think we're being watched?'

'You mean by hidden cameras?'

'No, but don't dunk your biscuit in your tea, or sip it too loudly.'

'I never do.'

'Yes, you do. I've heard you at work.'

A petite elderly lady who had a badge on her lapel saying *Volunteer* brought us a tray of tea and a plate of biscuits. Five minutes later Priscilla returned wearing a pair of plastic gloves, carrying a cardboard box which she put down in front of us.

'This is it,' she said, placing it gently on the table and removing a layer of cling film before handing each of us a small sealed packet. 'Please don't touch it until you've put on these gloves.'

It was only about eight inches high, with a ten-inch circumference, made of bronze. Around the top was a Flemish inscription that said 'I was made in the year 1510'. I had expected it to be a much more impressive piece; the size of it was quite underwhelming.

'What is your first impression?' asked Priscilla.

'Well, Mike,' I said, 'over to you. Give us your professional opinion.'

'Do you mind if I pick it up?' Permission was given, and he proceeded to inspect its entire surface inside and out. He was certainly playing the part of one in deep contemplation. On the drive down, I'd told him to act it up a bit; I just hoped he wasn't going to overdo it.

'Yes,' he said eventually, 'I don't see why not. I think we should make a skin mould of silicone and hold it rigid in a gelcoat jacket.' Brilliantly and convincingly delivered, demonstrating that he knew exactly what he was talking about.

'What about the patina? Can you match it precisely?' asked Priscilla.

'I think so,' I said. 'With our new techniques, we should be able to replicate it perfectly.'

'You know it will have to be acceptable to Margaret Rule.'

'Of course.'

'When can you start, and how long will it take?'

'We've got a VAT inspection next Tuesday. How about the following Thursday?' It had to be then, after the Bath market and before I went to the Portobello Road.

'Well, organise it with the Trading Company and I'll put it in the diary.'

As we drove back to Puckmill I told Mike this was the beginning of a new era in his life.

'What do you mean?'

'Leaving home, staying in a hotel for a couple of nights, all paid for by the Mary Rose Trading Company.'

'Are we going to be sleeping in the same room?'

'Yes,' I said. 'We can get a double room with two single beds.'

'I've never slept away from home before.'

'There's nothing to worry about. Bring your teddy bear if you want.'

'How did you know I had one?'

'It was a joke, Mike.'

I would never agree to carve a facsimile of someone famous again, not after the Gary Sobers fiasco. The MCC Cricket Museum had commissioned us to make the statue; twelve inches high, all padded up and standing on one leg, his bat raised in his left hand, having just hit an off drive through the covers. I'd given the job to Andrew Wood, a local sculptor who lived in Kingscote and was well known for starting the Prema arts centre over in Uley.

I took the bronze statue of the great man up to the museum at St John's Wood, quite relaxed about the whole thing, confident I would get their approval and a nice order to follow. Half a dozen people sat around an oval table, passing, or rather pushing, it from one person to the next. For five minutes there was no reaction from anyone, they just stared at it. No one uttered a word.

'Sorry,' said the distinguished chairman, for that's who I took him to be, sitting at the head of the table. 'Did we commission you to carve a statue of Gary Sobers?'

'Yes, you did.'

'Well, unless my eyes deceive me, this is not him.'

'I'm afraid I have to disagree with you. To me that is obviously Gary Sobers.'

'Rachel,' he said, turning to the only woman in the room and the head retail buyer, 'your opinion please.'

'Well, it didn't actually leap out at me and say I'm Gary Sobers.'

'So who did leap out at you? Perhaps you could let us all know.'

'My first impression was Lionel Richie.'

'Lionel Richie. Is that what you all think?'

No one answered.

'Perhaps you would like to resubmit it. I'm afraid we can't accept what you've offered us today.'

Five hundred pounds down the drain. It didn't look anything like Lionel Ritchie.

When I showed it to Simon Fisher, who was a cricketing buff, and asked his opinion, he immediately said, 'Isn't it Clive Lloyd, the West Indian captain?'

I gave up then, and never bothered with it any further, especially after Rob said it looked like Viv Richards.

I hardly slept the night before the VAT inspection, coming and going out of a disturbed slumber. I felt guilty, imagining I'd been discovered after being under surveillance for some time. As I drove Thelma to Puckmill she told me I had nothing to worry about and our bookkeeping was squeaky clean. She might be, being the treasurer of an Anglican church in Bath, but what about me? I suggested that maybe she could slip into the conversation with the inspector that she kept the books for the local church, or as an afterthought mention that she sang in the choir.

My brand new wooden shed looked as if it had been put up yesterday, which was practically true, Mike having been concussed playing football on Saturday morning and suffering from double vision. I'd got Tom Minety to come and build some shelves and put in a bench top that ran the length of the shed, and bought three new chairs and an electric kettle. There were mugs for tea that had never been used. The whole thing looked as though it had been stage-managed purely for the inspector's visit.

To further raise suspicions, there were three cars in the farmyard which all looked likely to fail an MOT test. One of them was Johnny Allard's newly acquired Deux Chevaux, covered in painted butterflies. Across in the barn the two goats were bleating. I had told Thelma not to wear high heels, but she hadn't remembered and made her way across the yard in a most ungainly way, avoiding a few piles of horse droppings. I was almost tempted to carry her, but she was a little on the heavy side.

'He'll be here in ten minutes,' I told everyone. 'Johnny, you're going to have to move your car, it makes us look like a bunch of hippies.' Ade Tucker asked me if he was to address me as sir. 'We don't have to go that far,' I said. 'Let's go for Mr Perry.'

Thank goodness everyone had combed their hair and shaved. It was the best we could do; I handed myself over to the fates.

Driving into the yard in his Austin Maxi, he couldn't have been anyone other than a VAT inspector. He was almost a caricature of himself, exactly as I'd imagined, wearing an off-the-shelf suit and heavy-framed glasses. We'd already rehearsed a few things, one being to look extremely busy, which wasn't hard because we were. As he got out of his car, Rob walked past carrying a Guinness toucan down to the stockroom.

'Bill Little from the VAT office in Gloucester.'

'Pleased to meet you, Mr Little. Welcome to Puckmill.'

'You're certainly hidden away down here. I had to get directions from the pub up in the village.'

'Please come to my office. Our bookkeeper, Thelma, is waiting to go through everything with you.'

After I had made him and Thelma a cup of tea, I left them to it. 'Don't hesitate to call me if you need anything. I must get on with the *Mary Rose* bell. Can't keep His Royal Highness waiting.'

He stayed a painfully long hour behind the closed door of the shed. I listened outside but couldn't hear what was being discussed. The suspense was too much, so I interrupted them, making the excuse that I needed to check the price of a kilo of rottenstone, which Thelma tracked down in the purchases file.

'Seven pounds fifty,' she said, believing it to be a genuine request.

'Thank you, Thelma.'

I left, and then turned back and popped my head round the door. 'Sorry, is that including VAT?'

When he eventually emerged, carrying his briefcase, he had a smile on his face. My heart rate returned to normal then; he wouldn't be smiling if he'd been suspicious of anything.

'What an interesting business you have. I've never seen anything like it.'

I searched for the appropriate cliché. 'Well, at the end of the day, you have to do your best.'

'Now, I must make use of the Gents before I leave.'

'Ah, now that's a bit tricky. It's behind an air compressor at the end of the building. It can be a bit noisy in there.'

He didn't reply. I crossed my fingers the compressor didn't charge up, but it gave me the chance to go and have a quick word with Thelma, who was in the shed putting on her lipstick.

'Are we in the clear?' was all I wanted to know.

'We underpaid one pound twenty-three pence in the last quarter.' I kissed her and dislodged her glasses. 'Stop it. I don't know why you were so worried about it.'

'You only know the half of it, Thelma.'

'And that's the way it's going to stay.'

It couldn't have gone any better, until we stood in the yard and he said, 'So you keep goats as well,' and as I was about to explain the agricultural look of the place Haggler walked on to the scene with what appeared to be a woman's swimming costume in his mouth.

'Nothing to concern yourself about, Mr Little, but I suggest you get into the car straight away. Very nice meeting you.'

I'd had enough. As soon as he'd left I walked over to the Booths'. Haggler followed me, refusing to let go of the swimming costume. I knew Chris was on a week's holiday, and found him up a ladder tying back the wisteria that covered the front of their beautiful house.

'It can't go on any longer,' I said. 'If he'd come over two minutes earlier he could have attacked the VAT inspector.'

'He's bored. He thinks life is much more exciting over there with you. I'll have to padlock the gate.'

I took Thelma out to lunch at the Crown, and as I stood at the bar ordering our drinks Ivor joined us. In front of Thelma, he said, 'Well, have you caught that adder yet?'

'No, we haven't seen it. It probably moved on ages ago.'

'Not adders. They stay where they're born.'

Then Ron the postman threw down a pile of letters on the bar counter, saying, 'I've got something for you, Nick. Shall I bring it in now?'

'I'll come out with you,' I said, passing Thelma the menu. 'Ivor, no more talk of adders, please. This is my bookkeeper, by the way. Thelma.'

Ron gave me a handwritten envelope; it had been posted in Plymouth. Was it a response to the letter I'd sent addressed to *Beryl Cook, Plymouth*? I read it before I went back to join Thelma. It was a warm invitation to the artist's house in Athenaeum Street.

By the time I got back Ivor was in full flow, Thelma in a fixed position of disbelief, her glass of apple juice held halfway between the table and her open mouth.

'Yes, that was back in the long hot summer of 1976. I tried to suck the venom out of his ankle, but I couldn't. They had to rush him to Stroud hospital.'

'What happened then?' Thelma asked.

'They injected him with some antidote. Do you know, to this very day you can still see them curled up in the sun in the same spot. I can show you if you like.'

The sleep I slept that night was the sort one only slowly wakens from. Belah tried several times to get me up, reminding me I was taking her swimming in the outdoor pool in Cirencester, but it was Ros who got me rushing downstairs; Kase was on the phone from Amsterdam. All the musical instruments were now hanging from the ceiling of the Pink Cowboy, a nightclub in New York. 'Make me another six of each,' he said.

It was endless, the diversity of work we took on, and as if what we already had wasn't enough, Rod Holt wanted us to work with him on a themed bar in Leicester Square called Little Havana.

Rob and I drove down to Rod's workshop on Button Farm near Brentwood. He was renting a huge barn which was filled with the pieces he had made over the years for Fortnum & Mason's window displays. It was a storeroom of complete make-believe: great leaping horses, unicorns, figures contrived in Rod's imagination. It made me wonder if he'd taken a lot of LSD in his life, but he assured me he'd never gone near the stuff. In amongst this museum of incredible relics was a giant iguana, over twelve feet long, and so lifelike it appeared to be crawling towards us.

'Who on earth did you make that for? Surely it's off a film set?'

But I was wrong. The iguana, which had been carved in polystyrene and weighed just a few kilos, had been commissioned by a design outfit in Oslo. Rod and his team had driven it to Norway on a flat-bed lorry and then had to fix it to the outside of the company's building. Spotlights lit it up, and on the club's opening night the effect it had on the traffic passing below caused a spate of minor accidents. The police closed the road and the authorities forced them to remove it immediately. So the following day Rod had no alternative but to drive the iguana back to Brentwood, where it remained. 'At least I was paid for the job,' was all he said, this self-effacing man whose diverse talents included not only sculpting, but making moulds and painting the most intricate pieces.

We spent all day with Rod and his team and, five minutes before we left, he sketched on a sheet of brown paper what he wanted us to make for the Little Havana bar. It was a three-foot-high figure of a girl in a bikini standing on the world with her arms outstretched, a cornucopia of fruit in her hair. She was the centrepiece to be displayed on the bar below a sign saying *Welcome to Havana*.

I delivered it an hour before they opened, when everyone

was rushing about with brooms and paintbrushes, cleaners polishing floors, electricians still putting bulbs into chandeliers. Rod was calm, while all those around him were in a state of panic.

'It always happens,' he said. 'Finishing touches, before the opening.'

I had a drink sitting beneath the artificial palm trees Rod had made, the branches wafting in the breeze created by the ceiling fan. He suggested we had supper in the Lebanese restaurant next door, and as I waited for him at a window table, a queue started to form outside the Havana. Invited guests in their dinner suits, expensive dresses and jewellery waiting patiently to be let in.

From where I sat I could see the doors being opened, and as the guests filed in Rod emerged, squeezing past them with a ladder over his shoulder, a bucket swinging on the end of it, and a cloth draped over his arm. The man who'd created it all looked like a window cleaner amongst the glitterati.

'What an exit, Rod. Never have I witnessed one so understated.'

'They did invite me, but I'd have to hire a dinner jacket for the night. The job's finished; now let's eat.'

It was two years to the day since I'd started Puckmill Studios, and what had I achieved? Well, I was nowhere near becoming a millionaire, and I knew why. I was the root cause of all my undoings; there was no doubting that. Every business needs to consolidate at some stage, not just keep on expanding. It's obvious one has to build a solid foundation, but unfortunately for me I was constantly having to respond to individual customers who all had their own projects.

At one time I'd thought that Walter Pepper would make the perfect partner, that he'd level me out. But no, old Walter had metamorphosed into another creature altogether. I realised my prediction of becoming a millionaire in three years wasn't going to happen and regretted telling Ros and the children about it, although I'd believed it at the time. Well, I wasn't, and that wouldn't change.

What I needed to change was myself. I needed to play another role, but what that was I didn't know. Maybe I should employ a workshop manager and just develop products, keep away from the everyday running of the business. And yet . . .

Bath and Birmingham markets were worlds apart when it came to what they sold. Bath was mostly high-end top-quality antiques, Birmingham the other end of the scale. I'd see some of the same faces at both, and they were all after the same thing: a quick profit. The early morning rush of dealers at Bath usually calmed down at about 10 a.m. Then the public gradually drifted in, most of them casually strolling about the place with no intention of buying anything. Most stallholders had already made their money and would have been happy to pack up and be on their way. But we weren't allowed to. The agreement with the management was that we stayed until 5 p.m., and if we didn't, we lost our pitch.

London dealers also came to Bath, searching for expensive pieces of English furniture, or buying on commission for Americans. I once heard one such agent talking about a lovely pair of cabriole legs. 'Mind you, Dolores, they don't compare to the smoothness of yours.'

'No, honey, and mine don't get woodworm either.'

The man's name was Marcus Wesley, and I'd seen him several times with his American buyers. With his olive skin, he looked Spanish, but was in fact Maltese. You could describe him as good-looking, one of those types with rugged features that I knew appealed to women, and he could naturally talk the talk that I was now so familiar with. It went with the job of selling antiques, especially to an unaccompanied middle-class woman. The smooth, honeyed tones, the soft sprinkling of flattery – not too much, otherwise she'd spot it, but said in passing – 'Yes, only a discerning eye would appreciate the craftsmanship in those clawed feet', making her feel that he recognised the value of her opinion; subtle comments that would eventually have her reaching for her cheque book. Then, of course, stressing the rarity of the piece: 'It's a wonderful opportunity, because they don't often come up for sale nowadays.'

Marcus Wesley had perfected the technique as he escorted his Americans around the markets and antique shops of Bath. He offered a complete service, picking them up from the airport and then running them all over the southwest of England. He arranged their accommodation and planned their whole itinerary. For this he was well paid, and the other perk, of course, was the kickbacks from their pre-planned visits to certain specially selected shops. For every pound they spent there, a percentage found its way into Marcus Wesley's pocket. He scored on all fronts, but he never did any business with me. His Americans were after furniture and genuine British antiques, not replicas, no matter how good they might look.

That's why it surprised me when Marcus took a little detour from the party he was showing round and slipped a business card into my hand. 'Give me a call,' he said. 'I might have something of interest to you.'

As he left, Quentin Saffell came over and told me his fears had been confirmed: he did indeed have subsidence.

'Well, you seem to be walking okay to me,' I said, which wasn't funny, and as soon as I'd said it I apologised. It was a cheap joke.

'We'll have to sue the surveyor.'

'Aren't you covered by your house insurance?'

'No one knows at the moment. It means major structural repairs. It looks as though we'll have to move out and close the shop.'

'Saff, if there's anything I can do, let me know.'

'Well, you might be able to help.'

'How?'

'Give me a job.'

11

It was March 1983 and I was standing outside Beryl Cook's house in Athenaeum Street. Getting here had been a long journey on a slow train, stopping at station after station; deserted platforms in cold sleeting rain. Most of it had been spent sitting opposite an obese woman with her head buried in a word-search magazine.

John Cook, Beryl's husband and manager, opened the door. With thinning grey hair, he was probably in his mid-fifties.

'Come in and warm yourself up,' he said, taking my raincoat, which was dripping wet.

'I think that's the longest train journey I've ever been on,' I told him. 'I feel as though I've travelled to another country.'

'I know it only too well. When we leave Devon, I have to prepare myself psychologically; it takes us seven hours to get to London.'

I noticed in the corner of the sitting room one of the Snooty Foxes we'd made, wearing a top hat, a red riding jacket and black leather boots. I made it when I found out there were over two thousand pubs in England called the Snooty Fox, convinced there'd be a market for them. Another of my ideas that hadn't been properly thought through: we'd only sold about twenty so far, because I just hadn't had enough time to get in touch with two thousand landlords.

'We love it. We buy a lot of your work from the Barbican Antique Centre. All those old advertising figures are very amusing. Beryl will be down in a minute; she knows you're here. Now, what would you like to drink?'

I'd heard that Beryl was a bit of a recluse and shunned publicity. She didn't give interviews and would never go on a chat show. When I'd mentioned in my letter that I was keen to sculpt a figure from one of her paintings, I'd doubted she would reply at all. So I had no idea what to expect, having never even seen a photograph of her.

Beryl introduced herself and sat on the sofa opposite me. She had short, almost white hair and black-rimmed glasses. There was a natural friendliness about her, a warmth in her eyes and the hint of a gentle smile as she spoke about her art. I explained that I wanted to sculpt some of her most popular characters. Without a moment's hesitation she said I should begin with Ruby Venezuela, a transvestite and close friend who did a drag act in Madame Jojo's in Soho. She showed me a picture of a large redhead looking back over her shoulder at the top of a flight of stairs, with a pouting mouth painted with bright red lipstick. She was wearing a blue, tight-fitting dress covering a sizeable bum.

I stayed for an hour and had lunch with them as we talked about the financial arrangements. It was agreed I'd make a limited edition of five hundred pieces and that Beryl would sign each one and provide a certificate of authenticity. John was happy with ten per cent of the sale price.

Only one thing remained to sort out, then the project could go ahead.

'You need to get Roger's permission.'

'Who's Roger?'

'He's Ruby Venezuela,' said John. 'He lives in Blackheath. We'll put you in touch with him.'

'When we've finished sculpting the piece, will you come to Puckmill? It would be easier than bringing the statue all the way here by train.'

'Yes, of course. We can combine it with a trip to see our son, who lives in Bristol.'

So I left Beryl and John and the screeching seagulls of Plymouth, the clouds clearing, a setting sun in patches of blue. I bought a copy of the *Antiques Trade Gazette* and sat in the station café for over an hour waiting for the next train. As I ate my lardy cake, I came upon a photograph of our Bruno Zach figure, *Girl with a Riding Crop*. Derek had done it again and entered one of our Art Deco replicas in a top London auction.

After I'd finished at the Bath antiques market I went to meet Marcus Wesley in Lansdown Crescent where he had a ground-floor flat.

'I'm going to roll a joint. Do you smoke?' was the first thing he said.

I told him I did occasionally, but mostly at weekends.

'I've known about you for some time; you've always interested me,' he said, turning his head to blow the smoke away from me.

'You mean what I do interests you.'

'If you want to put it like that, then yes, it does.'

'I've heard how you work those Americans you bring round the markets.'

'You let people hear what they want to hear.'

He told me he had a client who was paying huge insurance premiums on rare bronzes in his Belgravia flat and wished to put them in a bank vault and replace them with replicas. I had no difficulty in saying I could take on the job. The sticking point, as always with these one-off jobs, was the price.

'He's a retired colonel, worth a fortune in bricks and mortar, but having to watch every penny.'

'Well, I could meet him after I've finished in the Portobello Road.'

'No, don't worry about that. You'll be dealing with me. I'll bring the pieces over to your workshop.'

'Of course. It's only half an hour away.'

As I wasn't in a hurry, I decided to call in on Quentin in the London Road on my way home. Quentin had become a friend, someone I knew would be around for years, like Rob, but that day I walked into his shop for the first time: a bygone world full of tins and old enamel advertising signs, bread bins and brass-plated jelly moulds, with shelves of original packaging of famous brands such as Bisto and Atora suet. The Dickensian atmosphere was enhanced by the subdued light and the low, moulded ceiling. It felt as if I had stepped back into Victorian England. I could hear the stairs creaking before he appeared and greeted me, wearing a burgundy velvet smoking jacket.

'Quentin, I'm almost lost for words,' I said.

'That I can't believe.'

'Is it really you, the same man I've come to know?'

'I dress up for the job. It's in keeping with the mood I'm trying to create.'

'Well, it certainly works.'

'The American dealers love it, and of course it's by appointment only.'

'You clever bugger.'

'Let's have some tea, and then I'll show you round a subsided house.'

And he did, all three storeys of it. I could detect something, the dipping floors that made me correct my balance as the room seemed to slope away beneath me.

'We've had a second opinion now, from an independent chartered surveyor, and it's not looking good. We're going to have to move out.'

'How much is it all going to cost?' I asked.

'Thousands, and the chap who wrote the original report for the mortgage company is denying negligence. I think we'll have to sue him.'

I had booked us into the Victory Hotel in Portsmouth for two nights. We had a double room with twin beds. Mike wanted the one nearest the window, because it led to the fire escape. He'd read the notice on the back of the door, *In Case of an Emergency*, and told me that all residents had to gather in the foyer.

'Look Mike, don't worry. There's a smoke alarm right above you. Besides, I'm a light sleeper,' which I wasn't, especially after a bottle of wine.

He'd brought his teddy bear, which he propped up on his pillows. Then he laid out his pyjamas on the eiderdown and put a glass of water on the bedside table.

'It's only seven o'clock. Let's go and find a restaurant. Remember, the Mary Rose Trading Company is paying for all this.'

We found an Italian place, Luigi's. Mike wanted to eat something he'd never tried before and unfortunately chose the spaghetti bolognese.

'Mike, most of it's on your face. There's a knack to eating it: you need to turn it around your fork.'

'I'll cut it up into little pieces.'

'You can't sit there like that. You need to go and clean yourself up.'

I spent the next two days being nothing more than Mike's assistant, which meant doing all the menial tasks involved in mould making: cleaning the electric drill after he had mixed the silicone, soaking the paint brushes in acetone, adding the catalyst to the gelcoat resin and passing him various tools like a nurse in an operating theatre. Thankfully, everything went without a hitch. Mike concentrated on the job in hand and was only nervous when someone came into the room and stood behind him watching him work.

Luckily, when Margaret Rule came to see how we were progressing, she didn't introduce herself, but walked around the table several times and eventually said, 'Do you think you will have it finished today?'

I suppose it could have happened to anyone. Without looking up, Mike uttered a word you wouldn't find in any dictionary. 'That's an impissibility.'

It was a painful moment, which grew into a long cruel silence that hung in the air. I did everything physically possible to suppress the laughter bubbling up inside me. Mike just carried on working and Margaret Rule showed remarkable self-control. I had to leave the room; I couldn't bear it any longer.

The bell was finally moulded and cast in a bronze powder and then aged up with a gentle coating of copper sulphate. Mike dried the surface with a hairdryer and the job was complete. It was a remarkable achievement, to have kept his nerve under such close scrutiny. He slumped back in his chair, staring at the ceiling. Then we looked at each other, and went on looking, waiting to hear what the other had to say.

'Go on, then,' I said.

'You say it first.'

'I'm happy with it. We can't improve on that.'

'I need a break,' Mike said.

So we took an afternoon stroll through the dockyard and breathed in the sea air. The place had its own peculiar atmosphere, surrounded as we were by ships of all sizes and giant cranes loading military hardware. And then, aghast, I saw a huge American aircraft carrier, towering above a row of terraced houses, a monstrous leviathan that seemed to be gliding silently past the side streets that led down to the quayside.

We stood amongst all that naval history, hundreds of years of it, and walked around the *Victory*, both of us bent double, breathing in the smell of the timbers. They must have cut down a forest to build it.

'Hey, I wonder if it's got a bell we can mould?'

'Who knows? I haven't seen one.'

'I suppose we ought to get back and get it over with,' I said at last.

Our work now completed, the moment had arrived. We placed the two bells, the original and our replica, side by side on the table. Margaret Rule came in and pulled up a chair, accompanied by Priscilla, the Keeper of Collections. Neither said a word, but I did. I told them that the bells weighed exactly the same, and the only difference between the two was that if you struck the replica there would be no metallic ring.

'You have done a fantastic job,' said Margaret, getting to her feet and coming to shake my hand.

'It's Mike's hand you should be shaking, not mine,' I told her, so she did, and so did Priscilla, who no longer looked down her nose at us.

'So,' I said to Margaret, 'you really cannot tell the difference?'

She paused for a moment before she gave her answer.

'It's an impissibolity.'

I sat in my garden shed in the candlelight, smoking a contemplative roll-up, stroking Silo the rabbit with one hand and holding a human skull in the other. Well, a replica of one that we had made for Beatrice. Whose skull it was I did not know; 'Alas, poor Yorick!' Beatrice had sent it by parcel post to Puckmill. She was expanding her company, Bones and Other Things, and was so keen to get me involved that she was prepared to offer me shares if we took charge of her product development. I realised that perhaps for the first time in my life a sensible streak was making itself felt. I was tempted, and thought long and hard about it, but when I imagined the chaos all those bones would create around the workshop I knew it was the last thing we should do. We'd be up to our necks in bones. I'd have to tell Beatrice.

We'd had a bit of publicity recently, because of the work we'd done on the *Mary Rose*, and what I called conventional businesses had started to take notice of us. The Malmesbury parish council wanted us to make a replica of a gargoyle that had been smashed on the Market Cross. I said yes and handed the job to Rob, because he lived there. I told him they might give him the freedom of the town and let him graze his sheep on the common.

'Our deputy managing director will come to the council offices and discuss the matter with you,' I told them on the phone, Rob standing next to me.

'Can't we drop these silly job titles you've given us? Everyone knows that there's only one.'

'What's that then?'

'Dictator.'

I gave Quentin a part-time job when he had to close his shop so the subsidence work could be carried out; it was a difficult time for him. He drove over to Puckmill in his VW camper van three times a week. Despite Rob's ridiculing me for giving everyone a job title, I made him Assistant Finisher to Ade Tucker, who looked after all the scrimshaw, netsukes and now Tom Greenfield's prayer balls. What I called the bread and butter department of Puckmill Studios. We sold hundreds of these pieces every week, not only at the markets, but also to wholesalers.

Quentin brought an air of calm to Puckmill and was looked upon as an intellectual. He was a solid, diligent worker who moved at the same speed throughout the day, and worked methodically on finishing the fiddly pieces, dipping a cotton bud into acetone to remove the excess stain from the intricately carved prayer balls.

'You can't leave your balls alone, can you, Quentin?'

In his lunch hour he read the *Guardian* and did the crossword. If he happened to finish it early, he'd come and play frisbee with us out in the field behind the workshop. Being slightly rotund, he lacked the graceful movements of Johnny Allard, who liked to show off by hurling the frisbee well beyond his reach, just to see him on the run.

I hadn't planned it, so it was lucky that we all seemed to get on together and work well as a team. Everyone took pride in what they did, and it certainly helped that a lot of our customers liked to walk around the workshop to see for themselves the skill that was on display. The one recurring comment as they left was genuine disbelief that hidden away on a farm in deepest Gloucestershire a motley bunch of artisans could be producing works of art in such basic conditions.

We had our fun moments, just to break up the routine, when we would dress up in the costumes I'd bought from Sifta in the rag market. We looked like characters from a macabre pantomime and danced in the yard beneath the viaduct so that the passengers and drivers on the passing trains would get a full view of us. One week we did it at the same time every morning and the train slowed down to a crawl, with passengers crowded at the windows. By the Friday they were all ready for us, leaning out of doors, waving and taking photographs. When we eventually had enough of giving these performances, the driver actually stopped his train on the viaduct, sounded its whistle, and shouted down to us, 'Has the show closed? What's happened to the pantomime?'

Marcus Wesley had kept in touch. He drove into the yard in his Renault estate and opened the boot to reveal, wrapped in blankets, some of the finest bronzes I had ever seen. Classical representations of Hermes and Apollo, and a beautiful sleeping lion. They were all cast with the finest definition, showing the minutest detail. Whoever had produced work of such quality was indeed a master. I knew as soon as I saw them that they were worth thousands; no wonder the insurance premiums were so high.

'Can you do it?' was the first thing Marcus asked.

'They're exquisite. I've never seen the like before,' I said. 'The patina takes your breath away.'

'But can you reproduce them? That's what I need to know.'

'I can replicate whatever we take a mould from, but it's the patination that's going to be the challenge.'

I called Mike out to have a look at them; he was now our expert in bronze finishes. Walter had written down the recipes for electroplating all the subtle variations from around the world. We kept the book under lock and key.

'What do you think, Mike? Can we match the patina?'

Mike always deliberated whenever I asked his opinion on anything. He liked to ponder for a while, as everyone around him held their breath.

'It's not an impissibility, is it, Mike?' He was never going to live that one down.

'I'd say initially yes we can, but it's not definite.'

'I'm not sure what that means,' Marcus muttered to me.

'I think it means maybe.'

Marcus had other concerns to discuss, which I found hardly surprising after he whispered to me that the bronzes were worth fifty thousand pounds. 'What's your security like? Have you got an alarm system?'

'Not really, just some very strong padlocks.'

'Anyone could break in here in five minutes.'

'Why would they want to do that?'

'To steal fifty thousand pounds' worth of bronzes.'

'How would anyone know they were here?' I asked him. 'Look over at the barn. What can you see?'

'Two goats, two donkeys and a Shire horse.'

'Precisely. Just what you'd expect to find on a farm.'

'You need to get yourself insured. One dropped cigarette end, that's all it would take. We've both got too much to lose.'

I'd never thought about it before: the value of all the finished stock, or the masters that I kept in my 10x4 foot shed, secured by a three-pound padlock. If someone did decide to break into the place, all they'd need was a crowbar. We weren't insured, not even against fire, and most of the paints and stains we used were highly flammable. We could go up in smoke, and there'd be nothing left of my empire but the smouldering remains as I kicked over the ashes.

When we had our lunch break, I told everyone that smoking in the building was now forbidden.

I hadn't realised that show business types go to bed late and sleep most of the day, which explained why I had failed to reach Roger, alias Ruby Venezuela. He never answered his phone, because he probably didn't get home till the early hours of the morning. So I rang him at half time during the televised match between Spurs and Manchester United in the FA Cup. Sam, Seth and I followed Spurs closely. After all, I'd been supporting them since the 1950s.

'Dad, you've got fifteen minutes till the second half begins.'

'I know. I'll be back in five. I've just got to make an appointment to meet a transvestite.'

At last he picked up the phone. 'Is that you, Roger?'

'It might be. Who am I talking to?'

'Nick Perry. Beryl Cook gave me your telephone number.'

'Oh, yes, she's told me all about you. It's very exciting: you want to sculpt me.'

'Can we meet and discuss the project?'

'When were you thinking? I don't get up until the afternoon.'

'At five on Saturday, after I've finished in the Portobello Road?'

'Come to my flat in Blackheath.'

'I'll be there. I've got the address.'

'You sound adorable. Are you in a relationship?'

'Yes, married with four children.'

'You wicked boy, turn to stone, turn to stone.'

With that he put down the phone and I went back to watch the match with Sam and Seth.

'What's a transvestite?' Seth asked me, just as they were kicking off for the second half.

'That's going to take some explaining. Do you mind if I tell you at the end of the game?'

'It's a bloke who dresses in women's clothes,' said Sam.

'Is it, Dad?'

'Yes.'

'But why, if he's a man?'

'And he wears make-up and stockings and high-heeled shoes,' continued Sam, who seemed to know rather a lot about the subject.

'Does he varnish his fingernails?' Seth wanted to know.

'We're missing the game. Let's talk about it later.'

It was Belah's first day at school and Ros wanted me to go with them. I realised why when Belah refused to take Miss Dibbin's hand and join her class at Powell's kindergarten in Cirencester. We couldn't reason with our daughter, who was clinging to Ros's neck. The mother and child separation, painful tears in the playground. Horrible as it sounds, I had to break her grip, and we left quickly without turning back, listening to her crying in the September air. As we walked down Dollar Street towards the town centre it felt as if we'd committed the most heinous crime, and maybe we had, emotionally.

'God, what am I going to do if this happens tomorrow?' said Ros.

'She'll be all right. It always happens on the first day. Don't you remember what Seth was like? He locked himself in the loo.'

On our way home, we walked past the Brass Rubbing Centre where my brother Jack still worked. I couldn't remember the last time I'd seen him. Through the small office window I caught a brief glimpse of him, his hair a lot shorter, clean shaven; not at all how he looked when he was a shepherd in North Wales.

It's strange how people can drift apart, not through a falling out, but when the gaps between seeing each other simply get longer, which was the case with me and my brother. We had had a close friendship up in those Welsh hills, but not since he'd become a married man; these days we lived in the same town but didn't bother to keep in touch. My mother said it was because he was a father now as well as practically running the Brass Rubbing Centre.

At last I'd managed to get Walter into Simon Fisher's office in Stonehouse to sort out repaying the money the business owed him. Not once in three years had he ever asked me to settle the debt.

I could tell Simon was somewhat taken aback by Walter's appearance, the ponytail and the old biker's jacket. I still remembered so clearly the day I first met the immaculate chemist in his white coat behind the counter of his shop. However, I'd noticed recently a gradual waning in his enthusiasm which I'd wanted to bring up with him, but I'd never felt the time was right to delve into something so personal.

In Simon's office, he made it clear that he didn't want to call in the debt. What he had contributed should be considered a gift.

'Well, if your mind's made up, that's exactly what we'll do. I shall enter it in the books as cash introduced,' said Simon, turning to me and telling me what a generous benefactor I had.

'I cannot put into words how grateful I am,' I said to Walter.

'You've clearly played a big part in the development of Puckmill Studios,' Simon said. 'With the electroplating shop up and running, what are you working on now?'

'I think I've reached the end of the road. My work is done.'

Here was the reason for the melancholia I'd sensed in him.

'Of course not . . . no, Walter. There's plenty more to do,' I said.

'I've done my bit. You have all the recipes, you know all the techniques, how to apply the patinas, and now that the plating shop is ready it's a young man's game, not for me.'

And with that he got up and shook Simon's hand. Then he turned and looked at me.

'In all my life, I've never had so much fun.'

12

December 1983, the first snowfall of winter, and although they had gritted the main road from Cirencester to Stroud, trying to drive into Frampton Mansell was definitely for the reckless and foolhardy, while the final winding descent to the farm had already become impassable. Any vehicle that got stuck down there would have stayed put, unrecoverable until the thaw arrived. Only Ivor was on the move, having fitted chains on his tyres. Winding down his window as he passed, he shouted out to me, 'One of us was wise, the rest were foolish,' like one of those smug know-alls from the Bible.

Everyone who worked at Puckmill abandoned their cars above the church, before the road narrowed, and walked down from the village, which was treacherous enough. All of us, that is, except Johnny Allard, who skied down the snowy slopes like someone competing in a downhill slalom. He had style, I'd give him that, but he was nothing but a huge show-off. Rob found it hard to be around his inflated ego for long, and I told him that being vain required its own commitment and was extremely time-consuming. On one occasion Ade Tucker had brought in his guitar, which he'd been learning to play for several months, paying for lessons; Johnny had picked it up at lunch time and given us a perfect recital. After he had finished his performance and handed the instrument back to Ade, he said, 'By the way, I wrote that myself.'

But that was Johnny, and now, with the snow falling all day, he sat in the barn with a paraffin heater sculpting Ruby Venezuela. I'd eventually got the go-ahead for it, after what was best described as an unconventional meeting with Roger in his flat in Blackheath.

'I can give you half an hour, my love, that's all,' he said, answering the door wearing his make-up. He was on the large size, not fat but bulked out a bit. 'I think it's lovely what you're doing. I'm sure you'll sell a lot of them to my adoring fans at Madame Jojo's.' He opened the wardrobe in his bedroom, holding a sequined dress out in front of him. 'Would you like to see me in it? I make them all myself, you know.'

'Yes, all right,' I said nervously. 'By the way, what shall I call you? Ruby or Roger?'

'You can call me Roger, sweetheart.'

He'd put on a white petticoat and stuffed some false boobs down his front, wriggling for a few moments and making exaggerated noises as if he was a chicken about to lay an egg.

'A woman has to feel comfortable. Now zip me up, you naughty boy.'

'Can I remind you why I'm here? We talked about it on the phone: the photographs for the sculptor.'

'Oh yes, photographs. I've got so many.'

'I only want the ones of you dressed as Ruby Venezuela, for the detail. It's most important.'

'Why don't you put the kettle on and I'll go and see what I can find.'

He eventually found them, and many more, all of him in dresses that he had made himself. As he sat drinking his tea, leaving smudges of lipstick on the rim of the cup, he finally talked seriously about the project. Like Beryl, he wanted ten per cent for the right to use the image of Ruby Venezuela. My profits were diminishing rapidly. As I drove back down the M4 to Cirencester I knew there was no money in the job. I should have walked away, and would have done but for Walter Pepper. I felt I owed it to him; he had been so enthusiastic. On the long drive I turned it over in my mind, but kept reaching the same conclusion: we wouldn't make a single penny. I decided to see Walter on the way home. It was nine thirty on Saturday evening. On the kitchen table was the *Times* crossword, half finished, and a steaming bowl of soup.

'I was just having my supper. Join me, please.'

'No thanks. I've only called in for a minute. I've been up since five this morning.'

'Of course – it's Saturday. Your Portobello Road day.'

'I thought you might be interested to hear about the Ruby Venezuela job. We've got the go-ahead.'

'Well, good for you, after all you've put into it already.'

'I wondered whether you would unveil the piece and present it to Beryl and Ruby? There's going to be a lot of publicity; it will be your moment in the spotlight.'

He didn't answer me, but his lips broadened into a warm smile. I waited, but still he said nothing.

'Say something, Walter. I hate long silences.'

'It's because I don't know what to say.'

'Well, say something like "I'd be delighted to".'

'Sit down for a minute. Let me tell you what happens when a man stumbles into old age.'

So I listened as Walter told me about his withdrawal from the mainstream of life, the point he'd reached which, as a young man, I couldn't imagine. 'And why should you?' he said. 'You're in your thirties, with a lot of life still ahead of you.'

Helping me build up Puckmill Studios had been his final fling, was how he put it. In the three years since walking away from being a pharmacist he had reinvented himself.

'I've lived without restraint, with a freedom I've not felt before.'

'I still don't see why it has to stop now.'

'Because it's done. Surely you can see that? Already you're looking for things I could do, and unveiling a statue of a transvestite is not one of them.'

At which point our laughter got the better of us and I left him to reheat his soup and finish his crossword.

'You're not done with me yet, Walter,' I said, closing the door behind me.

That winter lay heavy in the valley below Frampton Mansell. Most of January the temperature never got above freezing. Huge icicles hung from the arches of the viaduct like glass spears in the blue, sunlit days. The snow-covered fields showed not a single tuft of grass, only the tracks of wildlife, most probably the fox on its way from Baker's Mill where Daphne and Martin Neville lived.

The workshop was never warm, despite the infrared heaters I'd had installed, and the extractor fans in the painting booths sucked out what heat there was anyway. All of us wore as many clothes as possible, which restricted our movement, bundled up as we were in thick coats, bobble hats, scarves and gloves, all of which were covered in paint.

At lunch we boiled up vegetable soups on the Aga in Sheila Booth's kitchen across the road, queuing up with our bowls like prisoners of war. We shared the warm room with Haggler, no longer a serial escapee, being now confined to barracks and putting on a considerable amount of weight.

The winter months were more severe in the valley, the sun only reaching us in the early afternoon, as if the seasons had stopped moving on and we were suspended in a lost world. No visitors came to the workshop, and the only way we could get deliveries to our customers was by paying Rex Horton, the dairy farmer, to come down with his tractor and trailer and take them up to the village, where we loaded them into my van.

All the pipes were frozen, so we had no water and of course the lavatory was out of order. Johnny said if conditions carried on like this for much longer, we'd need counselling.

'Yes,' said Ade, 'cannibalism could break out.' He had recently read the book about the Andes plane crash survivors.

Mike suggested we build a sledge that could seat at least four of us and so we did, out of various bits of wood lying around the place. The field behind the workshop sloped steeply from the viaduct down to a barbed wire fence. To make it more exciting we built a ramp of snow halfway down the field so that we would take off and sail through the air for a few feet.

Unfortunately, no one calculated the speed we were going to reach, so we were blind to the impending disaster. We started impressively enough, our style similar to that required in the bobsleigh event in the Olympics, four of us running beside the sledge and then jumping on board and huddling together. But the first time we went over the ramp we flipped sideways and crashed through the barbed wire fence, causing cuts and bruises for all of us and two broken fingers for Ade. He made a meal of it, and because I knew his mother Jennifer well – she was the manager of the Crown and bent a few rules when it came to closing time – I walked him over to Chris Booth for an expert opinion.

When he confirmed that he thought Ade had indeed broken a couple of fingers, I knew I'd be in trouble with Jennifer. She was over-protective of her only child and would pop into the workshop from time to time to say hello to him. On one occasion, she found him not wearing his face mask, something I was constantly reminding him to do. He didn't like putting it on, because he said he couldn't breathe properly and felt claustrophobic. In the summer we could work with the windows open and didn't notice the fumes, but the windows were shut the day Jennifer walked in and she accused me of killing her little boy. What was she going to say to me now, playing the fool with my employees on a sledge and leaving

Ade with two broken fingers?

The snow lasted a week, and every lunch hour and at the end of each day, even in darkness holding torches, we were on that sledge. Poor Ade, all he could do was watch. He pleaded to be allowed to join in, but he was accident prone; two broken fingers now and already the top of his forefinger removed by a scalpel blade.

Quentin wanted to speak to me about the saga of having to cope with his subsidence, so we went up to the Crown for a chat. He was reaching a state of despair.

'It's all those heavy juggernauts rumbling through the Georgian streets. I don't understand why the council allows it.'

As we continued our conversation, which I called the ruination of Bath, Jennifer came over and stood in front of us with her hands on her hips, giving me an ironic smile, which was enough to tell me she knew what had happened to Ade.

'Do you remember you asked me if we stocked pine nuts?' she said, addressing herself to Quentin.

'Yes.'

'And then you said do we sell pumpkin seeds.'

'Yes.'

'And I said no.'

'Yes.'

'Well, someone came in yesterday and asked if I had any.'

'Had any what?'

'Pine nuts.'

'And what did you say?'

'I said you're the second person who's asked me that this year.'

'Is that it?'

'Yes. I thought it was interesting,' said Jennifer, returning to the bar.

'One never tires of the intellectual conversation you get in a country pub,' I said to Quentin.

Just as we were about to leave Ivor sidled up and sat down next to us.

'Before you go, I'm looking for some exciting stories for the parish magazine. I'm guest editor for next month's edition.'

I could only think of one thing. 'What about the transvestite we're carving from a painting by Beryl Cook?'

'Is that one of your jokes?'

'No, Ivor, it's a statue of a great big voluptuous woman, who in real life is called Roger. Now that's exciting.'

'You could put it on the front cover,' suggested Quentin.

Ivor admitted it would cause quite a stir in the village. 'But we couldn't use it. What about the children? And besides, the vicar reads it.'

'Okay, we could always fall back on the story of the work we did for the *Mary Rose*.'

'Yesterday's news. Everyone knows about that.'

'They're the only interesting things I can think of.'

'A little bird,' said Ivor, tapping the side of his nose and leaning forward to speak in a barely audible whisper, 'a little bird has told me that you're thinking of making skeletons.'

'Where did you hear that?' I asked, genuinely surprised.

'Don't forget I run the Neighbourhood Watch scheme.'

'What's that got to do with it? So, you have a mole working at Puckmill Studios, do you?'

'My lips are sealed. Please don't make me reveal my sources.'

'I don't need to. It can only be Ade Tucker.'

'How did you know!'

'God, Ivor, I don't need to be Hercule Poirot to work that out. He's the only one from the village and just happens to live two doors down from you.'

Ivor looked deflated and changed the subject.

'Could you set next month's crossword, now that Betty Langley's in hospital?' he asked feebly.

'That's impossible. Though that could be something for you, Quentin. You spend most of your lunch hour buried in one.'

I had supper with Chris Booth that night; over the years of being our neighbour and also my GP we had become friends. He thought it would be a good idea to include the village more in what we were doing at Puckmill. Although his surgery was in Minchinhampton, a lot of his patients lived in Frampton Mansell and had often asked him what we got up to under the viaduct.

'You need to involve them. Apart from the pub, you're the only business around here.'

The importance of what he was saying had never crossed my mind.

'You know, some of them complain about you, the way your boys drive through the village.'

'Do they?'

'And on these lanes, it would be polite if they reversed, rather than just wait for an elderly lady to manoeuvre herself out of a tight spot.'

'I didn't know any of this was going on.'

'Hasn't Celia ever mentioned it to you?'

Celia, our dear landlady; the title made her sound old, when in fact she was younger than me. We only ever saw her briefly in the mornings, speeding up the farm track past the workshop, taking her two daughters to Westonbirt School.

'No, she's never said anything.'

'She told me some time ago that she followed a vintage Daimler that sounded its horn continuously as it drove through the village.' That was Derek Tindall and Archie, alias

Rent-a-gob, on one of their visits. 'And Eileen doesn't ride her horse to Chalford until she knows you're all at work.'

I knew Eileen well. A retired midwife, she had never said a word to me.

That conversation with Chris made me decide to do something to improve our standing in the village.

I knocked on Ivor's door just as he was about to start his school run, taking children to Deer Park in Cirencester. Before I got a word out he said, 'I've just got back from Heathrow, dropping a banker for a six o'clock flight to Frankfurt.'

I ignored that. 'Ivor, we're going to have an Open Day at Puckmill Studios. Everyone from the village will be invited. It will be on June the twenty-first, the summer solstice. There'll be a buffet lunch and we'll give the people of Frampton Mansell a guided tour of the workshops.'

'That's very generous of you. We can have a raffle.'

'Yes, and I'll donate the prizes, pieces made at Puckmill. It's your scoop, Ivor. Now take it to the printing press.'

'We haven't got a printing press. Gillman's in Cirencester do it for us.'

'I know that, Ivor. It was a form of speech.'

'Guess how much I charge for a trip to Heathrow?' he asked. As if I wouldn't believe what I was about to hear.

'Fifty pounds.'

'Ninety. Not bad for three hours' work.'

It was one of those occurrences that happen once in a lifetime. Planets must have aligned somewhere, causing their two paths to cross. Not only Derek Tindall turned up at the workshop but also Kase, unannounced and within an hour of each other. Derek had come on his own, with Archie in the States organising the unloading of a container in Boston and then distributing everything into various auctions.

These two standing in front of me were the twin peaks of my business empire. Maybe that was an exaggeration, but they certainly kept the cash flow running through its veins. They were their own people, and when I had introduced them to each other I thought it was in their best interests, not to mention reasons of customer confidentiality, that one should leave the stage now. So Kase, who'd travelled up from Ardingly in Sussex after selling his jukeboxes at a trade show, went and booked a night in the Crown. 'I left a message with one of your sons,' he said as he left. 'You obviously didn't get it.'

That left me alone with Derek, and the first thing I said to him was I knew about the Bruno Zach figure, having seen what it had sold for in the *Antiques Trade Gazette*. It brought everything to a head and this time I wasn't going to hold back.

'It has to change, Derek. I'm not going to be deceived or exploited by you any longer.'

'You're making money, so stop coming out with all this moral crap.' He blamed it on Archie, of course, an easy get-out, but even if it was true, it didn't let him off the hook.

'I'm feeding your greed and I'm not going to do it any more.'

'So, what are you going to do about it?'

On the long train journey back from Plymouth I had given it a lot of thought. The answer I'd come up with was to glue a small disc saying *Puckmill* on to the base. They wouldn't be able to remove it without ruining the surface, and, besides, it advertised our business.

When I told Derek that this was what I intended to do, he couldn't suppress his rage, nor get a word out. His cheeks swelled like someone blowing on a trumpet, and his temples bulged trying to cope with the extra flow of blood.

'You look like you're going to internally combust.'

All this happened in the yard, just as Celia was returning

from picking up her daughters from school. The rent was due and I had it in an envelope for her; someone else who always liked to be paid in cash. Her timing couldn't have been better; I think Derek was about to punch me. It also helped that her two girls, Fenn and May, came over with her.

The moment had passed, and Derek took a six-inch cigar from an aluminium tube and occupied himself by walking over to the barn, where two Anglo-Nubian goats were standing on their hind legs leaning over the stable door and bleating continuously.

When we were alone again he was still seething with anger and began prodding me rhythmically with his finger, emphasising every word he delivered. 'You are pushing yourself into a corner, my boy.'

I knew I was, but things couldn't go on as they were. I was lining their pockets by making the replicas they sold under false pretences, and they were getting rich. These were dark moments, and for the first time since Puckmill Studios had begun, I felt its future could be threatened.

'So, your mind's made up, is it?' were Derek's last words as he drove out of the yard. He never told me the reason for his unexpected visit. I knew he'd be back; he had to. We were still making thousands of pounds' worth of Art Deco statues for him.

I felt depleted when I went to meet Kase at the Crown, after I had gone home to change my clothes. I would never go out in what I'd been wearing during the day; the smell of resin was off-putting to those who were not used to it. I couldn't shake off the sense of foreboding that engulfed me, but I needed to show some enthusiasm to Kase. A bottle of red wine and some light-hearted conversation would help.

Ivor was there, huddled together with some locals, one of whom was PC Slinn, over from Sapperton, the neighbouring village. Kase was full of energy, Jennifer having recently woken him, and ready for a long evening, which I wasn't sure I could cope with.

'I'm sorry. You did leave a message with my eldest son.'

'I would never turn up without letting you know first.'

I told him Sam had become unreliable since he'd fallen in love, and spent most of the evening on the phone.

'Listen, I have a lovely job for you. Right up your street, as you English say.'

'I could do with some good news. I've had a crap day.'

'Well, this will cheer you up.'

He went on to explain that a chain of night clubs financed by Hollywood celebrities was opening across the States. He was supplying all the music memorabilia, which would include a thousand gold discs.

'They're to be mounted on black velvet and framed. All you've got to do is cast some old LPs and spray them with a gold paint. I will supply you with the record labels to be fixed in the centre.'

'You mean they're just decorative pieces?'

'Yes. They'll be hung on the walls.'

'Kase, that is indeed good news. Let's open a bottle of wine.'

'You know, there would be a big market for these here in the UK.'

'You're right. I could probably sell them to our wholesalers.'

'Well, if you pay me some commission, we could come to an agreement.'

After a bottle of wine and two hours with Kase, I'd forgotten about Derek. We ate chicken Kiev and chips, followed by Jennifer's speciality dessert 'Death by chocolate', finished off with a double brandy.

'Hope you're not thinking of driving home tonight,' said the ever-watchful Ivor.

'Of course I'm not.'

'You can stay with me. There's a single bed in my room,' suggested Kase.

'I'd better ring Ros and tell her.'

'I'll run you back for fifteen pounds if you want,' said Ivor.

When I got through to Ros, she said, 'You'd better speak to Sam. He's been on the phone for over an hour. It's too late now to ring your mother back about Sunday lunch. Oh, and Derek called.'

'What did he want?'

'It was a very bad line. All I could make out was the word mincemeat.'

The following night, after we'd eaten, Sam and I had a chat in the sitting room. I told everyone to leave us alone for twenty minutes, which annoyed Lysta because she wanted to watch *Top of the Pops*; she had a crush on George Michael. 'Don't worry, I'll wake you up before we go go,' I told her.

'Dad, I know what you're going to say, and I already know about puberty and hormones. We're taught it all at school.'

'What about hogging the phone all night, and not considering others?'

'I'm in love with Tess. I just want to be with her all the time.'

'Can't you see her for an hour after school? Go and have a milkshake in the Wimpy Bar.'

'Everyone goes in there. I want to be alone with her.'

'Well, bring her back here. Take her up to your room.'

'What about homework?'

'You'll have to do it after supper.'

Here was my son growing up, condemned to it rather than choosing. It comes upon you like something to be endured, its power causing the pained expression on his face. It sweeps away everything before it, including the feelings of others, all under the name of love.

'Dad, five minutes then I'm coming in,' said Lysta through the door.

'I've got an idea. Why don't you bring her down to the Portobello Road one Saturday? You could spend the day going to the museums.'

'Okay. That would be good.'

'You'll need to get her parents' permission.'

Johnny had finished sculpting Ruby Venezuela and was insisting he be allowed to sign it, which I refused. He claimed he was responsible for a great work of art and should be recognised for it. I reminded him that he had not originated the idea but had carved a facsimile of someone else's creation. He wouldn't accept this, and when he realised I wouldn't change my mind he demanded he be paid a royalty.

'I've paid you for carving it, and you're employed by Puckmill Studios. Let's leave it at that.'

'Well, if I carve original pieces I have the right to sell them to whoever I want.'

'Not on my time you don't.'

'Then I shall create my own work in the evenings.'

'What you do in your own time is up to you.'

It was getting difficult with Johnny. I'd hardened up since the showdown with Derek and wasn't going to be taken advantage of any more. Johnny was becoming disruptive and it was probably best for all of us if he went on his way. Students from the art colleges were getting in touch all the time, wanting to submit their work. Some would bring their portfolios to Puckmill, hoping for an opportunity to get on to the first rung of the ladder in a competitive world. It suited me to have an in-house sculptor as part of the team, but Johnny's ego had outgrown us, and Rob agreed when I told him I thought his days were numbered.

After Mike had moulded Ruby, and Rob had matched the colour of Beryl's original painting identically, I rang the Cooks to invite them to come and view the finished piece at the workshop. I knew Beryl had a weakness for strawberry sponge cake, and when I told Jennifer in the Crown who was coming for tea, she immediately offered to make one for her.

We had a big clean up the day before Beryl and John were coming. We hid all the empty drums of resin under the viaduct and I parked my van in front of them. I got the skip taken away by Valley Trading, we cleaned the barn windows, and, most important, we all promised to have a shave and get rid of our stubble.

'And you, Ade, get rid of that bum fluff on your chin.'

'It's not the queen that's coming.'

'It's as good as, and we must create the right impression.'

'Do you want us to wear ties?' asked Johnny sarcastically.

'No, but you could wash and comb your hair.'

When Beryl's car pulled into the yard, I had everyone lined up ready for inspection: it really did feel like a royal occasion as I introduced them to 'the staff', which I had decided to call them on the spur of the moment. Rob even bowed his head when he shook hands with them, while Quentin, who was blessed with a distinguished voice and had the air of a courtier, said, 'Madam, it is indeed a pleasure to meet you.'

It was a pity Beryl wasn't carrying a handbag on her arm, because it would have completed the scene. They were given a guided tour of the workshop and we explained the processes involved in making the finest quality replicas.

'They really would fool anyone, they're so convincing,' Beryl said. I almost told her that some people did pass them off as originals, but I thought mentioning a certain wide boy's dishonesty would tarnish the day.

At last the moment arrived to show them the finished

article: Ruby in all her glory, which Johnny was to unveil in front of our honoured guests. It was only right to let him have his moment and be recognised for the work he'd done. And although I had warned him in advance not to overdo it, he, of course, took full advantage of being in the limelight, letting Beryl know the difficulty he'd had getting the precise feel for the piece, capturing Ruby's cheekiness and humour. 'I came back to it time and time again until I was happy with it. And I think you'll agree, even though I say it myself, I've made one or two improvements to the way you've portrayed her in the painting.'

Johnny's ego taking flight was deeply embarrassing and I immediately stepped in and made light of it. 'Oh, don't be so silly, Johnny,' I said, mouthing the words 'you bastard' and showing him my clenched fist.

Whatever John and Beryl were thinking, they certainly didn't show it, and Beryl gave a dignified response. 'Well, I think it's absolutely marvellous, don't you, John?' Her husband nodded his head in agreement. 'It's astonishing the work you do here, in this converted cowshed.'

'Stables, Beryl. When I started the business I shared the place with a Shire horse.'

'Well, I can't thank you enough for your wonderful welcome. You've made me feel like a queen.'

Over afternoon tea at the Crown, Beryl tucking into her strawberry sponge cake, I thought all that remained now was to get Roger's approval, the rest just a formal confirmation of everything we'd already agreed. I hadn't expected what came next and it ruined what until then had been a highly successful day.

'You know, of course, that this all has to go through the Portal Gallery in London,' John suddenly announced to me.

'What do you mean? I don't understand.'

'There's no problem, it's just that they have the rights to Beryl's work. But I'm sure you can do a deal with them.'

In that instant any profit to do with Ruby Venezuela vanished without trace. If I had previously had doubts that there was any money in the job, I knew now we would make a serious loss. Beryl was taking a cut, as was Roger, now the Portal Gallery. There was nothing left in it for us.

As I sat there, anger welled up in me that took all my will to suppress. I could tell John didn't have a clue what a devastating effect his words had had upon me. Why only mention this now? He should have told me when we first met in Plymouth. All this went through my mind as Beryl ate her cake and Jennifer came to the table to make sure everyone was enjoying themselves.

If I'd added up what we'd already spent on the project, I couldn't have stayed sitting there. And opposite me, the lovely Beryl was blissfully unaware of the significance of John's passing remark.

'I've had the most wonderfully interesting day. I can't thank you enough.'

'I shall look forward to hearing what Roger thinks of his little statue,' John said, shaking my hand warmly.

Jennifer came and stood next to me as we watched them drive away.

'I bet you're very pleased with the way that went,' she said.

'Couldn't be happier.'

'You look terribly fed up. What's wrong?'

'You'll never know, Jennifer. Things are never quite what they seem.'

'By the way, your tea and homemade strawberry sponge cake.'

'What about it?'

'The bill's eight pounds. Do you want to pay it now, or shall I put it on your tab?'

✦ 13 ✦

Rob came and asked me whether I'd been over to the barn and seen Johnny, who was airbrushing a gold saxophone that was going to be hung in the entrance of a record shop opening in Tottenham Court Road. I said since the Beryl Cook incident, when he'd tried to steal the show, I preferred to see as little of him as possible.

'Well, he's over there smoking a joint, so you'd better go and do something about it.'

'You're joking.'

'Can you see a smile on my face?' he said. 'I've known you a long time. You always put off dealing with things when they get unpleasant.'

'That's a complete exaggeration.'

'He's making a mockery of you and knows he can get away with it.'

'Not any longer. I've had enough. I'll go and tell him.'

'And don't worry that we can't survive without him, because we can.'

'Okay, Rob, you've made your point.'

Everyone had complained about Johnny at some time. Quentin, who had an impressive command of the English language, could defend himself quite easily with off-the-cuff responses. But Johnny directed his sarcastic ridicule mostly at Mike and Ade, soft targets for a bully because of their local accents. I'd never witnessed it, being away a lot of the time, but I'd been told.

When I walked into the area of the barn we had converted into a workshop, I was hit by the smell of marijuana. A blue cloud of smoke floated around the bare light bulb hanging from one of the rafters. Johnny had never shown me any aggression, but he always let me know he knew the answer

172

to everything and believed I should consider him my right-hand man. Unfortunately, his downfall was that he thought being a talented sculptor elevated him above everyone else at Puckmill. He would never be a team player, and such was the arrogance he'd shown in front of Beryl I had begun to wonder if there was not something pathological about his behaviour.

Now, as I stood in front of him, I knew it was the end.

'You know why I'm here, what we have to deal with, don't you?'

'You're going to give me a pay rise.'

'Nothing could be further from my mind.'

'You're not happy with what I rightfully said in front of Beryl Cook?'

'I think that performance showed you for what you really are.'

'Which is merely your opinion and therefore won't be worth listening to.'

'Well, in that case, get your stuff together and get out of the place now. You're sacked.'

'Are you sure you want to do that? It'll be your loss.'

'Yes, I'm sure, Johnny. We've all had enough of you.'

I didn't think he believed I was really going to say it. He silently put on his jacket and his hands were shaking when he lit a cigarette. He didn't look at me once the whole time he was gathering up his belongings and then brushed past me, flicking the butt of his cigarette into the air as he got on his bicycle. My last words to him as he rode out of the yard were, 'You need to go and take a long hard look at yourself.'

As I watched him disappear I wondered how long it would take to replace him. Firing him created a vacancy that we would have to fill; Rob might have been right when he said we could survive without him, but for how long? At our lunch break, I told everyone what had happened, and it was met with such unanimous joy that I added, 'Oh, come on, he wasn't that bad.'

'Oh yes, he was,' they said in unison.

When Frank Webb told me his mother had died on his birthday twelve years ago, I could tell he was going to follow the statement up with a heartfelt memory. I knew very little about him, except that he was an only child. Now, while Greasy Gadd was walking about the rag market in search of military paraphernalia, Frank opened up. When I say opened up, it was only for a sentence or two. He told me she had died at home, five minutes after trying to swat a fly with the *Reader's Digest*. Apparently, she had then sat down in her armchair to sip a cup of tea and it had slipped from her hand, derailing the *Pines Express* as it passed beneath her.

'For some reason, Frank, I feel there is more to this story.'

'It's my fiftieth birthday today.'

'Oh, I see. Happy birthday.'

'It never has been, not since she passed on.'

'Well, I can understand that.'

I suspected he had something else to say, but I never heard it, as Sifta turned up just then, signalling to me that he had a matter of some urgency to discuss. For those who scavenge in the markets it's all about seizing the opportunity as soon as it presents itself. It's the same for all wildlife on this planet: strike immediately or someone else will.

'Come on, Sifta, can't you see I'm talking to Frank?'

'I need a quick word, and a quick answer to something. Have you heard of John Betjeman?'

'Of course. He's the poet laureate.'

'Have you heard of "Betjeman's Bygone Britain"?'

'No.'

'Read this,' he said, taking from his pocket a leaflet and a certificate of authenticity. It was for a limited edition of silver medals depicting landmarks that had vanished from the face of Britain.

'Signed, they are, and I can lay my hands on a dozen of them.'

'Good luck, Sifta. Hope you know what you're doing.'

'I got done for bald tyres last week. This could pay for a new set.'

He was off then, and Frank had disappeared without imparting what I had felt was going to be something of great importance.

To my surprise, after months of not seeing her, Isobel appeared in the distance. Stylishly dressed as always, she had an Afghan hound on a lead and was making her way slowly down the aisle towards me, stopping at each of the stalls as if something had caught her eye. I was ready for her to walk past without acknowledging me, but as she got closer I saw a smile spread across her face.

'This is Sophia,' she told me, stroking the ears of her well-groomed companion, who raised her paw, hoping I would shake hands with her.

I almost asked her if the creature had her own personal hairdresser.

'Isobel, it's been so long. I can't remember the last time I saw you.'

'Oh, I've seen you several times, but not to talk to. You've always been busy.'

'And is there a reason you're here today, or are you just exercising the dog?'

'Yes, there is indeed a reason. And the matter must be discussed privately, in the strictest confidence,' she said seriously.

'You're not suggesting over supper, because that would be impossible.'

'Nothing of the sort. A very wealthy friend of mine is facing a dire predicament, which maybe you can solve, and I'd like to bring her to your workshop.'

'Surely you can tell me now? It might save you a journey,' I suggested.

'No, she insists on meeting you first, and my only involvement is to introduce you to each other.'

It felt genuine, so I gave Isobel my telephone number and told her to make an appointment. She didn't bother to look at anything on the stall and I watched her walk away, disregarding one of the homeless who stretched his hand out to her. At the last moment, I saw her take a quick look back at me.

Sifta returned with a beautiful boxed collection of 'Betjeman's Bygone Britain'. They were large coins depicting in the finest detail buildings that had vanished from the British landscape. Cast in sterling silver, among them were places I'd never heard of: the Alhambra Theatre in London, Fonthill Abbey in Wiltshire, the Crumlin Viaduct in Monmouthshire, the Peacock Hotel in Northamptonshire.

'How much, Sifta?' I asked. 'I'll certainly buy a set. I've never seen anything like it.'

'Would you pay a hundred and fifty pounds for one?'

'Probably. Being a limited edition, they're bound to go up in value.'

'Can you lend me five hundred to help me out and I'll give you a set?'

'For how long?'

'A week. I can get rid of some debts and put a new set of tyres on the van.'

'How much are you paying for them?' I asked, needing to know I'd be getting my money back.

'Fifty pounds each, and don't you breathe a word about it to anyone.'

So I lent Sifta the money; he'd always paid back every penny he owed me. And it was nice to be able to help him out of a hole.

Frank returned, as usual just as I was about to leave, not to say goodbye, but to see if I would be increasing my order for the walking sticks that he still made for me every week. This time, though, it was for a totally different reason. He asked if I'd give him a lift home to his house in the Hagley Road, which I drove past anyway on my way to the M5.

'I thought you might like to call in for half an hour and celebrate my birthday with me.'

'Why not, Frank? Your fiftieth will never happen again. Have you got anything special lined up?'

'Yes. After we've listened to my parents' favourite record, "The Laughing Policeman", I'm going to let you take the mail train down to Euston.'

'That would be an honour.'

'It's important to create the right atmosphere, so it has to be in the night.'

'But it will only be two in the afternoon.'

'I'll close the curtains and turn off the main light.'

'I won't be able to see what I'm doing.'

'Don't worry, I'll be following it with a spotlight.'

'Brilliant, Frank. You've thought of everything.'

'And then as you come into Euston station, you can sing "Happy Birthday" to me.'

'I can't wait. What a day to remember.'

Sunday lunch with my mother. Why is it that teenagers who always think they know better than their parents, are so well mannered and accommodating when they visit their grandmother? Sam and Lysta even laid the table and waited for her to finish serving before they began eating. Ros and I gave one another an ironic look. They didn't behave like that at home.

'Now, I've got some news for you all,' my mother began.

'Are you going to marry that man you went camping with?' asked Seth, who remembered that she'd once gone to Cumbria with Peter, the chap who wanted to buy the flat above her.

'Certainly not, and I never went camping with him. That was a silly idea of your father's.'

'Is there a man involved in this news?' I enquired.

'Will you please let me speak?'

Whenever my mother announced that she had some news to tell us, it was usually something life-changing. Like the time at Dyffryn when she told us she was going to marry a Greek fisherman. She returned two months later having realised she had made a terrible mistake. Luckily, they had not tied the knot.

'I've given up taking driving lessons.'

I was mystified. 'I thought you'd given up years ago.'

'I had, but I started again, in Peter's car. He was my instructor.'

'Oh, dear. So it's over with him, is it?'

'Not over as such, but he says he's psychologically damaged.'

'They say husbands and boyfriends should never teach their partners to drive.'

'It wasn't anything to do with that.'

'What was it, then?'

'It was the driving test I took last week.'

'You ran the examiner over.'

'No, worse than that. He said he'd never failed somebody before for so many mistakes.'

'How many, Mum? How bad was it?'

'Ten, and he asked me who my instructor was, because he certainly wasn't a professional.'

'So, what happened?' asked Ros.

'Well, as you can imagine, it's been difficult. Peter's been driving nearly thirty years and has never had an accident.'

'Granny, can we have some apple crumble now?' said Belah, who had been sitting patiently for the past five minutes.

'Gran,' said Lysta, 'you told me one of the lovely things about Bath was you could walk everywhere, so why do you need to learn to drive?'

'You're quite right, I don't need to. Now come and help me clear away the plates.'

I hadn't heard a word from Derek for two weeks, the longest period of silence since we'd met. I was sure he was waiting for Archie to return from the States, and rather feared they'd turn up at Puckmill and work me over, but that wouldn't really have been in their interest.

When I got the telephone call, which was after I'd had two or three glasses of wine, I had to jerk myself awake. My brain had mellowed out listening to Neil Young's *After the Gold Rush*. Derek was a fast talker and didn't believe in pauses between words; he verbally galloped like a runaway horse.

'Okay, we'll do it your way. We'll sell nothing in the UK. Everything will be shipped to the States.'

'Is that a promise?'

'Of course. I've spoken to Archie. Now you should be a happy man.'

When Marcus Wesley came over to collect his bronzes, I was genuinely proud of what we had done for him. Rob had suggested we should take photographs and keep a record of all our work, especially these classical bronzes.

'We should have an archive department,' said Quentin. 'All those one-off pieces that we'll never see again.'

'It's part of our history,' added Mike.

'What happens to the moulds, when you've only had to take one cast from them?' asked Marcus.

'Well, really we should destroy them,' I told him.

'But you don't, do you?'

'Only because you can't burn silicone. Too polluting.'

'Couldn't you go on producing them and sell them to interior designers?'

'We charge the customer for making the mould, so I suppose legally it's their property.'

I always did the cash deals privately in my shed with the door locked. Marcus counted out what he owed me, all four thousand pounds of it.

'Let me tell you something,' he said, 'for your ears only. Those bronze replicas you've just made weren't wanted because of the high insurance premiums.'

'What, then?'

He went on to tell me that the retired colonel was divorcing his wife. A part of the settlement was that she got the bronzes, all fifty thousand pounds' worth of them. Now she would be getting the replicas we'd made and would be none the wiser.

'Look, we're not here to pass judgement, or none of us would make a living.'

I was getting a bit weary of all the moral dilemmas people wrestled with, or rather didn't. All I had ever wanted to do was get Puckmill known for the excellence and diversity of our work. Dealers could make an honest living by selling on the replicas we made without any pretence about what they were.

Marcus was sniffing an opportunity. Everyone did; they couldn't help it. It was like living with a psychological condition that needed to be kept under control. It was the rush that came from making a profit, the buzz flooding through the veins. They went searching for it again and again.

Of all the people I'd met through the years, it was Marcus who moved in the right circles, awash with what he called old money. He knew many of the aristocracy with their inherited dosh, living out in the country in old houses, full of antiques. 'Some of your pieces would appeal to London's top interior designers, and they'd pay the right price.'

'I like it. It's so far removed from the world we deal in now.'

Chris Booth knocked on the door then, wanting to know if I needed any help for Saturday's open day. He was bringing his ninety-three-year-old mother, who was partial to tuna and cucumber sandwiches.

I wasn't nervous, but as soon as I woke up an image of Isobel was on my mind, walking around the rag market with her Afghan hound. She was coming to the workshop that day, bringing this friend of hers who was apparently in a dire predicament.

Ros often asked me about the people I met in the street markets; she was fascinated by them. I'd told her about Isobel some time ago, what an interesting woman she was and how she'd given me such a boost in those early days, buying from the stall every week.

'Are you sure it's only your netsuke she's after?' Ros had said once.

It was a warm summer's day at Puckmill and some of the airbrushing, thanks to our mobile compressor, could be done outside. Rob was spraying twenty of Kase's gold discs laid out on a long wooden table when Isobel and her friend arrived in an open-top Porsche. They were both dressed as if out on the French Riviera, wearing transparent silk chiffon blouses. Isobel's gold earrings sparkled in the sunlight.

'This is Delphine,' she said, introducing me to a lady whose heavy make-up was doing its best to hold back the years. She had an abundance of auburn hair which swept back from her forehead. Her green eyes had a touch of ice about them. When she smiled she was without wrinkles and her pale skin seemed tight. She had the assured presence of a woman who got what she wanted. I'd not met anyone like her before; she intrigued me, but there was something about her that made me feel uncomfortable.

'This is my pleasure, I can tell you,' she said, in a French accent. 'My, what a hidden treasure we have here,' she continued enthusiastically.

'This is my friend Rob. We used to farm pigs together in the Welsh hills.'

'Well, I'd heard they were alive with something, but never pigs.'

'Are you going to show us around?' asked Isobel.

'I'd rather not; you're too well dressed, and the fumes might affect you.'

'So, can we talk somewhere comfortable?'

'Yes. There's a lovely old pub in the village. You would have passed it on the way down. I suggest we go there.'

Jennifer was always a good host and knew whoever I brought to the Crown was there to talk business.

'Do you want to go up to the top bar where it's more private?' she asked when we arrived.

'*Très bien*,' said Delphine. 'Could we have a pot of tea?'

After Jennifer had served us we had the place to ourselves. Delphine took some photographs from her handbag and put them face down on the table.

'I ought to tell you about myself,' she said, 'before we get down to business.'

Delphine was born in Marseilles. She didn't say when, but it must have been fifty or so years ago. 'I had a few burning ambitions; one was to marry an Englishman.' She found her man, who had been to public school and made his money in steel. 'Can you imagine that?' Always outshone by her older brother, she had been determined to prove herself. She had an interest in art, and, having secured a rich husband, bought an art gallery.

'I exhibited the work of dozens of young artists and made them who they are today,' she said boastfully, filling our cups with tea and adding an artificial sweetener to hers. 'I always get what I go after.'

'So, what brings you here today?'

'You've got to understand, I'm well known in certain circles, so there are assurances I need from you before I can tell you anything.'

'Go on.'

'Everything you hear around this table today goes no further than the three of us. Can you give me your word on that?'

'Of course. A lot of the work we do is confidential.'

She then turned over the photographs and selected a couple which she handed to me, old black-and-white photos that had faded to sepia.

'Here. This one shows the artist driving the tractor and trailer to the site where it still stands today.'

'That's a very large piece. It must be twenty feet long.'

'And here she is applying the patina.'

She passed me several more, giving me a running commentary about the day when the world-famous artist put the finishing touches to her bronze sculpture of *Psyche Lying in the Arms of Zephyrus*.

'She's waiting to be carried away to a magnificent palace,' Delphine said.

One showed a JCB digging a moat around the artwork to create an island that Delphine could see from the veranda of her palatial house.

'So, tell me, what has all this got to do with me?'

'Isobel tells me you specialise in making replicas.'

'That's true, but this is well out of our league.'

'But that is defeatist talk. All I want is a copy made in fibreglass. Surely that's possible.'

'It's realist talk. We've never moulded anything as large as that.'

'There's a first time for everything, so give it a go.'

'It looks too complicated. How do we get all our equipment on to an island? And we'd need electricity.'

'I've got a rowing boat and have a handyman who can run a cable out there for you. I'll give you thirty thousand pounds, half of it as a deposit within a week.'

'It's not the money. This would be the biggest job I've ever taken on. If you want a replica made, what's going to happen to the original?'

'I can't tell you, and you've given me your word to remain silent.'

'If you're going to sell my copy as the original, I want nothing to do with it.'

'All right. This is what I'll promise; no one will be buying your copy. What I'm asking you to do is for me. I'm not going to make a penny out of your replica.'

'Give me a day to think about it. I need to speak to someone.'

After they'd gone I talked to Mike and asked him what he thought. He reckoned we'd need at least fifty kilos of silicone, more than a hundred kilos of gelcoat resin, and the whole job could take two to three weeks. I'd completely forgotten to ask Delphine exactly where she lived. Would we have to stay in a hotel somewhere? The greatest difficulty about one-off jobs was how to price them up accurately. It was always hit and miss; mostly miss, unfortunately. I'd learnt that on the Ruby Venezuela venture.

Once again I found myself back in familiar territory, the same old things fizzing around in my head. 'No, don't do it!' shouted a distant voice from the depths, only to be squashed by the dominant fool who sat at the helm: 'Go on, it'll be exciting. You haven't taken a risk for ages.'

It was time to go and sit in the garden shed, stare out of that little square window, put Silo on my lap and stroke his furry back, and ponder things. I hadn't seen the rabbit for a while and noticed how much heavier he was when I picked him up. Also, there was a cigarette end in the saucer I used as an ashtray; someone had been smoking a filter-tip.

As the sun went down that evening and the little square window filled with twilight, I gave in to the fool who stomps around just beneath the surface of consciousness. It was then the shed door suddenly opened and there stood Sam and his girlfriend Tess. I'd taken them completely by surprise.

'Dad.'

'Sam.'

'What are you doing here?'

'I was about to ask you the same question.'

'Tess and I come in here for a little peace and quiet.'

'Silo's put on a lot of weight since I last saw him,' I said.

'Well, you know why. He's overfed and doesn't get any exercise. Not since next door's dog got in and nearly killed him.'

'He doesn't have much of a life.'

'Lysta's lost interest. She's listening to Wham! all the time.'

'And whose is this cigarette end?'

'It's mine,' said Tess unconvincingly.

'It's ours, Dad.'

'How many do you smoke a day?'

'One, down here in the shed. I forgot to throw away the butt.'

'Does Ros know?'

'No, and please don't tell her.'

Over supper I asked everyone if they thought Silo had a good life shut up in a shed all day. Seth said it was better than being imprisoned in a hutch.

'I hate cruelty to animals and I don't like zoos either,' he concluded.

Lysta couldn't admit she didn't care about Silo any longer and excused herself from any responsibility, blaming the amount of homework she had to do. When Ros asked me where all this was leading, I suggested I took Silo to Puckmill.

'He can stay in my shed at night and have the freedom of the place during the day. All those in favour,' I said, raising my hand. 'Motion carried.'

It was the Puckmill Open Day, the temperature up in the seventies and a cloudless sky. Swallows, faster than the speed of sound, dived from the heights, zipping through the arches of the viaduct.

We'd spent most of Friday afternoon cleaning the whole of the workshop. The place hadn't been this tidy since Beryl's visit, and every room had been sprayed with air freshener. It smelt like a massage parlour, not that I've ever been in one. All of us who worked at Puckmill were there; it was strange seeing everyone dressed in their casual clothes rather than ripped overalls or torn jeans covered in paint. All the windows open, we were ready for inspection.

Tables had been put out in the yard and covered with white tablecloths, which were in fact sheets that Ros had finished ironing early that morning. I'd rented fifty glasses from the off-licence in Cirencester, which was a complete guess, because we'd no idea how many people were going to turn up. There were sausage rolls, and Sheila Booth had made all the sandwiches. Jennifer at the Crown had provided soft drinks and a few bottles of wine on a sale or return basis. I guessed the population of Frampton Mansell was about one hundred and fifty, and that those who were interested would meander down through the day. I'd only advertised the event in two places: obviously in the pub, and in the entrance to the church.

Of course, the first to arrive were Ivor and his wife Janet. Luckily, Quentin engaged Ivor in conversation, which I could overhear. Ivor told him about the history of the canal, the Puckmill lock gates and the price someone had recently paid for the lock-keeper's cottage. 'Money a man would never earn in a lifetime labouring in the fields.' Quentin was nodding his head continuously. 'Now this new breed is turning up from the cities, pushing up house prices, and what do they contribute to village life?'

'Not a lot, I suppose,' said Quentin.

'How can they, only coming at weekends? Now it's different with your friend here, Nick. He is part of the community, and helps the economy of the village.'

'Yes, he does.'

'Although some of those types he mixes with, I don't know what to make of them, with their long hair and untaxed cars.'

Daphne Neville, who liked to make an entrance, arrived with Bee the otter on a lead. I knew she'd come; she had an undying need to be centre stage. She gathered all the children around her and entertained them by reading from her book *Bee*, all of them taking it in turns to hold the otter. I'd often wondered why she'd never mentioned our interview and her audition for *Down Your Way*. Only Martin, her husband, referring to something else altogether, said that it can take the BBC years to reach a decision about anything.

Celia Foxton came with her American boyfriend who described himself as a graphic artist. After spending ten minutes with me, he offered to design a logo to put on our stationery and compliments slips. 'Who prints your invoices for you?'

I didn't tell him that I still wrote them all by hand, using carbon paper.

'You know what the next big thing's going to be?' he asked.

'Interstellar space travel?'

'Fax machines. Every business will need one.'

'Fax machines, hmmm. I think we're a few years away from getting one of those.'

Mike introduced me to his parents, Wilf and Min, who told me their son was a completely new person since he'd been working at Puckmill.

'In what way?' I was interested to hear.

'Doing that work on the *Mary Rose* gave him confidence,' said Min. 'He even leans over the fence and talks to the girl next door now.'

'Well, it was all down to him, no one else.'

Chris Booth turned up with the vicar, Andy, a name you don't associate with a man who has been called by God. The two of them showed great interest in what we were doing, wanting to go through each stage of manufacture from beginning to end, which we did for half an hour. I owed the day to Chris, who had often asked me to explain what Puckmill Studios was all about. On the few evenings I'd spent with him in his sitting room he'd always been on call, and every visit had been cut short, so he'd never heard the whole story.

Rob gave a demonstration on airbrushing an Art Deco statue and Ade raised his status in the village by de-moulding a whale's tooth and expertly showing everyone how we were able to give the piece an aged look with a bath in potassium permanganate. Ivor said we were 'a bunch of clever buggers', praise indeed, and then challenged me to make a replica of his grandfather's ivory letter opener, which he was still using every day in the post office.

By five o'clock we'd all talked to most of the folk of Frampton Mansell. That evening I told Ros they had asked question after question about how we managed to make plastic look like bronze and the history behind several of the pieces. Chris was the last person to leave, waiting for his mother, who had sat at the end of a trestle table for most of the afternoon, slowly making her way through her tuna and cucumber sandwiches.

The following Monday, as soon as I had settled Silo into his new home under the Formica shelf in my shed, I rang Delphine. After she'd greeted me with all her French effervescence for at least a minute, I said in that reserved English way, 'I've been thinking about things.'

'Yes, yes, you've been thinking about things. We've all been thinking about things. Now when are you getting over here?'

'Just a minute; hold on.' I'd got distracted by Silo, who had hopped out of the shed and disappeared into a clump of nettles. There were adders around at this time of year.

'Delphine, I'm coming tomorrow with my mould maker. We should be with you by midday.'

'So, you're going to take it on.'

'I didn't say that. I'm coming to take a look. By the way, where exactly do you live?'

'Would you like lunch?'

'Sorry, Delphine, I've got to go. My rabbit is about to be eaten by a snake.'

14

Ade Tucker, because he moved from job to job, had been given the nickname 'Floater'. He was the youngest member of the team and often complained that whenever someone didn't fancy doing something, they gave it to him to do. What's called taking advantage of the weakest. I had Silo in my arms when he walked into my shed, demanding that he be given more responsibility and reminding me he had now been working at Puckmill for eighteen months. Jennifer had already mentioned that her son was ready for promotion. 'I look after you,' she said. 'Well, you should look after him.'

'I could make you Head of Packaging and Despatch,' I said, passing him Silo as the phone rang. 'Puckmill Studios, how can I help you on this wonderful morning?'

It was Kase from Amsterdam but ringing from India; it sounded as if he was speaking to me in the middle of a traffic jam. I could barely hear him over the noise of car horns.

'Listen, I'm sending you a telegram with an address to deliver thirty Nipper dogs. Now, this is important: cut the heads off ten and send them loose, so I can glue them back on over here. Do you understand?'

'Sounds completely barmy.'

'I don't know what that means.'

And he never would; the line went dead. Cut the heads off ten Nippers? What was he up to?

'Now, Ade, as I was saying, your promotion would mean a wage increase of five pounds a week, but the role won't be full time. Whenever we need parcels wrapped and a courier booked, it will be your responsibility. Are you ready for it?'

'Is that all?' he said indignantly.

'What do you mean is that all? It's extremely important work. Have you had any experience using a felt-tip pen?'

'Not really.'

'Well, we'll have to train you up. You can spell, can't you?'

'Won't I just be copying out addresses?'

'Yes, I suppose so.'

'And bubble-wrapping everything, which I've never done before.'

'We'll go through it tomorrow morning.'

'All I need is a dummy run, someone to show me.'

Delphine's house was a beautiful Georgian mansion with a garden that could have been designed by Capability Brown. Large sculptures were dotted around the place, all perfectly positioned to lead the eye eventually to the circular island where *Psyche* basked in the sunlight.

Delphine was there to greet us, along with a pair of Doberman Pinschers who growled at us. She completely ignored them and didn't try to put them back in the house.

'If we have to run the gauntlet past them every morning, the price is going up.'

'They're guard dogs. They'll be fine once they get to know you.'

The only way to reach the island was by a rowing boat, which drifted on a rope tied to a wooden post.

'Which one of you is going to row?' asked Delphine. That's when Mike told me he couldn't swim and was afraid of water.

'Now you tell me.'

'I can get him a life jacket if you want,' said Delphine.

'It's only ten yards, Mike. Just close your eyes for a minute.'

'And I suffer from seasickness.'

'When was the last time you went near water?'

'When I was a child.'

'Well, you've probably grown out of it by now, so don't worry.'

I got into the boat first and helped Mike in. He looked full of trepidation.

'You're overacting.'

'No, I'm not.'

Delphine untied the rope and after only six strokes and fifteen seconds, which I counted out loud, we were on the island.

'That must have been the world's shortest ever voyage,' I said. 'I wonder if we'd get an entry in the *Guinness Book of Records*.'

Mike ignored me and was already walking round the sculpture, taking out a tape measure and running it the complete length of the marble plinth it sat upon.

'We must be quiet now,' I said to Delphine. 'He needs to assess it all; consider the pitfalls we might encounter.'

Mike took out his notebook and began scribbling things down. I liked it when he weighed up a job, especially in front of the customer. He had a naturally thoughtful expression and stroked his Adam's apple in deep concentration. The most important thing was that he looked like somebody who knew what he was doing.

'It's not going to be easy; in fact it's going to be damn difficult. Getting all the equipment here, for a start. And the weather; we're going to have to put up scaffolding and cover the whole thing with a tarpaulin.'

He was right: we couldn't work if it was raining. 'We need to get a vacuum pump out here, and electricity.'

'I've got a man who can help with all that,' said Delphine.

'That's good. And as I thought, we'll need about fifty kilos of silicone. I'll take a skin mould and then make a gelcoat jacket. I'm going to need an assistant. Maybe Ade can cut the fibreglass for me.'

'How long do you reckon? Ten days or so?'

'More like two weeks.'

On the walk back to the house, Delphine assumed that we'd made up our minds and would be there in the morning to get on with the job.

'Hold on, Delphine, it doesn't work like that. First we need someone to put up the scaffolding and a tarpaulin.'

'Then you'll come and complete the work in two weeks.'

'Hopefully.'

'Then please come to the house. I need you to sign a non-disclosure agreement.'

'What's that?'

'It's just a piece of paper preventing you from breathing a word to anyone.'

'What happens if I do?'

'I'll shoot you.'

'Sounds a bit drastic.'

I dutifully signed her piece of paper, which she then photocopied. She handed the copy to me in an envelope. 'So, we are in business. Now we'll see if you're as good as your reputation would have me believe.'

'I need half the money up front and the rest as soon as we've completed the job.'

'You have my word.'

The only person I'd have swapped my life with was Tom Greenfield. At the stall in the Portobello Road, he told me he had just sold the last of his prayer balls, each individually boxed, with a few words of historical text on a printed leaflet. I couldn't believe he'd sold them so quickly. It was all so neat and simple.

'And of course,' I said, 'they fit easily into a lady's handbag.'

'Yes, but not for a fiver.'

'How much did you sell them for?'

'Twenty pounds each.' He'd made ten pounds' profit on each one! 'That sees me off to the Caribbean for the winter. Sun, sand and sex for a few months.'

'What a life you have.'

'Yep, and it's just me. No overheads, no mortgage and, best of all, no children.'

How is it some people can just sail through life with the minimum of effort, while others are always struggling to keep their heads above water? Tom was not only blessed with good looks but had a natural charm that he turned on every time he was in the company of a woman. I'd had the stall next to him every Saturday for weeks and watched him at work, this sweet-talking guy who repeated the same spiel day after day almost word for word. As soon as someone picked up the one prayer ball he had on display the same line flowed from him: 'Curious, isn't it, and with a very interesting history.' And they were hooked. 'Some people believe that even today they have the same protective power.'

As soon as they'd gone, out came another ball to be placed in the middle of his tiered stall, which was covered in black silk.

Through those summer months he'd worn a collarless white shirt and a gold crucifix around his neck. His white linen trousers and sandals gave him the air of a traveller, someone passing through on his way to somewhere else. He'd been educated at public school and had the aura of someone from another part of the world in another time, when England had its colonies. On his last day he introduced me to Stephanie, who was taking over his stall to sell her Inca jewellery. I could tell straight away they were, or had been, lovers; she kept tickling him and giggling like a schoolgirl.

'Stop it. People are looking at us.' He tried to tell her how best to sell her pieces of jewellery. 'Tell them they're handmade in the traditional way in the mountains of Peru.'

'She doesn't need a sales technique,' I told Tom. 'She's got enough good looks to attract enough people to the stall.'

'Nick's right. Maybe you just need to wear what you're selling.' And she did, and took so much money through that Saturday, she thought she'd only have to work one day a week to enjoy a life of fun. Tom, of course, had sourced the jewellery on his travels through South America.

The last I saw of him was disappearing down the Portobello Road on his old Norton motorbike, with Stephanie sitting behind him, her arms round his waist.

If I hadn't been married with children, or running a business, or employing people, I'd have gone with him without a moment's hesitation. I was lost in these thoughts when I felt a gentle tap on my shoulder, then two hands being placed over my eyes. A voice came from behind me.

'You wicked boy, turn to stone.' I knew that voice, but when I turned round I couldn't place the person standing before me.

'It's me, Roger, otherwise known as Ruby Venezuela.'

I didn't recognise him without make-up or lipstick, his hair flattened down with a central parting. Only his voice gave him away.

'Roger,' I said. 'How marvellous to see you in men's clothes.'

'Not many people have said that to me before.'

'Well, it's the first time I've seen you not dressed as a woman.'

'Enough of me. Now, what's happened to our little statue? Why haven't you been in touch? Beryl says she hasn't heard a word from you either.'

'There was no money in it. Not a penny. The whole job was a complete waste of time,' I told him.

'But what about the statue? Can I buy it from you?'

'It was destroyed when we took the mould from it.'

'Now that is a crying shame. It would have looked lovely on my mantelpiece.'

'I'm sorry, Roger, but if I'd known all the facts from the outset I would never had begun the venture.'

'You poor boy, you must be livid. I'm heartbroken, I really am. I was just beginning to like you.'

When Susie Atherton walked into Puckmill carrying her portfolio and dragging a trolley across the stony ground towards my shed, I knew why she was here. She had a dishevelled look: loose-fitting clothes, blonde hair falling on to her shoulders, and dried paint on her hands, as if she had come straight from her studio. She wasn't the first to try her luck with us, young art students who'd finished their courses at Stroud College turning up unannounced, looking for a job.

You would think it was flattering, these artists searching us out. That our reputation was such that they thought working at Puckmill could help their careers. But actually it was the opposite. I'd not been able to offer any of them a job and the interviews had become emotionally delicate encounters which could break vulnerable young hearts and destroy any glimmering of confidence. All those who had come before Susie had presented three years of effort and had it rejected in five minutes; it can do untold damage. It's impossible to let someone down so gently that they can walk away feeling optimistic about their future as an artist. Most of them would have taken any job I offered just to gain the experience and find out about all the different techniques we used. But we had no vacancies at Puckmill, or none that I advertised. If I ever met the right sculptor to replace Johnny that would be a different matter altogether.

'Please, will you give me ten minutes?' she said as I picked up Silo, who had hopped over to be a part of what was going on. 'No longer, I promise.'

We went into my shed and I turned over sheet after sheet of her paintings, watercolours of landscapes and some charcoal drawings and portraits of farm labourers. Her work was better than anything I'd seen previously, but it wasn't what we needed at Puckmill.

'What have you got in your trolley?' I asked.

'Some sculpture I did in my final year.'

And at last I saw something that we could use. The quality of her work showed her natural talent. A piece depicting two entwined female figures on a rock was what convinced me that I should commission her to carve something for us.

Since starting to work with Marcus Wesley, we had been supplying works of art exclusively to trendy London designers. Limited editions of bronzes, each one numbered and so making larger profit margins. Marcus controlled what we made available to these clients, as he called them, who had more money than good taste, a derisory remark he applied to the wives of rich businessmen who spent thousands on doing up their houses. Some of them apparently visited their properties for no more than two weeks a year. He'd also mentioned several times that there was an untapped market in erotic art.

'The pink pound,' he said, 'that's where our future lies.'

Susie gave an embarrassed laugh. 'They're just a bit of fun, but I can carve anything really.'

'They're not just fun, I think they're brilliant.'

'Wow! That's terrific.'

'Let's go up to the Crown and discuss a few things.'

'Wow! That's terrific.'

'You just said that.'

'Sorry. I'm terribly nervous.'

'Well, let's have a chat.'

Any hope of an immediate exploratory talk with Susie disappeared as soon as we entered the Crown. There in the corner was Peter sitting with my mother, one hand stroking hers, the other stirring his coffee.

'Susie, you'll have to excuse me. Order me a glass of elderflower and whatever you want for yourself. I'll be no more than a couple of minutes.'

'Darling, we were just on our way down to see you. You remember Peter, don't you?'

'Yes, of course. It's been a long-standing relationship.'

'Quite right. Almost two years now,' said Peter, inviting me to join them.

'No, sorry, I can't. That girl you can see at the bar, I'm about to give her some work.'

'Well, that was why we were popping in to see you, about some work that needs to be done on Peter's roof.'

'I didn't know he had a roof. I thought you lived in a ground-floor flat, Peter.'

'That's right, I do. It's the roof of my garden shed. Well, it's a bothy really, and, would you believe it, it's a listed building.'

'There must be lots of roofers in Bath. Why do you need me?'

'The building regulations stipulate I have to replace like for like. So, I was wondering if you could make me some Cotswold tiles.'

'Oh, I see.'

'I've had a quote for nearly two thousand pounds and I can't afford it. I'm nearly a pensioner.'

'Please, darling, do it for your mother. It's just a shed where Peter keeps his lawn mower.'

'Well, measure up the roof and bring me some of the tiles, and we'll see what we can do.'

'Darling, there's not a bad bone in your body.'

In the half hour I spent with Susie, I told her she had a natural bent for gay art. I didn't see the funny side of that appropriate choice of words until I heard what I'd just said. I commissioned her to sculpt a semi-naked young man wearing a baseball hat, jeans and a pair of calf-high boots.

'Make him look like a singer in that pop group Village People, leaning back against a lamppost, with his arms behind his back. We'll put it on a marble base and convert it into our first piece of decorative lighting.'

'Shall I do some drawings first?'

'Yes, please.'

'I can't tell you how excited I am,' said Susie. 'I'll have some sketches for you tomorrow.'

'Make it the day after. I'm away tomorrow.'

When we arrived at Delphine's and parked the van outside her front door, I sounded the horn several times.

'I'm not getting out if those dogs are going to attack us.'

Ade was in the back amongst all the equipment, moaning that it had been the most uncomfortable journey. 'If my mother could see me now.'

'Well, she can't.'

'I've got cramp in my arse.'

'Delphine,' I shouted, 'we're not getting out until you've rounded up your dogs.'

They'd encircled the van, scratching at the doors. One of the maids came running out, gesticulating wildly, trying to get them back into the house.

'I told you the price is going up if we have to go through this every day.'

'The weather forecast is good for the next week,' Delphine said, closing the door on the Dobermans. 'Who is this young man?' She was pointing at Ade.

'He's our assistant. The work will take twice as long without him.'

'Is he sworn to secrecy?'

'Of course. He won't say a word to anyone.'

'Does he know I have a shotgun?'

'It quite slipped my mind.'

'I'll come with you,' she said.

'No, Delphine. We work alone or not at all.'

'Well, then, I'll be watching you through my binoculars.'

It took nearly two hours, and who knows how many crossings in the rowing boat, to get everything on to the island. Ade was working away from the workshop for the first time and soon showed a maturity beyond his years. Being Mike's enthusiastic assistant seemed to fill him with a sense of importance.

'Don't you think I'm part of the team now, after giving my demonstration at the Open Day?' he said. 'When can Mike start teaching me how to make moulds?'

'Soon. You've nearly served your apprenticeship now.'

Delphine appeared from time to time, shouting across to us, wanting to know what progress we were making.

'Everything's fine, Delphine. You don't have to keep asking me every hour of the day.'

'My life depends on this. You have no idea what's at stake.'

We had brought thermos flasks and packed lunches, and took a break lying on the grass in the late September sunshine. An hour later, after we'd been back at work for a while, we opened the tarpaulin. We had to; wearing a face mask in such an enclosed space, Mike had built up a sweat and needed fresh air. In the distance I could see Delphine on the veranda watching us through her binoculars.

'It makes me nervous,' I said to Mike.

'What does?'

'Her watching us all the time.'

'It does make you wonder what she'd do if anything went wrong.'

'You brought your camera, didn't you?' I asked Mike. 'Take photos of the sculpture from all angles before you paint the skin mould on.'

'Whatever you say, boss.'

It was painstakingly slow work, applying silicone rubber to the surface of such a large piece of bronze. Catalyst was mixed into the silicone using an electric drill with a metal propeller fixed to it, and the measurement needed to be precise. Then Mike began the laborious task of covering every square inch with a paintbrush; he estimated it would take at least two days. Each time he emptied a bucket of silicone he stopped for a roll-up and changed the cassette on his portable tape player, usually country and western music.

'Can I bring my Sex Pistols tape tomorrow?' Ade asked me.

'I don't think Delphine would appreciate punk rock blasting out over her genteel gardens.'

Ade cut two-inch squares of fibreglass for Mike to lay upon the silicone, gradually building up layers of gelcoat to form a rigid jacket that would hold the mould in place. I left them to it and went to look for Delphine to reassure her everything was going according to plan.

I wandered through her geometric garden, between box hedges and neatly trimmed pathways, and came upon a pagoda entwined with hundreds of passion flowers. Suddenly a peacock emerged from the centre and opened its fan of tail feathers. This was what Delphine surrounded herself with: exaggerated forms of beauty. Ahead I could see a waterfall splashing over perfectly placed rocks, the stream then flowing along a canal through reeds in which, half hidden, was a bronze heron. All around me was contrived perfection.

Everything was man-made, lacking the vital ingredient of any naturalness.

I eventually saw Delphine in the conservatory, her Dobermans lying at her feet as she sat in a wicker chair talking on the telephone. I didn't go any closer, not wishing to be attacked by the dogs, but as I turned to make my way back to the island I couldn't help but overhear what she was saying. She was obviously talking about what we were doing, and that we'd be gone in two weeks.

'I don't care how you do it, but it has to be gone by the twenty-eighth.'

She sounded angry.

'I'll get the plinth delivered here. There's plenty of space to land a helicopter on the lawn,' she went on, her temper rising.

So, on the twenty-eighth our replica would replace the original and no one would be the wiser, since it could only be viewed from a distance. It reminded me of what Derek Tindall once said: 'Give me something that looks good from twenty yards,' referring to lots that were held up before being auctioned. I hadn't understood the implication at the time; that was down to my naivety, which I had gradually lost along the way.

At five o'clock, as we made our way to the van, Delphine appeared with the Dobermans, this time on leads. I had been hoping we could leave without seeing her, but she demanded to hear how the day had gone, and whether we were going to be able to keep to the crucial deadline.

I gave a casual response, not wishing to raise the levels of intensity at the end of a hard working day, but unfortunately it obviously unnerved her that I could be so relaxed about the job.

'You have absolutely no idea,' she said, shaking her head from side to side.

'Why should I be as tense as you, Delphine? I've no wish to

have a heart attack at my age.'

'You would be if you knew the people involved.'

'Well, I don't, and the job's going okay, and we'll see you in the morning.'

When I got home that night, Ros told me Rob had rung with several messages that I needed to sort out urgently. Rob always denied he was my deputy managing director, because he said there was no management structure at Puckmill Studios, which he likened to a banana republic run by a dictator. He was a friend of twenty years, so he had certain perks; one was that he could get away with ridiculing me. But he never let me down and I could always rely on him to look after things if I wasn't there. I read his messages. The first was that fifty skulls which should have been sent to Beatrice at Bones and Things had actually gone to Miranda Sopworth, who ran a gift shop near Great Yarmouth. I had never met her and had only ever spoken to her on the telephone, but knew she was an elderly lady who liked to keep me chatting, mostly about trinkets she had bought at church jumble sales. Rob had told Ros that she'd been totally freaked out, thought the devil was at play and saw the whole thing as an evil omen.

So I rang her before we sat down for supper. I was starving, having eaten my sandwich at midday, because Mike and Ade liked an early lunch. She was indeed in a state of shock, which I completely understood. Anyone opening a parcel of fifty skulls they weren't expecting would have been. But before I could explain, she told me she had asked the local vicar to come round and exorcise the shop, and went on to say that a police constable had taken a statement from her and a detective had been informed.

'They're not real, Miranda,' I managed to get out. 'They're replicas, made of polyester resin.'

'Well, why on earth have you sent them to me?'

'There's been a mistake; they were meant to go to someone else. Don't bother to get the vicar. I'll send a courier to pick them up tomorrow.'

'I'm not keeping them in the shop. I'm putting them in the outside lavatory.'

It must have been the first parcel Ade had sent out. It was probably going to be his last.

'You'd better deal with this as well,' said Ros. Walter Pepper had rung the workshop from his hospital bed, where he was recovering from a hip replacement operation.

'I'll go tomorrow night. He'll be asleep now.'

'That just leaves Susie Atherton. She wants to show you her etchings.'

'That's not a joke, Ros. She really does.'

'Dad, if you want a really good sculptor working at Puckmill, it could well be me,' said Lysta, who'd been listening to me explain to Ros my interest in Susie Atherton.

'Why do you say that?'

'Because my art teacher says I'm naturally artistic.'

'Really? You've never told me that before.'

'He says I'm no academic, but have a unique flair, and an original creative mind.'

'Well, in that case I'll buy you a lump of clay and you can prove it to me. But I should warn you I'm only interested in nudes.'

'I've only ever done a rabbit.'

'You can't expect your fourteen-year-old daughter to sculpt a nude for you,' said Ros, frowning at the whole idea.

'I don't see why not. I'll get her one of those body-building magazines. They're packed full of male models for her to choose from.'

'You're joking, Dad. I know you are,' said Lysta.

'I might be, but I'm always on the look-out for new talent.'

15

We were listening to Otis Redding, Mike and I happily singing along to 'A Change Is Gonna Come', when at last he completed the task of cutting off the gelcoat jacket. It was done. Silence had returned to our island after a morning of incessant grinding.

'It's behind you now, Mike,' I said, knowing how demanding this part of mould making was; just one slip of the drill and you'd be through to the silicone. Now for the easy bit, peeling off the rubber, and then we could relax a little.

'Do you want me to make you a roll-up?' Ade asked, as Mike began to peel back the silicone. When Mike ignored him, Ade raised his voice and said again, 'Do you want me to make you a roll-up?'

Still Mike said nothing. It seemed as if some alien had taken possession of him; either that or he was staring into the afterlife, but I knew disaster had struck.

'Mike,' I said, with a terrible sense of foreboding. But he didn't answer. It was as if he'd had a seizure. Eventually, he spoke.

'It's the end,' he said, putting his head in his hands. 'We're never going to get out of this.'

'Get out of what? Tell me!'

'The patination has been absorbed into the silicone. We're buggered, completely buggered.'

'You mean it's gone? There's no patina left on the surface?'

'No, we've removed it. We're ruined.'

Gradually the shock and immensity of the catastrophe I was facing sank in. The unique patination, meticulously applied by the world-famous sculptor, had been erased, and in a rush of disembodied sensations I found it impossible to fill my lungs, almost unable to stand. In just a few seconds, we'd come to the end of life as I had known it. And then Walter Pepper's words came back to me, that what at first seems insurmountable, the mother of invention will find an answer to. 'Persevere with clear, calm thinking and a solution will be found.' I clung to those words now, as I could hear Delphine calling my name.

'What's the latest?' she shouted over to us.

'Couldn't be better, Delphine. Everything's slippin' along easy like fried chicken,' a line I often used from a Captain Beefheart song.

'You told me you'd have the mould off today. Let me come and take a look.'

'Tomorrow. A slight delay, nothing to worry about.'

'Delay? I hate that word. Now let me come over.'

I knew Delphine wasn't going to back off. My only hope was to tell her some kind of chemical reaction had taken place, which was precisely what had happened.

'If you insist. I'll get Ade to row you over.'

'How are you going to get out of this one?' whispered Mike.

'We'll blind her with alchemy. Just give her the impression we are on top of the situation, even if she goes up like a firecracker.'

'She's going to see right through us. She'll know you're lying.'

'No, she won't. Now go and help her out of the boat.'

The most successful animals on the planet are those who adapt the fastest when they find themselves in a life-threatening situation. It's important not to show your adversary any hint of desperation.

'What's the reason for the delay?' she barked at me. 'Show me, or I'll blow your brains to kingdom come.'

'Delphine, please! I do wish you'd modify your language. Ade here is a regular churchgoer and a bell ringer at St Luke's.

We all gather there every Sunday.'

She said something vitriolic in French that I didn't understand.

'For the last time, show me.'

'Mike,' I said, 'perhaps you'd like to explain to Delphine the stage we've reached and how pleased we are with the progress we're making.'

'I thought you were.'

'No, Mike, I think it's best that you describe in simple English how the patination can become absorbed into the silicone for up to twenty-four hours and that tomorrow, when you've sprayed on the hydro-sulphide solution, it reappears on the surface of the sculpture. Quite miraculously, in fact.'

'That's exactly what I was going to say.'

'There you have it, Delphine. Nothing for you to worry about.'

'If you're lying to me and the patination isn't there tomorrow, then say goodbye to your loved ones.'

'Delphine, we've been doing this sort of work for years. We're experts in our field.' I didn't know what else to say. 'Look, I don't want to bore you with the details, but what has happened we call in the trade "symbiotic repatriation".'

'I'm going to look it up in the dictionary.'

'You won't find it in there. This is esoteric stuff handed down by word of mouth for thousands of years.'

'Well, I shall ask my friend, a well-known antiquarian book dealer.'

On the journey back to Frampton Mansell, I searched in the depths for an answer.

'Mike, take the photographs to be developed. Pay the extra for that speedy service they offer.'

'My aunt Doris works there. I can get them done tonight.'

'Good. I'm going to pay a visit to Walter's bedside. He might be able to help us.'

'Ade, do not say a single word about this to anyone.'

'Can I tell Mum I'm a bell ringer and go to church every Sunday?'

'No, you cannot.'

'Why did you tell Delphine, then?'

'To portray you as an innocent young man.'

'By the way,' said Mike. 'What's symbiotic . . .'

'Repatriation.'

'Yes.'

'I don't know, but it sounded good.'

When I walked into the Apsley ward of Cirencester hospital, there was Walter propped up in bed, his head stuck in a crossword. He looked thin, his cheeks hollow, but he greeted me with a warm smile, immediately putting down the newspaper and saying 'You're in trouble'.

'How do you know? Is it that obvious?'

'I've been through a lot with you. It's the furrowed brow that gives it away.'

'I'm facing a complete disaster and I can't see a way out of it.'

'Tell me about it.'

'I feel guilty coming with my woes when you're lying here in hospital.'

'We can talk about that later. I want to know what's going on.'

So I told him, not just about removing the patination from the sculpture, but how Delphine had given us a deadline of the twentieth and if we failed to meet it oblivion awaited me.

'Ah, oblivion,' said Walter. 'The only thing in the universe that doesn't exist.'

'It's not really a comfort to know that.'

'Yes, but you won't be aware of it, so I wouldn't give it a second thought.'

'Walter, do you mind if we could concentrate on my earthly problem? That's what's staring me in the face.'

'I'm sorry. Lying in bed all day one cannot help but think about the span of life, the passing of it, but I can tell you this: nothing is really that important.'

'Walter, come back. I'm losing you.'

'No, no, you're not losing me. I think it's the morphine.'

'Am I doomed? Is there any way out of this mess?'

'Yes, I think so. There is one man who could help you. Unfortunately, he isn't a straightforward soul, but you'll find him living on a narrowboat on the Stroud canal.'

I listened to every word as Walter told me the biography of a penniless artist (is there any other type, I asked myself), Blair Boulting, who had learnt how to apply patinas when he worked at the Armadillo Editions bronze foundry near Stroud.

'I thought he would be perfect to run the electroplating shop for us at Puckmill, but he has trouble getting out of bed in the morning.'

'Where can I find him?'

'That's easy. Down at Old Wharf Bridge, in a boat called *What's Up Doc*.'

'I'm going there now. I have to talk to him today.'

'He'll only do it for cash. That's just how he is. And he'll need a lift.'

'Walter, I must go and sort this out. Thank you. I'll be back in a couple of days.'

It was my one hope, but although it only took me five minutes to find his boat, Blair was nowhere to be seen. It was six o'clock in the evening, the sun sinking in a cloudless sky, a murmuration of starlings overhead. Nearby, an angler fishing in the canal said, 'If you're looking for Blair, you'll find him in the Fur and Feathers.'

Which I did, playing billiards with a middle-aged woman wearing a multi-coloured kaftan and sporting a black eye patch, while Blair himself, whose dark beard must have been over a foot long, was leaning over the table lining up his cue. I waited until he'd taken his shot and finished drinking the last dregs of his pint before I went over and introduced myself as a friend of Walter's. I told him, trying not to sound desperate, that I had a day's work for him tomorrow if he fancied it, and Walter had recommended him. I explained the whole thing; that we had photographs of the original patina and there was five hundred pounds in it for him, but we had to leave at seven in the morning. There were two problems: he didn't have a vehicle, and how were we going to get the equipment he needed on site? I rang Mike from the pub and asked him to come over in the van, a half-hour journey for him.

'I'm just about to get into a hot Radox bath.'

'It's our only chance,' I said. 'I've found someone. We need to get everything into the van this evening.'

Then I rang Ros and told her we were going to have an unexpected guest staying the night.

'He can sleep downstairs on the sofa bed,' she said. 'You sound worried. What's happened?'

Briefly I told her we'd hit a snag, and the guy coming for the night was the only person who could help us. It was partly true. It was much more than a snag, but I always watered down what I told Ros when we were facing a crisis.

'Someone will have to sit in the back and stop the oxyacetylene tank from rolling around,' said Blair as we loaded up the van.

'Are you sure we've got everything?' I asked him.

'Why are you so anxious?'

'I'm not. It's just we'll be working out in the country, miles from anywhere.'

It was nearly nine when we got home. Sam's first words as I walked in with Blair were 'Your dinner's in the dog'. Having recently picked up this saying, he used it as often as possible.

'We haven't got a dog,' I told Blair. 'This is my son, Sam, the joker in the house.'

'How long is your beard?' Belah asked him.

'I don't know. I've never measured it.'

With the whole family sitting around the kitchen table, it was impossible for Blair not to face the inquisition of my children, who were intrigued by this stranger among us. He looked as if he slept in his clothes, or could have been living rough. I knew what was coming, and decided that before he faced any further interrogation it would be best to pre-empt an evening of embarrassment by telling everyone why Blair was staying the night, and that he led an alternative life living on a narrowboat. I thought I'd said enough and they'd go and occupy themselves in the sitting room, but no: Lysta wanted to know if there was a bath on the narrowboat and did he have a television. Before he had a chance to answer, Seth was more interested in whether he cooked his own food.

Then Ros said, 'You're quite welcome to have a bath here.'

'Can you travel wherever you want?' asked Sam. 'We're learning at school about the old waterways of England.'

'Yes, I can up-anchor any time and go wherever I like.'

'Dad, let's go for a holiday on a narrowboat on the Norfolk Broads.'

And so we talked on for an hour; I couldn't remember the last time we'd all spent an evening together in someone else's company. It was only broken up when Ros had to tell me about telephone calls, including the latest from Rob, who always rang before leaving the workshop to let me know anything I had to deal with.

When I got into bed with Ros and set the alarm for six o'clock, half an hour earlier than usual, she had some worrying news for me.

'I couldn't tell you downstairs, but Kase's wife Eartha telephoned to say he's been arrested in Calcutta by the Indian customs.'

'For what?'

'She didn't say, but she's going to ring when she knows more.'

I couldn't sleep, and never expected to, my mind playing out every possible scenario on the island. I looked at Ros, sleeping soundly, her breathing relaxed, glad she wasn't sharing my anxiety.

All too soon Mike was knocking on the front door, having picked up Ade, and I had only just managed to wake Blair, who'd slept the night on the sofa bed fully clothed.

'I'm a heavy sleeper, always have been. I should have warned you.'

'We're running late,' I said. 'We don't have time for breakfast; we'll have to get something on the way. Mike, you've got the photographs, haven't you?'

'Oh God, I completely forgot them.'

'What!'

'Only joking.'

On the journey to Delphine's, while Ade and I rolled around in the back holding on to the oxyacetylene tank, I told Blair who we were working for. An unpredictable French woman who spoke an exaggerated language was how I described her.

'She likes to frighten us with playful threats,' I said. 'An unusual lady with a strange sense of humour, but there's really nothing for you to worry about.'

'Except her shotgun,' said Ade.

'Her imaginary shotgun,' I added light-heartedly. The last thing we needed was Blair working nervously with shaking hands.

We were over an hour late when we arrived at Delphine's, because Blair said he couldn't work without having eaten a solid breakfast. By a solid breakfast he meant the full English, followed by three slices of toast. Of course, it was impossible for us to just sit and watch him scoffing the lot, so we all had one. It was hardly surprising, then, that Delphine was waiting for us, this time without her Dobermans. She'd finally acknowledged my feelings about the creatures; I could hear them barking and scratching at the front door.

'So sorry, Delphine, but if you knew the morning we've had . . . a jack-knifed tractor and trailer blocking the road.'

'You're here now. Just don't waste any more of my time.'

'Let me introduce you to Blair. He'll be working with us for the day.'

'Where did you find him? He looks like a prophet from the Old Testament.'

'Don't let appearances deceive you, Delphine. This man is a forerunner in his field.'

'It is indeed an honour to meet you,' said Blair, speaking as if he was addressing someone from the Palace of Versailles.

'Please,' I said, as Ade and I carried the oxyacetylene tank from the back of the van, 'enough of these niceties. We have work to do.'

'Why do you need that? It looks like a torpedo,' said Delphine, as a sudden gust of wind covered us all in a cloud of dust.

'We have to heat the surface of the sculpture, just to apply one or two chemicals. All under control, ma'am.'

'I'll be watching you. And remember: if you're not out of here by the twenty-eighth, you know what awaits you.'

What had begun as a single gust blew up into a gale as the morning progressed, lifting the tarpaulin, which we had to fasten down. Then the rain came; not a light rain, but a steady lashing from darkening clouds that I sensed were going to be with us all day. Ideally, we wouldn't have worked in these conditions, but we had to. There was no alternative.

'What do you think, Blair? You decide.'

'I need the money, so let's get on with it.'

'That's not the point. The work needs to be faultless, otherwise she'll go berserk.'

The next five minutes will be etched into my soul for the rest of my life and, who knows, maybe beyond.

'Get a cigarette lighter, and let's get a flame burning.'

It took just a half-turn of the torch to release the gas, no more than a flick of the thumb on the lighter, and then one fateful gust of wind that blew Blair's beard into the flame. In a blind panic, when an automatic reaction kicks in, the body disengaged from the brain, I pushed Blair into the moat. He went completely underwater and lay like a corpse with his hair floating on the surface, Pre-Raphaelite amongst the water grasses. Mike rushed over and together we heaved him out, dragging him on his back. Minus his beard, his face suddenly strangely pale, he looked nothing like the man who had stood here two minutes ago. Now he could have been at least twenty years younger.

'Are you all right, Blair? Shall I go and ring for a doctor?'

'No, I'm fine. Bit sore on the chin,' he said. 'What on earth happened?'

'A calamity. You're lucky it was only your beard that went up in flames.'

'I'll miss it. It's taken me years to grow it.'

'Thank goodness it didn't reach your hair. That would have given you third-degree burns.'

'Come on, let's get on with it,' he said. 'I'm bloody soaked.

I'm going to have to strip off down to my Y-fronts.'

'Let's hope Delphine's not watching through her binoculars.'

Blair meant what he said, and began taking off his clothes, right down to his Union Jack underpants.

'You can't work dressed like that. Delphine's got a handyman; he'll have some overalls you can borrow,' I told him.

'I'm feeling a bit dizzy. I'm going to have to sit down for a while.'

'Take your time, Blair. Here, put my raincoat on. You need to keep warm.'

'He might be in shock,' said Mike. 'I was watching a programme the other night about people suffering a trauma.'

'What do you mean exactly?'

'We need to ask him three simple questions. If he answers them correctly, he's probably all right.'

'What's your name?'

'Oh, for God's sake . . . Blair, of course.'

'No, something trickier than that,' said Mike.

'Well, you take over.'

'I know what we could ask him,' said Ade, wanting to get in on the act.

'This is a farce,' said Blair. 'I'm completely all right.'

'What day of the week is it?'

'Monday . . . no . . . Tuesday?'

'Who on earth is that man?' shouted Delphine, fighting a losing battle with her umbrella, standing on the bank opposite us. 'And why is he practically naked?'

'Absolutely nothing to worry about. He got soaked, as anyone would, trying to work in a force eight gale.'

'*Merde.*'

'Stay calm. Just leave us to sort everything out.'

'Yes,' said Blair, 'I need to work without any further interruptions.'

'You're ruining me. You're a bunch of frauds.'

'Delphine, things will only get worse if you don't leave us alone.'

'I'm coming back in an hour with a loaded shotgun. It's your last chance.'

And with that blood-curdling remark she turned away, walking into the wind, which had become so strong that her umbrella flew away, lodging itself like a flapping bird in the roof of the pagoda.

'You see what I mean, Blair? It's all down to you now.'

If he failed us we'd be ruined, and where would it leave Delphine and her sculpture worth hundreds of thousands of pounds?

'Bet you can't spell Mississippi,' Mike said to Blair.

'Why on earth are you asking him that?'

'To see if he's trauma free.'

'That's easy. M-i-s-s-i-s-s-i-p-p-i,' said Blair.

'Enough!' It was the first time I'd shouted, the pressure getting to me. 'Here, drink this black coffee, and let's get out of this pit we've dug for ourselves.'

'I feel fine,' said Blair, running his hand over his bare cheeks, and then at last relighting the torch. Working from Mike's photos he slowly, and with a steady hand, began applying the patina to the bronze surface.

After lunch the wind dropped, and as the clouds lightened a swathe of sunlight shone down upon *Psyche*. We hung our wet clothes from the tarpaulin, and as they dried etheric mists rose around us as if they had been discarded by ghosts. We sat patiently as Blair slowly brought the surface back to life, endlessly dipping his paint brushes into various solutions. He was indeed a skilled craftsman, working with intense concentration, not uttering a word, inch by inch without a break until at last he finished as the light faded. Such was the sense of relief, we hugged each other and then sat silently staring with blank expressions into the distance. For a while I was emotionally drained.

We tidied up everything and carried the oxyacetylene tank to the rowing boat.

'It's my turn to row,' said Ade.

'Make sure you secure the oars in the rowlocks.'

'Mind your language.'

As I waited for Delphine in the kitchen, her dogs now showing an interest in me and smelling my feet, I noticed a photograph of Delphine and her husband, a tall well-dressed man. He had an aristocratic Englishness about him; they looked happy, standing in front of the Eiffel Tower. I tried to imagine what had attracted him to Delphine, because in the time I had known her she had not shown me a single attractive trait. I didn't hear her come up behind me. She was wearing a white dressing gown, her skin glistening and bare of make-up, as if she'd just had a facial.

'Charles,' she said, picking up the photograph. 'My beloved Charles, an Englishman, with all the attributes needed to build the British Empire.'

'He's wearing an expensive suit,' I said.

'He has all his suits made in Savile Row.'

'We're leaving now. Despite your worst fears, we have finished making the mould and will begin to lay up the fibreglass in the morning.'

'So then, the day after tomorrow I will organise for the original to be removed.'

'I don't understand how that's possible. I'd have thought it was too heavy to lift and could well be damaged.'

'That is none of your business.'

'I won't be coming back for a couple of days,' I told her. 'But Mike and Ade are more than capable of working on their own.'

'You've shattered my nerves. After this is all over, I don't ever want to see you again.'

'You're so appreciative.'

'I can't tell you the whole story, but if only you knew what I've been going through.'

'Well, I never will.'

'And don't forget you have one more week. Then I'm having my gala evening, when your replica will be floodlit and seen by over two hundred guests.' She then rang a little brass bell and one of several maids we had seen over the past few days trotted into the kitchen.

'Please show the gentleman out.'

Mike dropped Blair and me at Chester Street and drove Ade back to Frampton Mansell. Blair looked a bedraggled sight in the light of the lamppost, the uneven remains of his sideburns, his blotched skin; what a day he'd had. I didn't invite him in, simply because of the children's reaction, and the endless questions they would have asked him.

'Wait here a moment, Blair. I'll go and get the money I owe you.'

When I dropped him back at the Old Wharf Bridge, he asked me to join him for a pint in the Fur and Feathers.

'Do you mind if I don't? It's been a long day. I'm surprised you don't want to just fall into bed.'

'You know I'm available, if you need any work doing.'

'Thanks. I think this might have been a one-off, but I know how to get in touch with you.'

We shook hands. An unusual man. I didn't think he had a girlfriend. He lived an uncomfortable life and it was hard to imagine anyone wanting to share it with him.

16

On Monday morning at the rag market all the familiar faces crowded round, wanting to know what had happened to me last week.

'Top secret,' I said. 'All very hush-hush, but I can tell you this much: the job was worth thousands.'

'How come you're driving a clapped-out old van then?' said Sifta.

'I've never been a man to flaunt it. And what would the taxman think if I suddenly went up in the world?'

'I hope you've brought some stick heads. I'm out of stock,' said Frank.

'Why didn't you ring me?' Greasy Gadd asked.

'Because you've never given me your phone number.'

'Do you want to make some Cigar Store Indians for Jane Plum, of Plum's Emporium?' Sifta wanted to know. 'She was here last week, came down from Preston and waited over an hour for you.'

'I don't suppose you took her details.'

'Yes, but they'll cost you a fiver.'

'That reminds me, Sifta. Where's the five hundred pounds you still owe me from "Betjeman's Bygone Britain"?'

'It's coming. You'll have it before you leave today.'

'By the way, that fancy lady with the posh dog was looking for you.'

'Isobel.' I wondered what she wanted.

'Baz and Chaucer from the pewter factory want to see you as well.'

'Sifta, how do you know all this?'

'Because I took over your stall last week, flogged some of my own stuff.'

'Did you pay the rent?'

'We'll split it.'

Later that morning, after the initial flurry of activity had died down and the trade buyers had finished walking the market, Aileen wandered over with her thermos of tea. I enjoyed our quiet little chats when she passed on her considerable knowledge about the markets she visited.

'Do you know what a franchise is?' she asked, as if she was about to reveal some dark secret.

'No. I've never heard the word before.'

'I'm not sure if you were joking, but do you remember several months ago you said that soon you'd be a millionaire?'

'Of course, and I wasn't joking.'

'So how are you doing?'

'That's a difficult question to answer.'

'I take it that means not very well.'

I didn't want to tell her, because the reality of its happening seemed to be moving further and further away. It felt now to have been such a hollow thing to say. I'd said it in the false belief it would excite Ros and the children, and they'd feel there was a purpose to our staying in Cirencester, when in fact I'd deceived us all. I knew it would come up again one day, but maybe I'd get away with it for a while longer, now the children were so wrapped up in their own lives.

'Sorry, Aileen, what's the point you're making?'

'You could offer people packages, giving them exclusive rights to sell your products in certain areas.'

'There's a lot going on under that bobble hat of yours.'

'Do you think you'll really make your fortune selling replicas in street markets?'

'Many big businesses began with just a market stall, Tesco for instance. But maybe it won't be Puckmill Studios.'

'You need to develop original products that you can copyright and protect.'

The very reason I'd commissioned Susie Atherton to sculpt a range of gay statues that we could convert into table lamps. And suddenly I realised I'd completely forgotten to ring her.

'Watch out,' said Aileen. 'The world's changing fast and they'll dump you without a second thought.'

'What are you talking about? I don't understand.'

'It's just starting to happen. It's only a trickle, but within the year it'll be a deluge and lots of dealers will be swept away.'

'God, you make it sound so dramatic! But I wish you'd spell it out.'

'Cheap imports made in the Far East, and they're good.'

'They couldn't copy what I do. It's not that easy to electroplate on to resin and match an antique finish.'

'You'd be surprised what the Chinese can do. I'm already being offered jewellery at a fraction of the price I pay local dealers.'

'No, I'm sorry, Aileen, I don't believe it.'

'Well, what about all your advertising figures that you say you sell mostly to wholesalers?'

'What about them?'

'How can you stop them getting made in China? For a start, they're not your products; you don't own the copyright. You're vulnerable.'

'You're right, but surely there is such a thing as loyalty? That must count for something.'

'Loyalty,' said Aileen, letting an ironic laugh tell me what she felt about that. 'I'm just trying to make you aware of what's coming. And whether it's netsukes, scrimshaw or bronze statues, you won't be able to protect yourself.'

Aileen was painting an exaggerated picture based on what she could see happening in her world of costume jewellery. Everything we made at Puckmill required a lot of skill, and no matter how clever the Chinese were they weren't going to be a threat to us.

What I did do, as soon as Aileen had finished giving me her stark warning about the future, was go and telephone Susie Atherton. I'd been so involved in the whole Delphine saga that I'd let her down. She didn't pick up the phone; my apologies would have to wait until the evening.

Throughout the morning I thought about what Aileen had told me. The economic experts on the six o'clock news were certainly hinting at the possibility of an approaching recession. But what did I know about international finance, and anyway it all happened in a world far removed from mine. How could it affect Puckmill Studios, a little business down in a valley below a sleepy English village, where sheep grazed the fields?

One of my regular customers came over, Peter Riley, who had an antique shop and guest house in Broadway, Worcestershire. He'd always struck me as an astute man who liked to express his opinion about what was going on politically. I tended to give credence to what emanated from a man wearing a deerstalker. Don't ask me why, but I associated that particular headgear with a certain level of intelligence, and imagined I might well have been talking to a university professor. It was a pleasure doing business with him; he never haggled, and always accepted the price I was asking. I mentioned it casually as I wrapped up a dozen scrimshaw and some bronze golfing figures, which he sold in his guesthouse to weekend visitors.

'So, Peter, do you think there's a recession on the way?'

'Well,' he replied, 'growth has slowed, unemployment is up, and they're all worried about inflation. So yes, we could be in for a rough patch.'

'Will it affect your business?'

'Of course, if the Americans stop coming. Broadway is on the tourist route for thousands of overseas visitors.'

'Do you think it could spill over into my business?'

'Probably. There's always a knock-on effect. Money's like

blood: it needs to circulate around the whole body. If not, you'll fall ill before too long.'

I'd never thought about such things before; I'd had no reason. Orders were coming in all the time, and there was no let-up at the workshop. And it went even further to the back of my mind when I saw Isobel, dressed as if she was on her way to a garden party at Buckingham Palace.

'Where's Sophia today?' I asked.

'She's having a shampoo and getting her nails clipped.'

'Of course. Are you entering her in Crufts this year?'

'Don't be sarcastic; it's beneath you. I need to talk to you seriously.'

'Is it about Delphine?'

'Yes, actually it is.'

'Isobel, before you begin, you need to know that Delphine is the most difficult woman I've ever come across. She's a nightmare, and I wish I'd never taken on the job.'

'Have you ever asked yourself why? Do you understand the position she's in?'

'She hasn't told me anything and has offered nothing but threats on my life.'

'Well, let me tell you a little about Delphine, and then maybe you'll have some sympathy for her.'

So Isobel told me the whole remarkable story, why no one should know about the work we were doing for her and how, if it were to get out, her reputation would be in ruins. 'A reputation that has taken her years to build,' she added.

Isobel's dear friend was considered by the art world to be a connoisseur of impeccable taste, much admired by exclusive gallery owners. Through her connections she brought the finest paintings to be offered for sale in the auction houses of London.

'I still don't understand why we're making a replica of the sculpture for her.'

'Because she and her husband have serious financial difficulties.'

'So she's selling the original, and replacing it with a fibreglass replica?'

'I've told you too much. She's in despair. You need to leave without a trace, as if you'd never been there, in time for her gala evening. You can imagine how I feel, having recommended you. Every day she's rung me, calling you incompetent fools.'

'I'm going tomorrow. I'll try to reassure her. But she hasn't helped the situation at all with her crazy temper.'

'Please don't mention that we've spoken. I've broken her trust, and if she were to find out it would be the end of our friendship.' With that she moved on, passing the rest of the stalls without giving them a second look.

Sifta slipped me an envelope, the five hundred pounds he owed me for 'Betjeman's Bygone Britain'. No sooner was it in my pocket than he was telling me about his latest moneyspinner.

'What is it this time, Sifta? And how much is it going to cost me?'

'A hundred Russian bearskin hats. I can get them for a fiver each.'

'What about the money you made on "Betjeman's Bygone Britain"?'

'It all went on four new tyres for the van.'

'Who's going to buy a hundred bearskin hats?'

'A hundred bald-headed men, and with winter coming I'll easily get fifteen pounds each for them.'

'In all the time I've known you this is your wildest idea.'

'You said I wouldn't sell those Barnardo's collection boxes.'

'That's true. So how much do you want?'

'Three hundred would see me all right.'

'You know, Sifta, you're the world's biggest chancer, and

really I'm no more than your banker.'

'When have I ever failed to pay you back every penny?'

'I just wish you'd get ahead of the game instead of sleeping in the back of a van and always searching for your next meal.'

'Don't worry about me. I'm a born survivor.'

As I was packing up, Frank Webb came by, carrying his golf bag full of walking sticks. I could always tell when there was something on his mind: he would blow his nose and slap his hat against his thigh.

'What is it, Frank? I can hear your brain working; all those cogs turning over.'

'It's a long shot, but it might interest you.'

'I won't know unless you tell me.'

'I want something out of it, mind you. Fattorinis, have you heard of them?'

'No. They sound like an Italian ice-cream maker.'

'Amongst other things, they make ceremonial swords.'

'Why would that be of interest to me?'

'Do you know what shagreen is?'

'It's shark skin.'

'Fattorinis are wanting to replace it on the cutlasses they make. You might be able to help them.'

'Have you got a contact name?'

'Yes. Baz and Chaucer, those two pewter boys from Digbeth.'

'I was just about to go round to see them now.'

'Well, if anything comes of it, don't forget me.'

I wasn't sure what Frank was playing at, because when I sat down with Baz and Chaucer the first thing they said was they'd been approached by Fattorinis to do some work for them, including replacing the shagreen hilts on their cutlasses. Did Frank really think he deserved to get a cut from my contacts who'd come looking for me in the rag market in the first place?

They gave me a sample of the hilt, about five inches long, which had to fit perfectly into the silver handle. Mike always hated such precise work, because there was the problem of shrinkage with polyester resin that we could only estimate; we hardly ever managed to get a tight fit.

After delivering the latest batch of inserts for their whisky flasks, I thought our business was done for the day. But I happened to mention that while we'd been sitting in their office I had seen someone chucking boxes over their wall from the crisp factory next door.

'Oh, that. It goes on from time to time,' said Chaucer.

'They're seconds. Imperfect crisps not fit for sale,' added Barry.

'What constitutes an imperfect crisp? I'm interested, that's all.'

'Broken bits. The staff here take them home. Crisp manufacturing is completely mechanised, and if the vibrations are too strong you get nothing but broken bits.'

'You learn something every day, don't you?' I said.

As I was about to open the door, I noticed a pile of boxes with *Marco Spinetti, Awaiting Collection* written on them in black felt tip.

'That's the guy I put you in touch with. Car mascots.'

'That's him. A fantastic contact. Now we're making trophies for him.'

'I'm glad it turned out well for you. I was happy to offload the work.'

Back at the market, I finished packing up the van and, as usual, sat my Bavarian bear walking-stick stand on the front seat, securing it with the seat belt. It was a beautiful wooden carving, except it wasn't wood: we'd made it in resin in the tumble caster. It was about four feet high, standing on its hind legs with its paws curved out in front. I used it to display

Frank's walking sticks on the stall each week. This time, I didn't bother to remove the flat cap Aileen had put on him, which I thought added to his character.

After a few miles down the M5, I noticed the driver of the car on my inside gesticulating to me to get into the slow lane. I smiled, but ignored him, until the chap sitting in the back seat held up a sign saying, *If you want to sell him, pull into the services.* Which I did.

They wanted my Bavarian stick stand for their hairdressers in Tewksbury. So I sold it to them in the car park, and why not? We made them every week.

The first thing I did when I got home was ring Susie Atherton. Before she could say a word, I apologised profusely for my rudeness and told her I could offer many excuses, but none of them was worth listening to.

'Why don't we get together tonight? Where do you live?'

'In Stroud. We could meet in the Fur and Feathers.'

'I know that pub. I was in there recently. How about eight o'clock?'

'I've done a few drawings, showing some ideas for lesbian sculptures. Shall I bring those too?'

'Yes, bring everything you've got.'

The house was unusually quiet, with only Ros in the kitchen preparing supper. She told me that Sam had broken up with Tess, who had rung twice in the last hour in floods of tears.

'He won't talk to her and they've been going out for nearly a year now. You need to say something to him.'

'Like what? I've only met her a few times.'

'He needs to end it properly; she doesn't know where she stands.'

'Where is he?'

'Well, if you remember, he works in the Friar Tuck on a

227

Monday evening, serving fish and chips.'

'And where are all our other children? I can sense we're alone.'

'Seth is out at Kemble practising his sponsored parachute jump. Belah is round at the Millers', timing how long it takes Debbie's tortoise to cross the sitting-room floor, and Lysta's got netball practice.'

'And how's my lovely wife? What are you up to?' I said, putting my arms round her.

'Me? Watching our children growing up, trying to keep the house running smoothly and seeing you from a distance, completely absorbed in your work.'

'Not a lot then . . . I'm only joking.'

'And I'm still your bookkeeper, sending all the invoices to Thelma every month so she can complete the VAT return.'

'Ros, I've got a confession. It's been playing on my mind.'

'You're having an affair and that's why the romance has gone out of our lives.'

'No, of course not. Nothing like that.'

'Well, tell me. Because we hardly ever talk nowadays, except about work or the children.'

'I'm nowhere close to becoming a millionaire.'

'Is that all?'

'It's a pretty big thing to admit. You make it sound as if it's not important.'

'I don't know whether to laugh or cry, I really don't.'

'Do neither, but why are you saying that? I promised you we'd make some money and begin our travels again and explore the world. I feel I've let you down.'

'Do you remember when we bought Dyffryn, the picture you painted to me then? The idyllic life we were going to lead, growing all our own vegetables, living off the land? The mountain air, the children running around the farm? Baking our own bread, watching those glorious sunsets over the Irish Sea?'

'How could I ever forget?' And I meant it.

'But that was not the reality. There were only moments when you had the time to lean over a gate and breathe in that wonderful landscape. Every day you were full of financial anxiety.'

'When I think back on those times, the image that's always stayed with me is not of the hardship we endured, but of walking back to the house across the fields in the late evening. The smell of hay in the air, the faint outline of the Wicklow hills, the sun sinking into a calm sea. That's the old romantic in me still going strong. So you're happy to stay here, without making any plans?'

'The children come first. We need to see them through school with no more upheavals, and then we can think about the future.'

'You know, Ros, we could always take a weekend away together. My mother would be happy to come and look after the children.'

'We should. Everything between us seems to have drifted into a tedious routine. We need to make some time for each other.'

And on that note, just as we were speaking optimistically, I told her that I had to go to Stroud to meet Susie Atherton.

'She seems to be coming into your life more and more.'

'I need her. Not like that – as a sculptor to replace Johnny Allard.'

Ros stared into the distance with a faraway look and sighed.

'I promise you, it is nothing but work.'

'Sometimes I wish I'd married a man who worked from nine to five, had weekends off and more time for his children.'

'No, you don't. Now come here and give me a thumping great kiss, before I ride out into the night to conquer the world.'

'Please talk to Sam about Tess. He needs to understand her feelings.'

I sat down with Susie in the Fur and Feathers, and of all her charcoal sketches I still preferred what she'd drawn of my original idea, the semi-naked young man leaning up against a lamppost. He didn't look overtly gay, but as Marcus Wesley had told me, we needed works of art that might appeal to the pink pound.

A couple of her other drawings, two young men wrestling in their swimming trunks and two gymnasts, one standing on the shoulders of the other, would have been difficult pieces to make. She wasn't the slightest bit embarrassed about showing me two lesbians lying naked on a rock kissing one another passionately.

'This is a whole new direction for us,' I said. 'I really haven't a clue if there's a market for them. I'm being led by someone who moves in those circles who's certain they'll sell. So I'm going to commission you to go ahead and carve the guy leaning on the lamppost. I can pay you a thousand pounds for it. Are you happy with that?'

'I'm delighted. This is my very first professional job. You've no idea what it means to me.'

'Would you like an up-front payment of five hundred to keep you going?'

'Could you? The rent is due this week.'

I'd made somebody happy, and as I drove back to Cirencester, instead of going home, my guilt got the better of me. I had to go and see Walter; I'd promised to visit him again in hospital and then I'd found out he'd been discharged and sent home. Walter had given so much for so little in return and never complained once. As I sat with him in his house in Dollar Street, the first thing I noticed was that he'd lost a lot of weight.

'Walter,' I said, 'what do you eat? You look so thin.'

'I've never been a great eater. Mostly soup and bread.'

'You're neglecting yourself. I know I sound like your mother, but you need three meals a day.'

He just laughed, saying he didn't have an appetite and the last thing he wanted was someone coming from Meals on Wheels, which had been suggested by the hospital.

'So you're planning to just fade away,' I said.

'No, certainly not; far from it. I'm going to book a cruise to Cape Town when the surgeon's signed me off and visit my sister in South Africa.'

'That's more like it. You need something to look forward to.'

'I really don't know why you worry so much about me. Now be on your way; I've got a crossword to do.'

It was ten o'clock when I walked into the kitchen at home. Sam was on the phone and as I sat down I heard him say, 'We'll meet at four and have a coffee.'

'I'm glad to hear that. After a year, you need to end it amicably.'

'Mum's told you, then.'

'Well, of course she has. You can't just dump Tess or refuse to talk to her. That leaves her up in the air, not knowing what's going on.'

'It's hard to tell her. She's become so possessive, I just want to get away from her.'

'Finish it tomorrow. She'll get over it; you're not the only boy in Cirencester.'

'That wasn't Tess I was talking to. It was her sister.'

'God, Sam, now you're getting yourself into a mess.'

I went to bed at midnight, after I'd psychologically beaten up my eldest son. He'd promised to back off Tess's sister, Kim, for at least a month. That's how long we both agreed it would take Tess's broken heart to mend. I didn't really know whether he'd keep to it and hoped Ros hadn't overheard our conversation. I was so tired, the last thing I said to Sam was 'We're a couple of fools. No one knows how long it takes to mend a broken heart.'

I didn't wake up when the alarm went off at 6.45. Ros began by shoving me gently in the back and then started trying to roll me out of bed. Belah walked into the bedroom and knelt down to say into my ear, 'Dad, please can I have a tortoise?'

Before I could answer, Ros raised her voice. 'You're meant to be going over to see your favourite woman today.'

And that was it. Delphine's face loomed up in front of me, and I was out of bed, half dressed by the time Mike pulled up outside, shouting to me from the pavement.

'You haven't got time for breakfast. Delphine's expecting us before nine.'

'I can't keep going at this pace,' I said to Ros. 'I'll never see fifty.'

'You haven't reached forty yet.'

'God, I don't even know my age any more.'

I leant out of the bedroom window and told Mike, 'I'm not leaving until I've made a thermos of coffee.'

I relieved Sam of two pieces of toast, drank Seth's orange juice, and Ros stuffed a KitKat in my pocket.

'Dad,' Belah cried out, 'can I get a tortoise? I'll take it for walks every day.'

'You mean to the sofa and back,' I said, and left the house.

As we drove out of Cirencester, I insisted we listen to the news. Mike and Ade weren't interested, both waiting to hear last night's football results. It was mostly about the Northern Ireland conflict, kidnappings by some South American drug gangs, and the Education Secretary's concern about falling standards in English secondary modern schools. Then Manchester United beating Everton brought a reaction of pure joy, and Mike and Ade mocked me as Spurs lost at home to West Ham.

'United! United!'

It made me think how sheltered they were, these two Gloucestershire boys, living in a beautiful part of England, most of it still unspoilt, just as it was a couple of hundred years ago. Ade, born and brought up in Frampton Mansell, his mother running the pub, and he now making his living in the village's only business. His world was fishing with his friends down at Baker's Mill on summer evenings after an early supper, or tea as it was called, or flirting with girls in the village. They were cocooned in a little pocket of old England and didn't give a second thought to all the worries and fears people had about the way the world was drifting.

What stuck in my mind from that eight o'clock news was that unemployment was rising, the pound was weakening and the economists were still warning of a recession.

17

Mike told me as we drove along the Burford road that the day before hadn't been without its incidents.

'Please don't give me any bad news, or tell me Delphine's going to greet us with a shotgun in her hand,' I said.

'Let me take you through it step by step.'

'And then I'll tell you my version,' said Ade, butting in from behind me.

'Obviously something went wrong, otherwise you wouldn't be talking like this.'

'All the fibreglassing should be finished today, and then we can start sanding down the whole thing,' Mike told me.

'Okay, so what was the problem?'

'The surface hasn't cured as quickly as I'd hoped. It was a bit tacky when we left last night.'

'And we know what causes that, don't we, Ade?' I said.

'I put in exactly the amount of catalyst that Mike calculated. It's not my fault.'

'Maybe you didn't mix it properly.' That was probably what had happened.

'If it hasn't hardened when we get there, I'm going to have to run a hairdryer over it for the morning,' said Mike.

'More time lost. We've got two days. I'm going to have to cancel going to Bath tomorrow.'

'There's something else you need to know.' I could tell by Mike's expression that there was far worse to come. 'Ade got bitten by one of the dogs.'

'Is that all?'

'One of the maids gave him first aid, and she went further than sticking a plaster on his ankle.'

'Her name's Darina,' said Ade. 'It means precious in English.'

'So, what's the problem?'

'The problem is Delphine overheard her ask me if I knew where she could get a job. She's been working there for two years and wants to improve her English and go to college,' said Ade, looking somewhat guilty.

'And what did you tell her?'

'I gave her the Puckmill Studios phone number and said you might have a job.'

'Thanks, Ade. That's all we need.'

'Delphine went into a rage and ripped up the piece of paper I wrote the number on.'

'I suppose you fancied her and couldn't help yourself.'

'She's beautiful compared to the girls in the village.'

Delphine was surprisingly calm, or appeared to be, standing in the courtyard with her gardener, when I pulled up next to her Range Rover. She had her sleeves rolled up and was wearing gardening gloves. The day was bright, with patches of blue sky between the changing shapes of white cloud. The last of the swallows perched in a line along a length of cable that stretched from the house to a converted barn, where two vintage sports cars were parked.

As I walked towards her, she approached me and grabbed my upper arm, the way a policeman does before leading away an arrested man for questioning. Which was precisely what it felt like. 'I need a few words alone with you in the house.'

'Carry on, Mike. I'll catch up with you in a few minutes.'

'I can't wait to see the back of you, I really can't,' she said, seemingly at her wits' end. 'You're like a dark shadow that has come into my life.'

'What is it now, Delphine?'

'I can't believe Isobel could have spoken so highly of you.'

'If you don't delay me we'll be finished in a day or two.'

'They're coming to remove the sculpture in forty-eight

hours, at seven in the morning. You cannot be here.'

'Delphine, you have to lower your anxiety levels. It would help if you put me in the picture. So many things don't add up.'

'What are you talking about?'

'Where's the marble plinth to mount our replica on, for a start?'

'It's coming as soon as the original's removed.'

'And how are you proposing to do that? The thing weighs a ton.'

'By helicopter, you fool.'

'Oh, of course, by helicopter,' I said. 'Stupid me. I should have realised.'

'I've noticed your sarcasm before. What the English call the lowest form of wit.'

'I'll charge you if we have to work an extra day,' I said, knowing she would explode.

'How dare you suggest such a thing? Have you any idea how much it costs to hire a helicopter?'

'I'm afraid I don't know what a helicopter does to the gallon.'

'All I get is your flippant remarks. God, everything you've put me through, and yesterday that dumb boy of yours trying to steal Darina from right under my nose.'

'He fancies her, that's all, and if you'd kept your dogs under control they'd never have met.'

'This has been the worst period in all my fifty-two years.'

I left her; she was impossible. She blamed me for everything. No one could behave as she did and have a friend in the world. And yet, as I made my way to the island, Isobel's words came back to me, and I suddenly felt a touch of sympathy for her. She was facing the loss of reputation and esteem within a circle of art connoisseurs she'd known for years. I didn't know why she'd fallen on hard times; maybe her husband's steel business was failing because of cheap Chinese imports. Having to sell her major asset, and the fear of being found out . . . well, the stress could be too much to bear. If only she had told me from the beginning what she was up to; but she couldn't. It would have been involving me in a terrible deceit. It flashed through my mind that maybe when the job was done she'd aim her shotgun at my head and blast me to kingdom come. It was a possibility. She was a woman who had everything to lose.

'It's okay,' said Mike. 'Panic over. The resin's cured overnight.'

'You see? I told you I'd added the right amount of catalyst,' said Ade.

Now we had to assemble and lock together the three segmented pieces of the sculpture and cover the whole thing with a layer of gelcoat mixed with a bronze filler powder. Then Mike, using a sanding disc to get rid of the seams, could create a uniformly smooth cast. Then all we'd have to do was apply the patination and spray on a matt lacquer to give the piece a bronze sheen.

Every hour throughout the day, Delphine screamed over to us, not wanting to know how we were doing, but how much longer it was going to take. We eventually finished at six o'clock, and in a flurry of autumn leaves falling into the moat I rowed her to the island to look at the *Psyche and Zephyrus* replica.

She walked around the piece in complete silence and then took a few steps back, gazing at it.

'And what about the patination?' she said.

'We'll do that tomorrow, and then the job's done,' I told her.

'Aren't you pleased?' Ade wanted to know, while Mike said nothing, sitting with a pair of goggles pushed back on his forehead, smoking a roll-up.

'Delphine doesn't give compliments, Ade. Anyway, we should be pleased with what we've achieved, considering this whole project has been an endurance test from start to finish.'

'What *you've* had to endure? *Mon dieu!*' And immediately her face reddened. 'You . . . you . . .'

As she searched for the words, I suddenly wondered how we were all going to get off the island. You could only sit three in the boat, and I couldn't let Delphine row back on her own. I wouldn't have put it past her to leave us stranded there. It was a puzzle I got tangled up in, and as she continued to rant I tried to work out the best way to solve it, which obviously was that I should row her back, and then come back and pick up Mike and Ade.

'Delphine, we have to go. It's a long journey to Cirencester.'

'I'll row myself back. I need to think about things,' she said.

'No, you need to come with me.'

'But I don't want to.'

'If you stay here, someone will have to come back and get you.' Even Mike, who was no logician, could see what I was trying to say.

'Please, let Ade row you back, Delphine. Then he can come back for Mike and me.'

'Why do you have to complicate everything?' she said.

'I'm not. I'm trying to do the exact opposite and simplify everything.'

'We will never see eye to eye,' she said, at last getting into the rowing boat.

'That's the first thing you've ever said that I can agree with.'

When I got home that night, Ros told me Rob had rung, as he usually did, to let me know what had happened during the day at the workshop. Before I returned his call, I said to Ros, 'Do you know the whole of my life is nothing but work?'

She stopped what she was doing and sat down beside me. A look of such warmth came over her face that I wondered if she'd been waiting a long time for me to recognise it for myself.

'What has made you suddenly say that today?' she asked.

'Delphine, I suppose. All that effort without any gratitude.'

'It can't be just her. There must be other reasons to say such a thing.'

'I've lost my sense of fun and I blame myself for it. Maybe I try too hard and, just like Dyffryn, it's all going to end in failure.'

'Would you like to know what I think?' said Ros.

'Of course. After all, you have to put up with it every day.'

'You need to bring something else into your life. You know what they say, don't you?'

'Please, not a hackneyed old cliché.'

'All work and no play makes Jack a dull boy.'

'Ros, how could you, of all people? You know I'm a founder member of the anti-cliché party of Great Britain.'

'The only member, I believe.'

'I'd become a poet, but there's no money in it.'

'Why don't you put a manager in to look after the workshop?' she suggested.

'Who could run a business like Puckmill?'

'There must be someone out there. What about Marcus Wesley? You've always said he's a smart talker, full of the flange, as Derek Tindall would say.'

'He's the only person I'd consider.'

'Talk to him,' said Ros. 'See what he says.'

'My problem is I suffer from a rare condition that medical science doesn't even know exists.'

'And what's that?'

'I'm addicted to excitement, a particular excitement one gets from discovering things for oneself. I don't know if that makes any sense, but that sums it up.'

I rang Rob, who began by saying, 'This isn't a joke.'

'Which means it is,' I said.

'I've just told you it isn't. Alton Towers want an eighteen-foot bar of chocolate made for their hotel.'

'All because the lady loves Milk Tray.'

'It's not a joke. It's to do with a Cadbury wing in a hotel they're refurbishing.'

'Could be interesting. What else has happened today?'

'Eartha, Kase's wife, rang. She didn't sound very happy.'

'I wonder what's happened to him. We haven't heard from him in months. I'll give her a ring.'

'She said she'd ring back. One more thing, which also isn't a joke. Do you want to buy half a racehorse?'

'Which half?'

'There you go again. I'm being serious. A friend has a share for sale.'

'Now that could be exciting, I need a distraction.' Well, we were making more than enough money. Ros had been hinting that I was becoming dull, with only one thing ever on my mind. Work.

'I'll put you in touch. He's an old friend of mine; we used to share a flat in Ladbroke Grove.'

'Rob, I'm only going to ask you this once, and never again.'

'The answer's no, I can tell you already.'

'If I paid you an extra five thousand a year, would you become my workshop manager?'

'I told you already, the answer's no.'

'But why not? You'll be a father soon and need more dosh.'

'Because *you're* Puckmill, the driving force behind everything, and one day you'll run out of energy and that will be the end of it. That's what happened at Dyffryn, if you remember.'

'Hang on, Rob. The pigs were wiped out by Chicago Vomiting and Wasting disease. There was no way back after that. We were finished.'

'You're probably my oldest friend; I know what you're like. I give Puckmill another two years, and then you'll burn yourself out.'

'Definitely not. I'm only thirty-five. I know a receding hairline might make me look forty, but we've only just begun.'

'Isn't that a line from a Carpenters' song?'

'No, but I have asked myself why do birds suddenly appear every time you are near?'

'I'm going now. Danny Draysey, DD as we call him, will ring you.'

'Who's he?'

'The guy with the racehorse.'

Rob might have thought he knew me, but it didn't mean he held the answers. What he'd said had been based on things from the past. I was a lot younger then; I'd got staying power now. The only doubt I had was how to protect myself from world events over which I had no control. Ever since Aileen came over to the stall that day in the rag market, I'd started to feel vulnerable.

The phone rang, and it was Eartha. At last I got the whole story of what had happened to Kase in Calcutta. He had been arrested after Customs officials had found a quantity of marijuana inside ten Nipper dogs. He'd been detained for two months without trial and was now being released, the authorities having decided not to press charges.

'So he's a free man,' I said. 'You must be delighted.'

'He was innocent, although he had to pay a high-ranking police officer several thousand dollars.'

'When will he be home?'

'In a couple of days.'

Was he innocent, or had he been caught and got himself off by paying a bribe? I doubted I'd ever know, unless one day Kase told me what really happened.

'Belah has put in a special request for her father to tuck her in and say goodnight,' Ros told me when I got off the phone.

'I'm honoured.'

'Dad,' said my youngest daughter, clearing away the collection of animals that covered most of her bed. 'You don't have to make up a story for me. I want to ask you something much more important.'

'I thought you liked my stories.'

'I do, but I really want a tortoise and I promise I'll look after it every day.'

'It's not something you can really cuddle and play with is it?'

'Debbie Miller's got one. And a stopwatch, so we can race them against each other.'

'What are we going to do when you've lost interest in it? They live for a hundred years.'

'I won't lose interest, and Miss Dibbin says I can take it to school, to our nature class.'

'You know I still have Silo running around at Puckmill, all because no one was taking any notice of him.'

'Dad, please, just for me.'

'All right, you can have one if you can say Ken Dodd's dad's dog's dead.'

'Ken's dad's dead and Dodd's dog died.'

'That's near enough.'

Back downstairs I gave Marcus a ring and told him I'd commissioned Susie Atherton to sculpt a range of gay lighting for us, which set him off at a rate of knots.

'You really never cease to amaze me.'

'What do you mean?'

'I mentioned it to you once, and now you're getting on with the job.'

'Because I think it's a good idea and, as you said, there's a gap in the market.'

'And we're going to fill that gap,' he said.

'There is one thing, Marcus: I'm being led by you on this. I wouldn't want to give people the wrong impression.'

'What's that?'

'Well, that we're a gay business, because we're not.'

'But I'm going to offer these as exclusive limited-edition pieces. You'll have to sign them.'

'Susie would be more than happy to do that,' I told him.

'You don't have to distance yourself from this. Take my word for it, we are entering a growing market,' Marcus said, full of confidence that we were ahead of the game. 'I'm going to an interior design show in Paris next week; most of the buyers are gay. I'll come back with an address book full of contacts. This is the direction you should be taking. Those replicas might have built your business, but now it's time to move on.'

'Okay: I could do with a change. I was talking about it to Ros earlier. But I'm not going to give up the street markets or selling to the reproduction wholesalers.'

'You don't have to. That's your bread and butter, but you must build new layers on that solid foundation and broaden your customer base.'

He was right; and something else I realised, listening to him in full flow, was that Marcus was clearly not the man to be my workshop manager. He was a salesman, a man of vision who could open doors for Puckmill Studios, and he spoke fluent French, another thing that impressed me. Not that we had any French customers, apart from Delphine.

It was, we all fervently hoped, the last day we would have to make the journey to Delphine's. Although I was tempting fate, I was already composing my farewell speech to her, arranging the words in my head. As soon as she handed over the outstanding fifteen thousand pounds she owed me I wanted to be able to tell her just what I had learnt from the past two weeks.

No longer would we have to queue to get on to the Oxford bypass, or past the temporary traffic lights, stuck in a tailback of traffic that stretched for at least three miles. My heart went out to all those who suffered these delays every day and I marvelled at the patience they showed, the lost hours of their lives, just to keep a roof over their heads. But not for us, not after today. It felt as if we'd served our time and were about to be set free.

'What's been the hardest thing for you to bear?' I asked Mike as, bumper to bumper, we moved a yard every ten minutes.

'I think it's been Mum not waking me up with my cup of tea in the morning.'

'The same for me,' said Ade, who I'd expected to say having to kneel in the back of the van twice a day for two weeks.

'What's it been for you?' asked Mike.

'Can't you guess?'

'It wouldn't be Delphine by any chance?'

'It would, and after today she'll be just a memory.'

'Do you think we should celebrate?' Ade said.

'We could go to the Chinese restaurant in Burford we've passed every day on the way home,' I suggested.

'I've never eaten Chinese,' said Mike.

Neither had Ade, who had whatever was left over from the menu at the Crown.

'Pete, the chef, heats it up for me in the microwave.'

'I suppose for your mother it's a convenient way to feed you.'

'Yes, but it means I don't eat until ten, after the kitchen's closed.'

'Well, if all goes to plan, we'll eat Chinese tonight,' I told them.

'And if it doesn't?' asked Mike.

'Don't let's think about that.'

For the first time, Delphine greeted us with a welcoming smile, clapping her hands together. Her whole face had lightened up. Darina was there too, the girl Ade had taken a fancy to, who shot him a quick look and, coyly wiggling her fingers, gave him a little wave.

'The young ones,' said Delphine. 'Aren't they sweet?'

'I've not seen you like this before,' I said. 'Is it an act?'

'You see? Before I have even asked you into the house you accuse me of acting.'

'But you're a completely different person. What do you expect?'

'I have news for you. Darina, please make us some tea. We will be in shortly.'

I told Mike and Ade they didn't have to witness this charade any longer. 'Why don't you go and get started?'

Over a cup of lapsang souchong, beside a Japanese nodding doll that continuously bowed its head towards me, Delphine told me everything that had happened the day before, the day of the airlift as she called it.

'My beloved *Psyche* has flown away, and your marble plinth awaits you. At last, you can now finish your work.'

'And be paid the fifteen thousand pounds you owe me.'

'Following my final inspection, I will settle up with you. I am an honourable woman.'

By lunch time the fibreglass sculpture had been fixed to the plinth; being hollow and weighing no more than fifty pounds it was easy enough to manage. Mike drilled in several steel screws and sanded down the rough edges, so the piece sat flat on the plinth. I was happy; it looked exactly like the bronze original that had been cast in a Berlin foundry.

'Let's eat,' I said. 'Then all we've got to do is apply the patination before we head for home.'

We lay back on the grass, our heads propped up on our rucksacks; around us trees were shedding their leaves. With our shirt sleeves rolled up, we ate our sandwiches in the still warm air.

'We're enjoying an Indian summer,' said Mike, who always knew the weather forecast. 'Another three days, and then it all changes.'

'Ade, can you hear me?' called a slightly raised voice and Darina suddenly appeared on the bank, anxiously looking behind her. 'Ade, it's me.'

'Is that your love calling, Ade?' said Mike.

'Darina, don't let her see you. Go back.'

'She's doing a radio interview. Have you spoken to your boss about me?'

'I have, haven't I?' said Ade, turning to me with a pleading look.

'Yes.' What else could I say?

'When will we see one another again?'

'I don't know. Ring me.'

'Let me write down your number.'

Rather than be a part of this conversation I told Ade to row over to her, but whatever happened to be back within fifteen minutes.

'When are you going to get a girlfriend, Mike?'

'That's not going to be easy, because I don't think she exists.'

'What qualities are you looking for in a girl?'

'Someone who can chalk up the score in a game of darts.'

'You mean good at mathematics. Is that all?'

'Likes football and a pint in the Odd Fellows.'

'Anything else?'

'Doesn't mind listening to Johnny Cash.'

'I don't think that's a lot to offer a girl.'

'I know, but I'm not looking for one anyway.'

I certainly hadn't been expecting Mike to say that, but now was not the time to discuss what was probably best addressed to an agony aunt in the daily paper.

'You can't give Darina a job,' he said.

'I know that. And I'll ask Ade how he can possibly see her once we've finished here.'

'Which will be in a couple of hours,' Mike assured me.

We didn't need Blair Boulting to put the patination on to the replica because we didn't need to heat the surface. Neither was it necessary to follow a chemical formula. We could match the exact colour by using a blend of copper sulphates and quick air-drying stains, which were sealed by a colourless lacquer. Mike worked from the photographs he had taken and, using various sizes of paintbrush, had completed the work by four o'clock.

I hugged him, and so Ade didn't feel left out, I threw my arms around him too. We all stood in silence, as one does before an altar. The ordeal was over and I'm not sure what I really felt. Certainly much more than relief; that I had got my life back, perhaps. Yet there was no sense of achievement or inner satisfaction. In the minutes that followed, as we gathered our tools and tidied up so as not to leave the slightest evidence that we had been there, I had the thought, and not for the first time, that surely there must be an easier way to make a living.

Delphine inspected the completed job, walking around the sculpture at least three times, running her hands over it, getting down on her knees to make sure it sat flat upon the plinth. Her only acknowledgement that she could find no fault in our work was a gentle nodding of her head, and half a smile.

As Mike and Ade loaded up the van I counted out the fifteen thousand pounds in cash in her kitchen. The moment for my speech had arrived.

'Delphine, if ever there was a job carried out in the worst possible atmosphere it was this. Never have I worked for so long under such sustained tension, all of it created by you.'

'If there's a God then I have one prayer for him: don't ever let our paths cross again,' was her response.

'Did she pay you?' asked Mike, as we drove off.

'Yes. Now let's go and find that Chinese restaurant.'

18

Danny Draysey, who considered himself to be a man of the turf and bought the *Sporting Life* every day, told me that Barbara Waring was training a dark horse. Nothing to do with its colour, but a gelding with a lot of untapped potential. His name was Full Quiver and he'd only raced four times, being placed twice. Willie Carson had ridden him as a two-year-old, but Sheikh Mohammed, who owned him, had decided he wouldn't make the grade as a three-year-old and had put him up for sale for twenty thousand guineas.

I met Danny on the gallops at Lucknam Park one January morning, just after dawn, when the winter sun was rising over the high landscape that surrounds the city of Bath. He was probably in his mid-forties, full of self-confidence, projecting a casual, easy-going personality with his Brylcreemed hair swept back, the top button of his shirt undone and his tie loose around his collar. He had the hint of a smug grin that never broadened into a fully fledged smile, and a rolled up newspaper sticking out of a pocket of his sports jacket. We sat in Barbara's Land Rover, looking through our binoculars, as a group of racehorses appeared, silhouetted in the mist, snorting white plumes of breath into the coldness of the breaking day.

'Which one's Full Quiver?' I asked.

'The one that's just shot clear in the final furlong.'

After the jockey dismounted, we all huddled together and everyone agreed he was coming along nicely. My contribution was to walk around Full Quiver and say, 'Well, he certainly looks like a racehorse,' which no one responded to other than by giving me a blank look.

In Barbara's kitchen over a cup of tea, surrounded by rosettes and photographs of happy owners, she told me that in her opinion the horse would make a decent handicapper and was certainly up to winning races.

'How much does all this cost? I know it's called the sport of kings, which means it can't be cheap.'

'Your share of the training fees would be about five hundred pounds a month, but of course you'll receive half of any prize money, minus my percentage as the trainer.'

I didn't hesitate; it would be a distraction for all of us at Puckmill Studios and we could afford it now. I'd give Mike and Rob a share, call it a perk of the job.

'All I need, then, is a cheque and I can welcome you as an owner.'

After Barbara had left us and we were walking around the stables, Danny told me of his shrewd master plan.

'What we need to do is make friends with the work riders; they're the ones who are in the know.'

'Get some inside information, you mean?'

'Precisely. And then we can land a few gambling coups.'

'I usually only put a couple of quid on a horse,' I told him.

'You can forget about that. You're moving into a different league now.'

I decided not to mention that my first bet was two shillings and sixpence each way on a horse called Rice Pudding, which won at 13/2.

'Rob tells me you've got a successful business, so up the ante, become a playboy for a while. Let's have some fun. Do you know how to make money out of gambling?'

'Keep backing winners?'

'It's about contacts, and I've got them all over the country. Small trainers laying out horses to land a nice touch,' he said, tapping the side of his nose, which he'd repeatedly done, emphasising it was all hush-hush.

'Ah, contacts. Vital to any business.'

'Those yards that just have a few horses can't live on the prize money. Only the top stables can do that, the ones who train for the Arabs. We'll speak soon. And remember, whatever information I pass on to you is for your ears only,' he added, tapping the side of his nose yet again.

'Okay, Danny. I have a feeling exciting times lie ahead.'

'Hey, call me DD. Everyone else does.'

When I got back to Puckmill, Mike told me that George Ashley was still waiting for me.

'What do you mean, still?'

'You arranged to meet him an hour ago. You know, that sculptor who used to work at the Dummy Book Company in Tetbury.'

'Oh God, yes. I've been up since five; I thought I'd be back hours ago.'

'He's good, and we need someone if we're going to take on the Alton Towers job.'

'George, I'm so sorry to keep you waiting. I had to go out and buy a racehorse this morning,' I enjoyed saying that; it was my only opportunity. But George gave no response and looked thoroughly fed up.

'Why did you leave the Dummy Book Company? I heard they're doing well.'

'I was stagnating. Been there three years and my career was going nowhere.'

'Show me what you've done. I do have a job coming up, but we can't give you full-time work.'

George was the first sculptor I had seen who carved life-size statues, all of them done in his spare time. It was remarkable work, carved from large blocks of polystyrene, a process called hot wiring. He showed me pictures of some rock musicians he'd done, playing guitar and saxophone and other instruments, a complete pop group. They were highly commercial, and I could see them in nightclubs, and the themed pubs that were springing up everywhere.

'These are very impressive, George. I could sell all this work for you.' I'd immediately thought of Kase, sure he'd have customers for them. 'How do you fancy making an eighteen-foot bar of chocolate out of polystyrene for the Alton Towers hotel?'

'You're on. When do I start?'

'Soon. Give me your number, and I'll be in touch within the week.'

I had a day at Bath antiques market to look forward to and some good news for Peter, my mother's gentleman friend, as she called him. We had at last finished the first 8x4 section of his Cotswold tiled roof. It looked at least a couple of centuries old; we'd aged it with a coating of cow's urine and yoghurt before airbrushing it with a light covering of potassium permanganate. Then we left it lying out in a field for a week. It was surprising how quickly the forces of nature got to work. The job was never a priority and I was only doing it to please my mother.

'When you've found a builder to price up the job, let me know how many tiles you want,' I told Peter, who had turned up at the stall, waiting to meet my mother. 'I've done this as a favour really. I'm just breaking even; it's not the kind of work I normally take on.'

'I know. Thank you. A favour for someone nearly in the family, so to speak.'

'But you're not nearly in the family.'

'She might have turned me down twice, but third time lucky.'

'I don't think my mother will marry again. She prefers her freedom above anything else.'

'We will see. I've planned a holiday and I'm going to propose to her in San Francisco.'

Most of the overseas buyers at the market didn't give me a second look, but they knew who I was all right and when they wanted something made their approach was always the same, almost word for word: 'It's highly unlikely, but if there's a chance that you could make this, then we could do some serious business.'

As was the case with Stefan Seeley when he came to the stall. What Quentin Saffell didn't know about tins, Stefan didn't know about mother-of-pearl buttons. Half Bulgarian, the remaining fifty per cent English, as he put it, he had been born in Tunbridge Wells forty-six years ago.

'Who do you support, England or Bulgaria?' I asked.

'Italy,' he said. 'I married a very emotional Italian and I promised her. It was one of my marriage vows.'

Straight away I told him there was no money in buttons, unless you sold millions of them. And we didn't have a production line; everything we did was hand finished. 'But it's been very nice meeting you, and I'm sorry I can't help.'

'Please hear me out. I haven't reached the point of my premeditated visit.'

'Premeditated. I like that word. It suggests you've thought it all through.'

'We have a mutual acquaintance, Marcus Wesley. He holds you in the highest regard, and he told me there is no challenge you wouldn't take up. Of course, only if there was money in it.'

'So, Stefan, your premeditated point is?'

'I need a recipe to make mother-of-pearl.'

'You mean a liquid resin?'

'Precisely, and you can leave the rest to my factory in Bulgaria.'

'Well, that certainly is different. What you're after is the formula.'

'For me exclusively, all the exact ingredients, and for this I will pay you good money.'

'How much is good money?'

'First you must show me a sample, then we can negotiate.'

'Have you got a business card?'

'Of course.' He handed me one. *Stefan Seeley Ltd*, it said, and underneath, *More than just pearls of wisdom*.

My mother eventually turned up, half an hour after Peter had left, having been delayed at the hairdresser. The first thing I said was, 'You can't fool me, Mummy. I can see you've had your hair highlighted.'

'I have. Do you like it? Do you think it makes me look younger?'

'Yes, it does. At least ten years.'

'You are wonderful, do you know that?'

'No.'

'You'll never be a woman, but of all the changes she goes through, the hardest is coming to terms with ageing. Her beauty gradually deserts her, a cruel, slow process in front of a lonely mirror.'

'You're not the only one. Look at me, my hair flies away every day and it's not heading for sunny climes.'

'Oh, just listen to us. Now, have you seen Peter?'

'I have, but don't ask me where he is now.'

'He'll be waiting for me upstairs in the café.'

'Mother, as your eldest son who has now lived a bit of life, can I ask you, what is it you see in him?'

'That's simple, darling. What any woman wants: kindness, lots of attention and he flatters me.'

'Enough to marry him for?'

'Good God, no. Why do you ask?'

'Because I think he might be homing in on you again.'

I had a profitable day in more ways than one, including meeting an eccentric breeder of pedigree dogs, who lived in Minchinhampton in his aptly named residence, Pug House. He wanted two stone pugs to sit on the columns either side of the entrance to his Cotswold property.

'Of course we can do it,' I said. He told me he had an antique carving of the piece he wanted moulded and handed me a deposit of a hundred pounds there and then. Another one of those unexpected meetings; you never knew who you were going to meet working in the markets.

That night when I walked into the kitchen Ros handed me a postcard, saying, 'This has come from Walter Pepper. He's in Cape Town.' It was nearly impossible to read, all the words crammed together in minute writing. I literally needed a magnifying glass to decipher it. I missed him, and often wondered what he was up to.

'I owe that man so much and he never let me express my gratitude. He always rebuffed it and said he was the one who should be grateful.'

'Because that's what he felt,' said Ros. 'He told me once that he had never been so excited as he was working with you.'

Then the phone rang. It was a call I'd waited months for: Kase, his voice loud and clear, speaking from Amsterdam.

'You've made it home,' I said. 'Are you okay?'

'I got myself into a terrible mess, let's leave it at that.'

'So, what are you up to?'

'I'm staying put in Amsterdam. I've promised Eartha no more travelling for a while. I'm opening a lighting shop. It's time you did a range of lamps, instead of all that advertising stuff.'

'I might have something for you. I'm moving into new product ranges.'

'Like what?'

'Gay lighting, and that's not all. Erotic art.'

'This I could get excited about. Amsterdam has a large gay community.'

'They call it the pink pound here in the UK. According to a friend of mine, it's a growing market.'

'I wish I could come over, but I have a shop to set up here and a fragile marriage I need to repair.'

'Don't worry. I'll send you some photographs soon.'

Mike was putting L-plates on his old Subaru pickup, telling me he was going to give Ade driving lessons. The reason Ade was so keen to pass his test and get on the road was because of Darina. I hadn't expected them to keep in touch, but Mike said that somehow she managed to ring him every evening. Ade confided in Mike, seeing him as an older brother since working so closely with him at Delphine's. I'd hoped the whole Delphine episode was behind us, which of course it was; Ade's love life didn't really have anything to do with me or Puckmill Studios.

It would have been simpler if he'd taken a fancy to the French girl who had recently started working as a waitress in the Crown. Natalie was very different from the village girls; here for a year to learn English, and a keen footballer, she'd already joined the Cirencester Ladies football team as their goalkeeper.

'Take her out and give her some penalty practice on the common,' I told him.

'Amongst all the cowpats? No, thank you.'

'Well, get her to give you French lessons. You're not going to stay in Frampton Mansell all your life. It will make you much more appealing to girls if you can speak French.'

'Can you?'

'Of course I can. *Avez-vous de l'eau, s'il vous plaît?*'

'What does that mean?'

'Can I have some water, please?'

'That's not going to get me very far chatting up a girl.'

'It opens up a conversation that could lead anywhere.'

'I'll stick with Darina. She needs me.'

'She might just need you to help her find a job and get away from you know who.'

Harsh, though probably true, and as soon as I'd said it I wished I'd been more gentle, or made light of it in some way.

'You don't know what you're talking about. You just don't want to help because of everything that happened with Delphine.'

Stefan Seeley was certainly a man who didn't like silence. Every morning he rang me at nine to find out what progress I was making with his mother-of-pearl formula. It would have been the perfect job to pass over to Walter Pepper, but I had no alternative but to do it myself. Watching Ros put on her mascara one evening, I realised women's make-up might hold the clue. Blusher, eyeliner, rouge; those powders could be mixed with resin. And then it came to me: of course, nail varnish. So I got on the phone and eventually found a company that manufactured everything I needed. They supplied the ingredients to some of the most well-known names in the beauty business. Although they were protective of their customers, when I told them I only wanted a couple of kilos of their mother-of-pearl powder they agreed to send me a trial sample.

Now I was experimenting again, which I loved to do on my own, just me in the workshop, like those early Puckmill days.

I went on a voyage of discovery into the mystery of alchemy, mixing chemicals, looking for the consistency that would link the elements together. I'd completely lose track of time, and then with one quick glance at the clock find it was nearly midnight. Too late to ring Ros, and I knew I'd walk back into a darkened house to find a note on the kitchen table: *Your supper's in the fridge. Heat it up for twenty minutes if you're hungry.*

It took the rest of the week to find the perfect mixture of ingredients to blend the mother-of-pearl powder with the resin. To this day, Stefan Seeley still uses the formula to make his buttons, and he paid me ten thousand pounds to buy the exclusive rights.

Susie brought in the finished gay guy leaning on the lamppost, sculpted in a material called milliput. Mike thought it a tricky piece to mould; there were several under-cuts that required not only a steady hand with a scalpel, but the eye of a skilled surgeon.

'Let's call it "Leaning on a Lamppost",' I suggested.

We had to name not only each piece but the whole range. 'What about "The Gaylords"?' said Rob.

'Don't we need something a bit more subtle than that?' said Quentin, anxious not to limit its appeal.

'Well, what would you call this one, Quentin?' I asked.

'"Rebel Rouser" maybe, or "Blue Jean Boy".'

It was left undecided, but we went on calling it 'Leaning on a Lamppost' until someone came up with a better alternative.

DD rang me, having just heard some important news from one of his 'work watchers' who went by the name of Jack Whisper. He was a reliable source who spent most of his time wearing waterproofs and lying behind clumps of grass with a pair of binoculars watching racehorses tear past him at thirty miles per hour.

'Rainbow City in the 2.15 at Haydock this Saturday,' he said with hushed excitement. Then he put the phone down, without a word about Full Quiver, or when he was likely to run.

I went over to the electroplating shed where Mike was wearing a helmet with an inbuilt extractor fan, looking like someone who was about to go walking on the moon.

'Haydock, 2.15, Rainbow City.'

'I can't hear a word you're saying.'

'Oh, by the way, I'm giving you and Rob a share of the horse.'

'What?'

'Haydock, 2.15, Rainbow City.'

And then Celia Foxton skidded into the yard and announced she wanted to sell the barn, the workshop and the land as far as the wall that bordered the lane outside Chris Booth's house.

'I want twenty thousand pounds for it. I'm giving you first refusal and a week to think about it.'

'And what happens if I don't buy it?'

'I'm sorry, but I'll sell to someone else, and give you three months' notice.'

I asked Simon Fisher to come and see me about it. Over the years he'd not just looked after Puckmill Studios' somewhat colourful tax returns, he'd also become a friend.

'You know, if you were a more orthodox person, you could have built up a very successful business and have something to sell, after all the hard work you've put into the place.'

'It's the people we deal with; you could hardly call them conventional. None of them know what a cheque book is. Anyway, they're good for my cash flow.'

'I've told you before, you have a creative team around you.

Start doing the gift shows and meeting the buyers from the likes of John Lewis.'

'It would take all the fun out of it. Purchase order numbers, thirty days' credit . . .'

'You'll never change. I know I'm wasting my breath.'

'You're here to talk about me buying the workshop. All I want to know is should I, or should I move on?'

'First get another valuation and then find out if you could get planning permission to turn the barn into a dwelling. Then we'll decide what's the right thing to do,' said Simon, sitting in my shed with me, sipping a cup of tea. He hadn't noticed that during our conversation Silo had crept in and started to nibble at his trousers. It was only when I leant forward with a carrot that Simon saw him and pulled his leg away, horrified that there might be pee on his shoes. I picked Silo up and told Simon I was thinking of making him managing director.

'He's got all the traits one needs to get to the top: he's shrewd, he's a very good listener and he knows the time of day, which is exactly three o'clock when he gets his afternoon carrot.'

'You're mad. I'm going back to the office.'

Susie Atherton came in for a chat. She'd now completed four figures for our gay range, The Gaylords; the name had unfortunately stuck and everyone in the workshop used it. I admired Quentin's persistence; at some time each day he'd come up to me in the workshop with another suggestion.

'What about "Night Hawks"?' was the latest, which I liked and so did Susie, who was showing me another sculpture: two girls locked in a provocative embrace, their blouses loose on their shoulders, hands caressing each other's cheeks.

'Don't answer this if you don't want to, but are you that way inclined yourself?' I asked.

'Oh no, not at all. I'm a meat-and-two-veg girl any day of the week.'

'That's what I like, usually on a Sunday. I must say I prefer lamb.'

She looked slightly bemused, and then dropped a bit of a bombshell.

'I'm afraid I won't be available for any more commissions after we've finished this project, which is a pity, because I've really enjoyed working with you. I can't thank you enough for giving me this break.'

'You're going to travel the world,' I said.

'Oh no, nothing like that. I've been offered a year's contract designing for White Swan Gifts. They get everything made in China. It's a huge opportunity for me.'

She had no idea the effect this conversation had on me. It brought home the fact that the world I'd created was now definitely slipping away. It was just a matter of time. That night I returned to the garden shed and stared out through the little square window and contemplated my downfall. The only way we could protect ourselves was with bespoke work, one-off jobs with designers. I decided to ring Rod Holt in the morning. I needed to forge a closer link with him and see if he could offer us work on his Fortnum & Mason window schemes.

We'd completed a job for a chain of pubs called the Slurping Toad down on the south coast and now the product had to be delivered. I knew it was going to be an eventful journey; what else would you expect, driving three twelve-foot-high polystyrene toads down to Chichester on a flat-bed truck? They were an eye-catching trio, wearing great floppy hats and green jackets, each holding a glass of beer. It was a ridiculous sight and nearly every vehicle that passed sounded its horn;

some even slowed down beside me to take photographs. I had to keep my speed at a constant forty miles per hour, and although I had them roped together the police pulled me over. It was obvious from their expressions that they couldn't quite believe what they were seeing.

'There's a first time for everything,' said one to the other as they approached me.

'You need to make them more secure. They're swaying all over the place.'

'Sorry, officer. It's the side wind that's causing it; they only weigh a few pounds.'

'Where are you heading? A fun fair?'

'No, Chichester. I'll be off the dual carriageway in a couple of junctions.'

One of them climbed on to the back to make up his own mind whether it was safe for me to continue.

'The problem is that you're causing other drivers to drive without due care and attention.'

'I don't see what I can do about that.'

'We'll stay behind you, but keep at thirty miles per hour. We don't want to be seeing airborne toads over Sussex.'

So I was given a police escort until I turned off for Chichester. As I drove through the crowded streets, pedestrians waved and cheered until I eventually arrived at the Slurping Toad. Half a dozen people stood watching in astonishment as I carried the toads into the pub one by one.

'I'm not used to all this attention. I'm just the delivery driver,' I told them.

Sifta climbed into the van next to me while I waited for the doors of the rag market to open. He wanted to tell me that three vehicles back in the queue was a Welsh dealer up from Newtown who had just cleared out an old chemist shop.

'This is what I've waited for. This is it,' he said.

'Hang on, Sifta. I think we've been here before.'

'Beautiful Bristol Blue glass jars, boxes of them. Old bottles, carboys, and a black apothecary onion bottle. My day has come, I can tell you.'

'I don't think I've ever seen you so excited. How much do you want to borrow?'

'I can't tell you yet, but this will set me up, if only I can move quickly.'

'Are you talking thousands?'

'Maybe a couple of grand.'

'Okay. I'll lend you the money if you stop sleeping in the van and put something down on a room for yourself.'

'Okay, whatever you say.'

'It's for you, not for me.'

'I'm off. You're a pal, you really are.'

I'd been coming to the rag market for four years now and of all those I'd had dealings with, Sifta was the one who'd made the greatest impression on me. I sometimes wondered whether he'd have pulled off all those deals and managed to keep himself afloat if I hadn't been his banker. The energy and enthusiasm he showed never diminished; he zipped around the market like a sniffer dog, his nose close to the ground, always searching for the scent of a bargain. He'd probably have survived. Running to me just made it easier for him, and although every week I still gave him netsukes and scrimshaw to sell at Charnock Richard I would have helped him out anyway. I was fond of him in a strange way, and cared what happened to him. I admired him, always living on the edge.

And he'd never once not squared up and paid what he owed me. He'd only once briefly told me anything about himself; that he'd had a rotten childhood and was bullied at school because of his size.

Aileen came over for her mid-morning chat wearing a tiara she was trying to sell. She always wore what she was hoping to flog, and often one arm would be adorned with bracelets up to her elbow.

'You have to show them off to best effect.'

'I think you were right when you said we'd soon be overrun with cheap Chinese imports.'

'It's happening already. Do you know Ian Guise at Minster Giftware? He's a reproduction wholesaler.'

'I do. He's a customer of mine.'

'Well, only last week I saw a container being unloaded in his warehouse.'

'But he buys all my advertising figures and hundreds of Nipper dogs every year. He's worth thousands to us.'

'Well, he's the first, and the rest will have to follow. They won't be able to compete with him otherwise.'

As I was absorbing this catastrophic news and wondering how long it would be before it affected us, I saw Isobel with her Afghan hound walking towards me. I hadn't seen her since we'd finished working for Delphine and no doubt I was about to hear her friend's final damning comments.

'Before you say a word, Isobel, any job of that size is going to present unforeseen difficulties.'

'That's all in the past. I attended the gala evening. It was wonderful; the view of *Psyche* from the veranda was perfect. I was the only person who knew what had taken place and I'm certain no one could tell. And Delphine was so relaxed. She whispered to me, "Isn't it beautiful, lit up, just where it should be, in the spotlight."'

'Well, I'm glad to hear it. I've never had such a tormented two weeks.'

'It's a pity you'll never see her in different circumstances. She is the most charming woman and has helped so many young artists.'

'I'm glad she's happy, but please don't let's talk about her again.'

'We won't. Anyway, I'm off to India for a few months. I hope to see you when I get back.'

'I've done the deal,' said Sifta, suddenly appearing at the stall. 'And what's more he threw in six Victorian ear trumpets. Can't stop – I know the very person who'll buy them. I'll see you next week.'

'Who?' I wanted to know, as he was about to rush off.

'Jane at Plum's Emporium. You know, the girl you bought the phone box from.'

A subdued Frank Webb came over at the end of the morning, carrying his golf bag of walking sticks over his shoulder.

'What is it, Frank? You look fed up.'

'The world is changing; I'm getting left behind. I think I'll lock myself away and work on the railways.'

'You mean on your railway.'

'I've given it a name. It's called the WMR.'

'Which stands for what?'

'West Midlands Railway.'

'Sounds authentic. I like it.'

'I laid the track, built the bridges, I did it all.'

'And the stations. And it didn't stop there. You designed the villages, whole hillsides.'

'I could take it up as a full-time job if I could find someone to share it with.'

'Advertise. It could well appeal to a retired railway worker, sitting at home with nothing to do,' I said as enthusiastically as possible.

'Would a month's notice be long enough?' he asked.

'What do you mean?'

'Until I stop making walking sticks for you.'

'Really, that soon?'

'Do you know, the only person I've admired in my life is Isambard Kingdom Brunel.'

'I can understand why, Frank. You're a miniature version of the great man himself.'

We had finished the sample of the shagreen cutlass hilt for Fattorinis. As no one had chased us, Mike had fitted it in when he had the odd five minutes to spare. I told him not to make it a priority as I didn't think there would be any money in it. Rather than go around to their offices and waste half an hour, I dropped it in to Chaucer at the pewter company and asked if they would deal with it. After all, they were the ones doing the business.

'You know, it amazes me how you do it.'

'You mean how long it takes to deliver a sample to you? I'm sorry.'

'No, how real it looks, and it's certainly been worth waiting for. I can't understand why you're not a millionaire.'

He looked bemused when I couldn't suppress an ironic laugh.

Baz joined us, lighting one cigarette from the end of another that had burnt down to the filter.

'Yes, why aren't you a millionaire?' he said. 'Do you know, if you were really clever, you'd make a fortune out of what you've got between your ears.'

'You mean my face?'

'The knowledge you've built up; think about it. You drive to three different markets every week, up at the crack of dawn, for what? To make a few hundred quid in cash.'

'I get your drift,' said Chaucer.

'Well, I don't. What do you mean?' I said, suspecting this conversation was going nowhere.

'Write a book about how to make replicas. No one knows what you do.'

'Who'd buy it? A few antique dealers wanting to make fakes?'

'You're missing the point. Think of the museums, the film world, people restoring works of art. Start writing it all down: a manual on everything you know. Give me ten per cent and I'll be your agent,' said Baz; I could see he meant it.

'Well, if all these Chinese imports are going to flood into the country, I'll be looking for something to do.'

The Alton Towers hotel job had been signed off. It involved making a dozen flat-back images of two glasses of milk being poured into a bar of chocolate, the same as the Cadbury's TV adverts. They were to be fixed above the beds in each hotel bedroom and so we made them out of polystyrene. The eighteen-foot-long bar of Cadbury's Dairy Milk was the backdrop to the reception area in the foyer.

I sent George Ashley up there to oversee the job and work with the installers, a company called First Bite Design, whose manager rang and told me how impressed they had all been by him. As he wasn't in full-time employment, they were offering him a position in their art department.

First Susie, and now George. What was I doing wrong?

19

March, and although the daffodils brightened the gardens of Frampton Mansell, the wind still carried a vicious bite, the hedgerows giving no hint that winter could be softening into spring. Down in the Golden Valley everything lagged a few days behind; you could see it in the closed buds on the trees, while in the village the ancient chestnut outside the old school house was already unfolding its sticky leaves.

DD rang with the latest information on Full Quiver, letting me know he was going to have his first run of the season at Kempton Park the following week.

'How much are we putting on him?' I asked.

DD then listed a host of reasons why we were probably not going to put a penny on him. He wasn't fit, the going would be too soft and the distance was too short. But he still insisted we should go and have lunch in the restaurant at the course, which had a perfect view of the winning post.

'And, what is always a special moment, walking out into the parade ring to meet your trainer and jockey.'

'I must say, I'd enjoy that. I think I'll wear a homburg and smoke a cigar.'

'You'll be mixing with some rich Arab owners.'

'I'll bring Ros for a day out,' I told him.

After weeks of negotiating with Celia, I'd finally agreed to pay her eighteen thousand pounds for the barn and workshop. I'd never wanted to buy it, but it would have been impossible to find somewhere else nearby, certainly not in the village. We belonged in Frampton Mansell. To set up a new workshop, Mike estimated we'd have to shut down the whole operation for at least a month to move all our equipment and have three-phase electricity installed, if we were going to upgrade some of our machinery.

I'd applied for planning permission on the barn, which the council had not refused, but they wanted to see architectural drawings before a decision could be made. These would cost over a thousand pounds and so, before I spent any money, I asked Chris Booth if he would object to the barn's being converted into a house. He also wanted to see the drawings, so I took the gamble and got a firm of architects in Stroud to come up with some ideas.

Meanwhile, I'd noticed a gradual falling away of sales to wholesalers. Every other week we did deliveries to the north of England, as far as Andy Thornton who sold reproductions in Halifax, and then the following Friday we covered the south, mostly within twenty miles of London. One of the wholesalers we did a lot of business with was a young man called John Vaillant who had a warehouse in Birmingham. I knew him well enough to ask some direct questions, such as why he wasn't buying so much from us any more. His stuttering, almost embarrassed response was that the times they were a-changing.

'What do you mean? I want to know where I stand.'

'You're on wobbly ground, but don't blame me. We've all got businesses to run and everything comes down to price.'

'So, does that mean you're dropping us as a supplier?'

'It's coming in from China. The yellow peril's opening their factories to the West. They might not have the quality, but the price and the margins we make . . . I'm sorry. It's a cruel world.'

After I'd put the phone down, I rang Simon and gave him the glum news that probably in only a matter of weeks we would have lost all our wholesalers, the financial backbone of Puckmill. He could offer no hope, and when he said they represented seventy-five per cent of our business I had a sense of foreboding, as if no matter what move I made, it would be the wrong one.

'Come on. You'll find something else to fill the gap.'

I reminded him that I'd signed a cheque to Celia the day before to buy the place. It couldn't have happened at a worse time.

'Not if you get planning permission. That will add at least ten thousand pounds to the value.'

How on earth were we going to survive? I felt just as I had at Dyffryn when the vet told me the pig herd was dying of a wasting disease. There's little one can do when external events take over your world; this time the Chinese advancing into the West and wiping out British manufacturing.

Though everything else around me might have been falling apart, at least I had one perfect antidote to my crumbling life. I'd bought a racehorse and could now present myself to others as a playboy. I'd tell no one about the state of the business and show an extravagant optimism, greeting everyone as George Borrow had – 'Life is sweet, brother' – as he walked around Wales with unbounded exuberance. This eccentric Englishman's uplifting take on life must have been irritating in the extreme to some of those Welsh farmers who scraped a living from the land.

Nevertheless, I maintained this upbeat frame of mind when I walked into the kitchen and threw my arms around Ros and said, 'My love, life is not only sweet, but full of excitement.'

'What's wrong? Something's gone terribly wrong.'

'Nothing, absolutely nothing. The spring is springing, the twigs are full of birds singing arias, Full Quiver is running at Kempton next week, and you and I are going to have a wonderful day out.'

'I'm nervous,' she said.

'No need to be nervous. I'm going to sit in the shed for half an hour and indulge myself in a big think about everything.'

Was I going to have to start laying people off? This wasn't

a business with a workforce and a shop steward, it was me with a group of friends. But if we were going to stay afloat, something would have to turn up pretty soon. Rod Holt had said he'd give us as much work as he could, but each scheme for Fortnum & Mason was different and he couldn't guarantee how much he'd be able to pass our way. I just had enough coming in from the markets to pay the wages every week. Despite Marcus Wesley's enthusiasm for the gay lighting range, 'Night Hawks' was hardly going to replace the loss of revenue from our wholesalers.

For some reason I preferred to carry my anxieties alone. I constantly searched within myself, hoping for a moment of inspiration to show me a way out of the inevitable ending of another cycle in my life. Ros knew something was wrong and began questioning me about it.

'You can't hide it, no matter how hard you try.'

So I gave her a little of the truth, that Chinese imports were coming into the country and we needed to change direction, because it was impossible to compete with them.

Within a week, everyone at Puckmill knew what was happening; the orders weren't coming in. When I rang the wholesalers, people I'd dealt with for years, they didn't bother to return my calls. It just confirmed that there's no such thing as loyalty in business.

Lysta announced over supper that a girl in her class had been sent home from school for dying her hair green and purple. And then Sam told us that Pugh, the class show-off, had driven himself to school in his father's car.

'Would you like to make a contribution to this anarchy?' I asked Seth, who was two years below his twin brother and sister.

'Yes. Damian Purcell swallowed a goldfish at the funfair in

front of his girlfriend and then she was sick.'

'What is the world coming to? It's the end of civilisation. I give up; I'm losing the will to live. And Ros told me it would be all right to leave you on your own when we go to watch Full Quiver run tomorrow.'

'You go, Dad,' said Lysta. 'And I'll bring home what I'm cooking in domestic science for supper.'

Ros dressed for the occasion, wearing a black hat with a single yellow feather and a fitted purple coat which she reminded me she hadn't worn since her niece's wedding. She couldn't remember how many years ago that had been.

'Look nonchalant, as if we've done this many times before,' I said to her as we walked into the parade ring. Unfortunately, her shoe came off in the soggy ground and she had to lean on me as she tried to get it back on. There was quite a strong wind, so I had to hold on to my homburg and found it impossible to light my cigar. DD was already in deep conversation with our jockey, Nicky Howe, who was wearing red and white silks and about the same size as Sifta. When I introduced DD to Ros he gave us both a funny look.

'You're a bit overdressed. This isn't Royal Ascot, you know.'

'We have a natural inclination for style,' I said. 'I know it's only Kempton, but we're here to make a day of it.'

Then Barbara Waring appeared, wearing a modest white raincoat and what could be best described as a trilby. As we all huddled together, Barbara told us Full Quiver needed the run and that he shouldn't be given a hard race, because he wasn't fully wound up.

'So how much should I put on him?' I asked her, which seemed to take her aback, as if it wasn't the done thing to mention betting on one's own horse.

'It's not a day for gambling,' she said. 'Keep your money in your pocket would be my advice.'

DD pulled me to one side and whispered in my ear, 'I wouldn't say too much. Today we're here to observe, so leave it at that.'

There was obviously a racecourse protocol to follow that I was not aware of, so Ros and I made our way to the restaurant and waited for DD to join us to watch the race.

'I should have warned you, don't mention betting in front of Barbara,' DD told me as he sat down. 'She's never put a penny on a horse and she's as honest as the day is long.'

'What's dishonest about having a bet on your horse?' I asked.

'Nothing. With Barbara it's all about reading the signals.'

'I don't understand.'

'When she says the horse is very well and she's expecting a big run and the work rider has given us the nod, that's when we go in with a large bet.'

Full Quiver finished eighth, after leading for over a mile in a ten-furlong race. The jockey never used his whip, allowing him to come home in his own time. When they took off his saddle after the race and hosed him down, I could see he had a bit of a pot belly. I said to DD that even I could tell he wasn't fit, and he should be on a diet.

Ros told me the day had felt as if we'd been on a date and we weren't married.

'Really? Fancy coming back to my place for the night?'

I'd forgotten there would be a surprise waiting for us when we got home.

'Good evening, sir,' said Sam as soon as we opened the front door. 'Table for two?'

Which had been laid for a candlelit supper, with serviettes on our side plates and a bottle of red wine. Lysta poured me a glass to taste.

'It's delicious,' I said.

'I'm afraid we only have the set menu available tonight, but of course it comes highly recommended by our chef.'

Belah brought in a starter of prawns and avocado, while Seth put Ros's favourite piece of classical music, Albinoni's Adagio for organ and strings, on the record player. Lysta's chicken casserole was the main course and we finished with a crème brûlée.

The service had been excellent; I left a fiver under my plate and told Ros I'd certainly eat here again.

We raised our glasses and drank a toast to our children.

On the Saturday morning I drove to the Portobello Road. It had never been a market for dealers, and although it was quieter in the winter months there were always tourists looking for souvenirs. I was getting desperate to find a way to survive and somehow still enjoy what I was doing. It would probably involve no longer going to the rag market or to Bath, where I was dependent on business with the dealers and where the fun was. That would soon be falling by the wayside.

I had to acknowledge that although we needed to adapt to external events, my own failings had contributed to the situation we were in. Lately, when I woke up there were no aspirations flying like a flock of birds past my bedroom window. I knew the days ahead would be full of blunt hard-talking with Simon, trying to predict how long I could keep going.

I went to see Thelma and walked into her sitting room, where her underwear was hanging on the clothes horse as usual, drying in front of the convector heater. As ever, Chippy scratched at the door demanding to be let in, while Thelma went laboriously through the invoices, completely ignoring him. At the end of the afternoon, she handed me the VAT return for my signature, saying, 'Your sales are down quite a lot this last quarter.'

At last she let the dog in. He leapt up at a pair of her pantaloons and charged around the room with them, hoping Thelma would play the game and chase him.

'Thelma, do you ever walk Chippy? He always seems to be needing to burn off a lot of energy.'

'He doesn't get on with other dogs, never has, so I have to distract him with articles of clothing rather than take him to the park every day.'

'Yes, I've noticed he's fond of your underwear.'

'It's not mine, it belongs to Mrs Wilkins downstairs. He eventually tears it to shreds, but there's still a trunk of it for him to get through.'

'I don't think I've met her.'

'And you won't; she died three years ago. Now please shut the front door behind you. I don't want him following you down the street.'

20

May 1990, and, as the economy contracted and the country slid into recession, we launched the completed 'Night Hawks' range, six table lamps on marble bases. For the first time I employed a professional photographer and had leaflets printed for Marcus Wesley to send to his contacts in the interior-design world.

We had always agreed that the figures shouldn't be overtly gay, because it would limit their appeal to a wider audience. So when he insisted we be a little more explicit and the last in the series should be of two young men holding hands, I said, 'Well, that's subtlety gone out of the window.'

'I don't know why you're so frightened of it. This is a new emerging market; it's called coming out. Lots of people will identify with it,' was his reply.

What did it matter if 'Night Hawks' didn't sell? I doubted we'd be in business much longer. The phone wasn't ringing; all our wholesalers had disappeared, none of them getting in touch. People kept telling me they had seen a copy of one of our advertising pieces at half the price we'd been charging.

Everyone at Puckmill could see what was happening. In our lunch breaks I let it be known that I was looking at new product lines, trying to maintain an air of optimism, but the atmosphere had changed. No longer that zip of energy when you rushed to get orders out each week. The buzz you got working on those projects, staying on late into the evenings, and then sitting in the Crown until closing time after a hard day's graft. Mike knew the likely outcome, but put on a show of undiminished enthusiasm. Rob was working part-time now, and Quentin only came in on a Thursday. Ade was still doing a full week, because I could move him from job to job.

We'd quickly built up a range of resin souvenirs to sell in the

Portobello Road. Not only fridge magnets of famous London sights, but gargoyles in an old stone finish. They were cheap to make, with a good profit margin, appealing particularly to the Japanese, who bought several at a time.

DD rang, to tell me Full Quiver was now nearing full racing fitness.

'He's going to run on Tuesday next week at Sandown. Vernon rides him every day and says he's buzzing.'

'Ros and I'll be there. How much cash shall I bring?'

'Nothing. We're not going to have a bet on him. By the way, you don't have to dress up.'

'So he's not going to win?'

'No, we're going in big at Windsor on May the thirteenth. Keep it to yourself.'

It felt as if I was leading a double life, living on the breadline and watching every penny while owning half a racehorse and planning to pull off a gambling coup.

Simon suggested that by reducing my overheads and concentrating on the Portobello Road market, with the coming summer bringing thousands of tourists, I could maintain a level of cash flow that would pay the wages. So I had to let my mother know that I was giving up the Bath market.

'But what about me?' she said. 'What will I do with myself on a Wednesday?'

'Do something exciting.'

'Like what, row the Atlantic?'

'No, I was thinking you could write a book about your wartime adventures at Bletchley Park.'

'Out of the question. I swore the Official Secrets Act, I'm not allowed to say a word. Winston Churchill would turn in his grave.'

'Sell your story to the *Daily Mail*.'

'You know Peter proposed to me in San Francisco?'

'He dropped a hint he might.'

'I turned him down, of course, which put him in a bad mood for the whole week.'

'He should have saved it up until the last day of your holiday.'

'Precisely. He's always nagging me to join U3A. Perhaps it's time to sign up. Apparently, they do Scottish country dancing. I'd rather fancy that.'

Chris Booth invited me for supper at the Crown, which the two of us enjoyed together occasionally. He said our conversations were the antidote he needed to living a country doctor's life. Listening to everyone's symptoms morning to night would certainly have ground me down. Our lives were complete opposites.

'You have a very individual way of thinking about everything,' he said, looking at the wine list and choosing an expensive bottle of Bordeaux.

'Do I? Well, it's certainly not helping me now.' I was about to tell him I thought my days at Puckmill were numbered when Natalie, the French girl waitressing in the pub, came to take our order.

'How's the Cirencester Ladies football team doing this season?'

'We play very well. Last week I saved a penalty,' she said in her strong French accent.

'How do you ever get away from the place without a car?' Chris asked.

'I have a licence and Ade is learning to drive, so we can get about.'

'Are you teaching him French? It would give him the confidence to leave Frampton Mansell and see a bit of the world.'

Then Ivor came in with the quiz questions for the local derby that night, the Crown against their fiercest rivals, the Bell at Sapperton.

'Anthony Gascoigne's got a head cold so we're one short. Any chance you could make up the numbers, doctor?'

'I'm sorry. We're about to have supper and the two of us have plenty to talk about.'

I knew Ivor wouldn't leave us alone. After we'd given Natalie our order, he asked us if we'd signed the petition to put pressure on the bus company to increase the service to the village.

'Just two a day at the moment, one at nine in the morning and another at three in the afternoon. More cutbacks,' Ivor grumbled. 'They think everyone has a car, but what about the elderly?'

'We should all chip in and buy a community bus,' I suggested.

'And you could drive it, Ivor, and take more children to school than your taxi can carry,' said Chris.

'It's a good idea, but we'd need to raise a few thousand.'

'We'll come up with something. Why don't you organise a meeting in the village hall?'

'I will,' said Ivor. 'Glad I bumped into the two of you.'

It made me reflect on our years in Frampton Mansell. The village was changing; houses were being sold to people who worked in the cities and only came here at weekends. Rex Norton, the last remaining dairy farmer, complained there was no longer any money in milk production, the price of a pint being controlled by the supermarkets.

'My son won't follow me, and who can blame him?'

At least some hope of employment was being offered, as Adrian Linley, an ex-RAF man, had got permission to start a 4x4 business. There was no shop in the village, and Ivor had told me that the post office he and his wife Janet ran from their terraced house would close down when they retired. The old way of life in rural England was gradually fading away and there was nothing that could be done about it.

'You seem distracted,' said Chris. 'I can tell there's something on your mind.'

'I was just thinking about my time here.'

'You make it sound like it's in the past.'

'We've had our heyday, I know that. The world is shrinking, economies are getting tangled up together. We won't recognise this country in twenty years, and it's only just beginning. Soon the Chinese will swallow up the world's manufacturing. Puckmill Studios was here and gone in the blink of an eye in a little village in Gloucestershire.'

'That doesn't sound like the usual optimistic Nick. Do you mean it?'

'I suppose I was just wondering if we'd done enough for the village.'

'Well, you've certainly contributed to the Crown. And don't forget your Open Day and the gifts you've donated to local causes, including the hundred pounds for repainting the village hall.'

'It was a pity we couldn't have employed more people, not just Ade.'

As soon as I'd said it, I felt I was letting the evening slip into a melancholic self-indulgence. I changed the subject, helped by a second glass of the Bordeaux.

'Will you come on May the thirteenth to watch Full Quiver run at Windsor and bring anyone you can from the surgery? It's an evening meeting, so hopefully you can arrange it so you're not on call.'

'Let's do that. We can hire a minibus and bring the nurses, and maybe I can get Sheila to come.'

'He's going to run a big race, but only put ten pounds on him.'

How my last morning dragged on in the Birmingham rag market. No one knew, of course, and I preferred it like that, not wanting to explain all the reasons why I was calling it a day. I said nothing to anyone and was simply going to say goodbye after I'd packed up and loaded everything into the van.

At least Isobel wasn't going to be there. That would have been difficult; I knew she'd have played the hurt woman. I don't mean that unkindly, it's just the way she was with me. I was also hoping Sifta wouldn't need me to lend him more money on a last-minute deal.

Frank looked like a sad-eyed Barney Rubble and, without knowing it, delivered his words of farewell as if he'd stolen them from my own mouth.

'I'm packing it in today, but I'm not retiring, just changing my vocation.'

'Vocation, Frank. I like your use of the word.'

'I told Greasy Gadd that I was changing my vacation and he said but you've never been on holiday in your life.'

'So, I take it this vocation is taking a job with your very own WMR?'

'Yes. I interviewed myself, and as I was the only candidate it was an easy decision. I've worked out all the timetables and it's going to be seven days a week.'

'It sounds as if you're never going to leave the house.'

'I was hoping you'd drop by on Mondays after the market, just for a couple of hours.'

'Frank, my dear friend, this isn't easy to say, but it's also my last day. I'm not coming to the rag market any more.'

'What, never again?'

'No, I'm done with it.'

'Oh.'

Despite my hopes of being able to leave with the minimum of fuss, I lost count of how many goodbyes I said that morning, to the wheeler-dealers I'd spoken to every week without ever getting to know them on a personal level. No one talked about their wives or families but only about the incessant search, scouring the markets every day, all of them living on their wits, trying to end each week with a few quid in their pockets.

None more so than Sifta, who refused to compromise and was forever running on the spot, never getting to the point where he could manage to live in some modest comfort. He seemed unconcerned about his future. His life stretched as far as the end of each day, when maybe he sensed a little victory counting the cash he still had in his pocket. At least he'd come good on the Bristol Blue glass and made a sizeable profit on his Victorian ear trumpets. When I asked him if he had enough to put down a deposit on a rented room, he was blasé about it, saying that with the summer coming the van was good enough.

'I like to park up by a canal and feed the swans, and there's always a pub nearby.'

You can't change a man and his way of life. He has to do it himself, and Sifta wasn't ready to think about that.

Aileen was carefully putting her jewellery into the suitcase she padlocked around her wrist, a precaution she'd taken every week since someone had tried to snatch the lot from her as she walked to the car park. I went over to her.

'It's time to say cheerio, and I'll never forget our weekly talks.'

'I don't believe it – you're going! I won't have anyone to look at any more.'

You would never have thought a woman who always wore the same torn anorak and bobble hat, with those woollen mittens, could have been so perceptive. She knew a thing or two all right; she'd warned me the Chinese were coming. As for her idea to franchise what we made at Puckmill, maybe it would have worked then, but certainly not now. I told her briefly I was looking to take the business in a new direction and didn't bother to explain anything in detail. She was the only one who gave me her telephone number and made me promise to ring from time to time.

'Remember to get in touch if you ever come across a pocket watch. Time waits for no man,' was Graeme's parting remark.

I'd made my last journey loading the van and still hadn't seen a sign of Sifta, so I walked amongst the mostly deserted stalls, asking everyone if they'd seen him. So much for my swift goodbye, until at last I saw him pushing a four-wheel trolley, struggling with the weight of it, up a ramp used by the cleaners who came in at the end of each market to hose the place down.

'Sifta, let me give you a hand. You'll burst a blood vessel.'

'Yes, do. As far as that rented seven-tonner blocking the entrance.'

'Are you buying or selling? What's going on? Are you in the middle of a deal?'

'Let me tell you in a minute,' he said breathlessly, as we were joined in our efforts by Mossy, one of the homeless who shuffled round the market picking up dog-ends and scrounging money to buy cans of extra strong brew.

'It's a ballbreaker,' he said through his smoker's cough.

When we eventually shoved the trolley on to the grounded tailboard of the lorry and watched it being raised hydraulically, Mossy held out his hand and, with a look of expectation, said, 'I don't come cheap.'

'I'll get you a tea next week,' said Sifta.

'Come on, it's worth a quid.'

So I gave him a pound, which Sifta said was a hell of a rate of pay for a minute's work before disappearing into the cab of the lorry. When he returned he was stuffing a wad of notes into his pockets.

'Happy, Sifta? You've made some money, I hope.'

'Very rare, those speak-your-weight machines. Once seen on every station platform, but not any more. You can't put a price on nostalgia. People don't think about the cost when something pulls on their heart strings.'

'I remember there was one on Bournemouth West station when I was a child. I was standing behind an extremely heavy woman weighing herself and the machine said, "One at a time, please."'

'You think that's funny? I'm so light that when I got on one it said, 'Next, please. I'm still waiting.''

'Have you got time for a bit of lunch and a cup of tea?' I asked him.

'That's a first. What's wrong?'

'I've got a few things to tell you. Nothing serious.'

'Tell me now. I'm due in Droitwich to pick up some slot machines.'

So I did, in the street where I'd queued all those Monday mornings outside the rag market. It was all said briefly, without sentiment, and as I shook his hand I knew it was a final goodbye and I'd never see him again.

'You know,' he said, 'I've not used the word friend before, because I don't think I've ever had one. You don't make friends in this game, everyone just becomes somebody you wheel and deal with, but you were different.'

'One last word, Sifta.'

'And what's that?'

'Get yourself somewhere to live, and sleep in a comfortable bed.'

Ros and I went to watch Full Quiver run at Sandown, dressed in an understated way this time, in fact too understated because they wouldn't allow me into the members' enclosure without a tie. Which meant we couldn't get into the parade ring and see Barbara Waring, or have a chat with Nicky Howe. By luck, we saw DD queuing up at the non-members' hamburger stand where the riff-raff congregated, and I could explain why we couldn't join them.

'Go and buy a tie from the racecourse shop. You've got twenty minutes before the race.'

'It's not worth it; we'll watch from here. He's not going to win anyway.'

'No, not today. You know the plan, May the thirteenth at Windsor.'

All this was said within earshot of Ros, who understandably said, 'So why have we come all this way and wasted an afternoon when you know he has no intention of trying to win?'

'Tactics,' said DD, clearly taken aback.

I didn't buy a tie and Ros and I watched the race from the grandstand. Full Quiver finished tenth out of sixteen runners.

On the long journey home, Ros told me she wouldn't come racing again. Although she enjoyed it when we had time away from the children, there were things she'd much rather we did together, like walking in the countryside. Which led her to talking about getting another dog. We hadn't had one since Moss died, our Border Collie who had roamed the hills of North Wales with me.

Usually on a Saturday night Mike would turn up with a bottle of wine and a dartboard. He'd hang it on the kitchen wall and challenge anyone to a game, and the outcome was always the same: Mike victorious.

He and I sat alone, finishing the bottle of red while listening to Jackson Browne singing 'The Pretender', and that's when I came clean about the situation we were facing: what you would call the end of the road. Mike needed to know. He had discovered for himself so many skills through his years at Puckmill that would be of value, certainly to the Dummy Book Company over in Tetbury, or if he wanted to return to the Brass Rubbing Centre.

'You can't let what you've learnt go to waste.'

'I'll stay to the bitter end,' he said. 'And I don't believe we're finished. Rob told me the place would only close down if you got bored with it. And Marcus Wesley said the other day that "Night Hawks" will be the most successful range we've ever made.'

'That's what he's hoping. It's a world I know nothing about.'

'Sid, our postman, he's gay. And Tim, the lifeguard at the open-air swimming pool.'

'Well, that's two at least. I wonder if they're interested in buying a couple of table lamps,' I said, jokingly, but Mike was being serious and didn't find it the slightest bit funny. Instead he made a good point that I'd never considered.

'Mind you, do table lamps sell when the days are getting longer? You'd think the demand would be stronger in the autumn.'

He was right, and I'd just spent three thousand pounds on electrical components – cables, plugs, switches and five hundred sixty-watt light bulbs – and the same amount on marble bases.

'We'll see next week. Marcus is exhibiting them at the Interior Design Show in London. Then we'll know our future. Meanwhile, I want you and Rob to come racing at Windsor on the thirteenth of May. Chris Booth's organising a minibus; I'll reserve you a seat.'

'To watch that horse of ours, which Ros told me should be retired to a quiet field,' he said in a sarcastic tone, which was quite unlike him. 'By the way,' he went on, changing the subject, 'have you noticed the rabbits in the fields around Puckmill?'

'What about them? There's not an outbreak of myxomatosis?'

'No, they've gone two-tone. Silo's been out there enjoying himself.'

'Really? The old bugger.'

'I saw at least six of them above Chris Booth's house, grey and white. Definitely Silo's offspring.'

Walter Pepper rang from beyond the galaxy, or that's what it sounded like, his Dalek voice echoing in a telephone box. I hadn't heard from him for months.

'I'm in Cape Town and won't be coming back. I'm happy here and have my sister who looks after me. I hope the business is doing well and one day you'll visit me. I've taken up surfing, can you believe that at my age? The only thing I miss is Marmite. Goodbye, goodbye from South Africa.'

'Wait, Walter. Would you like me to put some in the post? I can send you food parcels from England. I doubt you can get Campbell's mushroom soup.'

'Goodbye from South Africa, and thank you for everything. Goodbye, my friend, goodbye.'

Ade came and told me he was taking his driving test in Gloucester the next morning. I wished him luck and told him to keep looking in the rear-view mirror. Examiners like that sort of thing.

'It's all about spatial awareness, being alert for the unexpected.'

But he wasn't interested in listening to my invaluable tips on how to pass a driving test. He wanted Mike to go with him and give him a kind of pre-test as they drove to Gloucester.

'So, that's both of you off for the morning,' I said, not that there was anything particularly urgent that needed doing. All the manic days of rushing to get jobs completed were in the past. We had resorted to taking on the most menial work, including electroplating a pair of baby's bootees in bronze for a doting mother.

'How much should we charge her?' Mike had asked.

'Get her to send a donation to the donkey sanctuary.'

May thirteenth, the day Full Quiver was running at Windsor, and I was having one of my monthly meetings with Simon. As he leant over his office desk he told me that having cut everything in the business back to the bone, I had achieved a certain amount of equilibrium. This was a word not normally associated with me and I asked him to repeat it; it gave me an inner satisfaction. This equilibrium was, in fact, running on the spot, in other words breaking even, but it showed Simon that I'd taken the necessary action and kept Puckmill Studios solvent.

There was a serious lack of reality going on in my life. The realisation washed over me after I had left Simon's office on that beautiful May morning. There was a warm softness in the wind as I drove up on to Minchinhampton Common where the cattle grazed and the golfers played, and walked amongst the cow pats, nervously considering whether I should risk taking the biggest gamble of my life. DD had rung the night before, to tell me that Full Quiver was ready. The going at the racecourse was good to firm, perfect for him. He also had little weight to carry, and the distance of one and a half miles was what he had been trained for. He was one of the outsiders and expected to be at least 25/1. When DD said he was going to put five hundred pounds each way on him, I was consumed by a cold fear. It was beyond my pocket; to lose that amount would have emptied the bank account. In my private little stash at the bottom of the wardrobe I had three hundred pounds in cash.

'Find a rails bookmaker, and as soon as he chalks up his opening show, place your bet,' he told me.

'Why so early?' I asked.

'Because as soon as the bookies know someone's had a bet of a monkey each way, the odds will tumble.'

Suddenly the evening of fun I'd been looking forward to had turned into something else altogether. There was no way I could have persuaded Ros to come with me, so I decided to drive to Windsor on my own. Everyone was there when I arrived at the racecourse: Mike and Rob, Chris and Sheila, the nursing staff and the physios. Even Amanda, the receptionist, had made it. None of them knew how I felt, my stomach knotted with anxiety. Only Rob noticed how tense I was, so I told him I was suffering with PRT.

'Pre-race tension. I always get it before he runs.'

DD kept appearing and then disappearing, feeding me vital information. Full Quiver was being saddled up, on his toes, which apparently was a good sign. In the parade ring, before the jockeys mounted, Barbara told me that she'd declared him to run in blinkers for the first time, which would help him concentrate.

'What odds did you get?' DD whispered to me.

'I haven't placed a bet yet.'

'You fool, I told you to get on early. You won't get twenty-five to one now.'

'I've got friends here. I haven't had a chance.'

'Go now. Have a bet with Johnny Derwent down on the rails.'

I searched for him amongst the crowd of punters, all trying to place last-minute bets, and spotted him just as the course announcer let it be known the horses were entering the stalls. In those last few seconds before the off, I froze in the panic of my own indecision. I really didn't know what to do. I heard the last horse was now in the stalls and then the announcement they were off and running. In that instant, I shouted, 'Fifty pounds each way Full Quiver.'

'I only do win bets,' Johnny said.

And the words just came out of me. 'A hundred pounds to win, then.' And he took my money. The odds were 33/1, better than DD's.

I ran to the grandstand, and by the time I'd heard Chris calling me and weaved through the crowd and managed to focus my binoculars, they were coming to the last two furlongs of the race. Suddenly I saw Full Quiver burst through on the inside rail, taking the lead, to race clear and win by four lengths.

What followed was a level of excitement that's hard to express in this physical world of ours. A great bursting of joy that could explode a fragile heart, with a rush of energy that would be hard to sustain before the body collapsed. All of us had our arms around each other; thank goodness my GP was with us, as I could have needed some treatment any minute. The look on everyone's face was one of total disbelief and happiness that we shared on one momentous night when Full Quiver romped in and lit up our world.

In the winner's enclosure, Chris took photos of the celebrations as Nicky Howe was lifted into the air by DD. I kissed Barbara, probably too many times, but I couldn't stop myself. As for Full Quiver, I'm sure he wondered what all the fuss was about as he was unsaddled, covered in sweat.

We didn't bother to watch any of the other races as we all drank champagne in the racecourse bar and gradually confessed to each other how much we had won. Johnny Derwent had counted out my winnings in twenty-pound notes, which I had to stuff into every pocket. I bulged with cash and looked like a suitable target for a mugger. No one from the Minchinhampton practice had bet less than ten pounds and most had been paid out at 25/1, so everyone was in the money. Mike had put twenty pounds on him so had won five hundred, while Rob kept quiet about his winnings, but had a broad smile on his face.

Before I left to drive back, DD came over to me. He was sober and had shown little emotion through the evening.

'So, you see it is possible to win at gambling. You've just got to know when to put the money down.'

'Does that mean he's not going to win again this season?'

'No. But we have to listen to what the work rider tells us, wait for the right signals.'

'Well, it was certainly worth waiting for.'

And on that evening of 13 May I headed into the night down the M4, having taken over three thousand pounds from my pockets and put it in the glove compartment. I drove on in a kind of dream state, constantly reliving the race: the faces of absolute joy; the elation when Full Quiver crossed the line; that moment when we all turned and a great 'Gosh' of disbelief flooded over us.

And still I drove on, way past Junction 15 where I should have left the motorway. When I eventually re-entered the earth's atmosphere and got my bearings, I stopped outside an off-licence, switched off the engine and sat staring into the night. I was engulfed by a wave of emotion and I laughed long and hard with some peculiar relief, the weight easing from so many things.

It occurred to me that life is made up of a lot of different phases, all of them little journeys that we have to take, and he who adapts the quickest lasts the longest. That's all we're doing as we live through our lives.

Driving home under a clear sky I turned on the radio and listened to Pink Floyd's *The Dark Side of the Moon* with the volume at its highest. What a way to end the night.

⚜ Epilogue ⚜

In the months that followed, I pinned our last hopes of survival on the success of 'Night Hawks', the range of lamps that was going to become fashionable and appear in all the Sunday supplement magazines. But it wasn't to be; although several lighting shops and interior designers placed orders and I waited by the telephone to hear about the tremendous response they had received, the calls never came. And no wonder, when I heard how much profit margin the retailers had put on, buying them for £95 and charging £225, which was far too expensive for most people. So they trickled out into a few sitting rooms and never did set the world alight.

As soon as planning permission was granted on the barn, I knew it was just a matter of time until I sold the place. Even if I'd got an overdraft set against the property, it would only have prolonged what could not be avoided. Over a few pints of 6X at the Crown on a showery evening with the rain sweeping in across the Golden Valley, I told Mike, Rob, Ade and Quentin that I was done with treading water and was going to close down Puckmill Studios. It was a relief to say it and they all knew it was coming. We raised our glasses and said to each other, 'The end of a little journey in our lives.'

There are too many people to mention who came and went in the years we worked underneath the arches of Brunel's viaduct; this book has only included those who played a significant part. It would take another volume to mention everyone, so to those of you who came into my life during the Puckmill years and haven't made it to the printed page, I'm sorry.

Mike was with me until the very end, when we sold the last piece of equipment and padlocked the workshop. I eventually sold Puckmill to a property developer and made a profit of

£7,000, having bought it from Celia Foxton for £18,000. It gave me a financial buffer, after I'd paid off all the outstanding creditors.

Mike and I still keep in touch, speaking to one another every week. He lives in the same house as he did with his parents, and is now doing back-breaking work building dry-stone walls around Gloucestershire. For a time Rob sold Bohemian art glass from the front room of his house in Malmesbury, while Quentin still has his shop selling antique tins in Bath. Ade learnt to drive a tractor and got a job on Rex Horton's dairy farm. Nothing ever came of his first love, Darina, but he's now married to a girl from the village. Daphne Neville still totters on down at Baker's Mill.

Walter Pepper never returned from South Africa, and my dear mother died in 2012. The last time I saw Peter, her gentleman friend, was at her funeral.

My children all have families of their own, except Belah who lives with her mother, and although Ros and I drifted apart, our friendship is strong to this day and we often laugh at the life we lived together and the risks we took without thinking of the consequences.

From time to time I return to Frampton Mansell. A Cotswold-stone house now stands in place of the barn at Puckmill. Little else has changed beneath the village, where you can follow the footpath down to the canal and take a beautiful walk to the Daneway pub below Sapperton village.

Do I miss any of it? No, and when I look back on those years what stands out are the conditions we worked in, the gruelling months of those hard winters. How we managed to produce such works of art astonishes me.

It was the characters I met that so enriched my life at that time, all of them living on their wits, individuals who came up with the most ingenious ways to put a bundle of hard-earned cash into their pockets. They are from a bygone era, for with everything now available on the internet who needs to be out at five o'clock on a freezing cold morning when you can find what you're looking for on a computer without leaving your bedroom?

Aileen kept in touch for a few years, and within six months of my leaving the rag market she told me Frank had died of a heart attack. The last time we spoke she let me know that Sifta was still zipping around the place, just one deal away from making his stash. That's what he believed, but in truth if removed from that world I doubt he would have survived. He lived on his adrenaline rush, all seven stone of him.

Marcus Wesley now makes his living selling second-hand cars in Bath. I bought one from him only six months ago. Derek Tindall retired to the countryside in Hampshire, and I'm led to believe Archie is still talking his way across America.

When Aileen told me to beware of cheap Chinese imports I had no idea how they would affect a little business hidden under a viaduct beneath a sleepy village in Gloucestershire, never mind that in the years that followed they would flood the whole world. It is now only in secluded pockets of England that you'll find craftsmen practising their skills in hidden sheds, preferably by a quiet river, away from the mainstream of life.

As for Full Quiver, he had one more night of glory, winning a handicap at Nottingham. When Barbara said his racing days were over, the stable girl who'd always looked after him took him to live out his remaining years in Cornwall. What a horse, and what an unforgettable night that was in Windsor.

ACKNOWLEDGEMENTS

My huge thanks to the following people who searched their memories and helped me to complete this book: Rod Holt, Mike Townsend, Rob Marshall, Mike Saffell, Mark Wilson, Jane Tully, Maureen Mosedale. To Mike Bunn for sending photos. Natalie and Buster. To Judith Mather, Nathaniel Mobbs, Ruth Cleaver and Sarah Gooch, and my dear friend Sharpie.

As always to Jan and my children, particularly Sam and Belah for their help. And to Arabella who worked painstakingly on every page.

And for all the support from Teresa, Alison, Nancy and Neville.